STAINED GLASS HOURS

STAINED GLASS HOURS

A Modern Pilgrimage

by

TOM DAVIES

photographs by

JOHN HODDER

foreword by

GERALD PRIESTLAND

NEW ENGLISH LIBRARY

Copyright © 1985 by Tom Davies

First published in Great Britain in 1985 by
New English Library, Mill Road, Dunton Green, Sevenoaks, Kent.
Editorial office: 47 Bedford Square, London WC1B 3DP.

Typeset by Rowland Phototypesetting Ltd,
Bury St Edmunds, Suffolk
Printed in Great Britain by
St Edmundsbury Press, Bury St Edmunds, Suffolk

British Library CIP Data

Davies, Tom, *1941*—
   Stained glass hours : a modern pilgrimage.
   1. Christian shrines—Great Britain
   2. Great Britain—Description and travel—1971
   I. Title   II. Hodder, John
   914.1'04858   DA632

ISBN 0 450 06053 5

CONTENTS

For all those holy pilgrims who shouldered wooden crosses to Walsingham; for those who sweated off weight on the causeway to Lindisfarne; for those who suffered from blisters at Lough Derg; for those bitten by dogs on the road to Knock; for those who all but froze to death at Holywell; for those caught in a storm on the summit of Croagh Patrick; for those seasick on the boat journey across to Bardsey Island; for those stung by nettles and torn by brambles on the road to Llantwit Major and for those who broke their hearts on the road to Canterbury . . . for all those who suffered in their search for holiness, this book is prayerfully dedicated.

FOREWORD

This is a book that I've thought of writing myself but I'm glad I didn't for I would never have done it so well. From the idea to the writing, the pictures and the design, it is a great joy to have and to read: as fascinating as a really good junk-shop, crammed with bizarre objects, lovingly polished and apparently offered for sale but with which the owner does not really want to part (even the ones he detests).

From the very first sentence – the road to Ely edged with carrots – this is an intensely visual book. Tom Davies looks closely at everything he encounters, thinks for a moment, and then jots it down in his notebook in a vivid phrase that brings it back to life in the reader's eye the moment you encounter it. Even when he kicks a tin can in Durham, it is memorable; and how much more so when he undergoes the awful austerities of Lough Derg, with pilgrims 'nodding off like drugged budgerigars', dawn coming up 'as dark as a hangman's stare', and poor Tom reduced to muffling a can of illicit Coke in his underpants, lest the spoilsport nuns hear it fizzing.

Yet it is far from being just a chain of wisecracks. It really is a pilgrimage in search of the living God who (in the true apophatic tradition) turns out again and again to be *not* this, *not* that, *not* the other. Tom rages splendidly against the commercialisation of piety, against bored priests, against the denial of intercommunion (which he very properly just ignores, as we all should). What is more, he has done his homework about the places he visits and the holy people who gave them their meaning.

John Hodder's pictures can sit proudly in this company. From tiny vignettes to human studies and grand views, they too are the work of a journalist who is also an artist.

Gerald Priestland

INTO THE KINGDOM OF THE QUEEN OF ICE

ELY·DOWNHAM MARKET·KING'S LYNN·WALSINGHAM·NORWICH

A strong north wind was blowing down over the Fens as I cycled along the road to Ely following a trail of half-eaten carrots. They kept on cropping up again and again on my Easter pilgrimage – long lines of carrots dotted every ten feet or so along the edge of the road. Occasionally a mouse, pancaked flat by a speeding car, broke up the orange line. Sometimes it was a mangled bird. Just by Deeping Fen a huge rat lay dead by the grass verge, its fat fleshy tail curled out behind it, a perfect smile of release twisted on its tiny white lips. Yet, quite soon, there were those carrots again.

All around me, in a vast sunken arena, lay the flatlands of the Fens; the finest agricultural soil in England, as you might have guessed from its deep black richness. The land lies so low you sometimes get the feeling that you are floating along in the air as you look out over the deep streams bisecting the black parallelograms of soil yet to yield the first signs of their crops.

This feeling of abstraction was reinforced by the sky; not so much one sky as three skies packed into one. All day those skies had swirled around me as I pedalled into the teeth of the north wind. Here was a deep grey sky, full of weeping and endless lament. Over there was a thick black sky, full of biliousness as it prepared to fling yet another shower of cold Fen rain into my face. Somewhere between the two was yet another sky which was neither sun nor rain, neither fish nor fowl – a nothing sky unable to decide what shape it was going to take.

The odd hunched tree broke up the flatness of the land; sometimes a line of poplars marched across the horizon, much as they do in the wine-growing regions of France. It began raining again and a lorry roared past me, buffeting my side with the damp smack of its draught, the spray dancing around inside its four wheels like a trapped and angry ghost.

And there it was again – the gaunt Gothic outline of Ely Cathedral, spearing through the packed Fen skies before disappearing into the rain mists again, haunting and elusive like a strange symbol in a recurring dream, huge and enigmatic, one great cannon for God.

All cathedrals have their own personalities. Some come on as sweet as a burst of applause, others have the aristocratic charms of an old and rather lovely lady. All too many are simply citadels of snootiness, a few even aspire to a teenage spriteliness. That rainy morning, though, each time I glimpsed her over the black fields and between the trees, Ely Cathedral kept changing her form. The nearer I got the more impressive she became, a massive Gothic birthday cake suspended from the rain clouds, a great Spanish galleon riding serenely before the squalls.

In a landscape so barren of detail, so empty of anything three hands higher than a duck's beak, it seemed almost unbelievable that such a massive structure should have found its way out here. As I toiled up the slope into the town she continued to work and rework her way through my imagination like a haunting melody. A face appeared at a window watching me, her features as indistinct as an old statue's in the tadpoling raindrops. Otherwise the streets were empty as I passed the Pilgrim's Parlour and Ye Olde Tea Shoppe until I finally came up to the cathedral's front door itself. If anything she became even more impressive close to and my back arched as I gazed up in simple wonder at the black cascading stonework.

This magnificent monastery was founded by Saint Etheldreda, Queen of Northumbria, in 673 A.D. She was a strange and beautiful queen of ice and flame, a woman of legendary unselfishness endowed with the gift of prophecy. She never washed in warm water and prayed from midnight until dawn. Even when terminally ill she delighted in the painful swellings which tormented her. But the most unusual aspect of her quirky character was that she did not believe in sex either before or after marriage. Despite two husbands, she remained a virgin and it was on this frigid reputation that her cult – and the cathedral – was built.

After the death of her first husband, Tondbert, a Fen prince, she came to Ely to devote her life to prayer. Five years later, however, her father forced her to marry Egfrith, son of Oswy, King of Northumbria. He too made unreasonable demands on Etheldreda's body and at one stage, complete with an army, he chased her right across Northumbria. She took refuge on a promontory and her virginity was saved by a week of storms which so discouraged the damp and sad Egfrith that he fully and finally gave up on her.

It is a singular story, vivid with threats of violence and thwarted lusts, and yet, just by stooping through the small wooden door of the cathedral and looking up and around at the awesome size of the brooding, pillared nave, I could immediately sense something of the ice queen's personality. The huge, dark-streaked spaces and high arches do not tell of the human failings of us ordinary people but of the vast, intangible mystery of God. There was not a trace of human sensuality in the flag-stoned floor, neither was there any warmth in the chilling little gusts of wind.

I moved past two people keeping warm next to a rumbling stove. Looking up again, my breath kept failing me; whether from feelings of fear or love I could not quite be sure. *My house is very big and you are very little*, those flaking walls told me. *I am very old and you are very young. You are in Etheldreda's house. Watch your step. Keep off the grass.*

Her shrine, like so much else that was holy, was broken up in the Reformation. Moving closer to the altar, I came to stand under the Lantern Tower and it engulfed me again – this sense of mystery and wonder – as I looked up at the shafts of hard, stellar light bursting in through the windows and coming together in a shimmering white starburst in the shadows of the distant rafters.

Just near the Lady Chapel I bearded Canon Murray McDonald, a precise and silky cleric with an accent wood-

smoked by public school. He explained that this was the mother church of the diocese of Ely; throughout the year, they had some hundred thousand visitors. Some three pilgrimages a week came from East Anglia; people were encouraged to concentrate on a part of the cathedral, study it and try to decide what it was saying to them.

He told me a bit about Etheldreda too, of how she was popularly known as Audrey and of the medieval fairs that were held in her honour on the seventeenth day of October. At such fairs, cheap trumpery – jewellery and suchlike – would be sold. This was identified as 'St Audrey' stuff, hence the modern word which came from this, tawdry.

I cycled back into the town and found a room in the White Hart Hotel, a most curious place full of sloping floorboards and passageways festooned with plastic flowers. There was a dog who went berserk with rage at the sight of a visitor and someone who seemed to be living rough on the floor of the residents' lounge.

It was dusk and the rain had stopped when I went back to the cathedral again, walking down past the school and the dean's house where the silhouettes of people moved, black on gold, in the light. From somewhere deep in the darkness came the sound of choir practice. All around in the cathedral grounds birds flitted past the spiky parapets and chipped gargoyles. The taste of newly mown grass hung in the damp air.

Wandering again around the cold shadowy interior, trying to second-guess the real nature of the place, I saw the urgent appeals for cash, the notices that all but commanded the visitor to donate a pound, the demands for more money for the use of a camera, the tourists milling about who would be hard pushed to tell the difference between a prayer and a poke in the eye. Etheldreda's house was in dire physical distress. On the noticeboard I read that the stonework at the east end of the cathedral was in need of repair, that the gable of the south transept had to be rebuilt. There were no financial reserves, we were told bluntly.

Ely Cathedral, legacy of Etheldreda, Queen of Northumbria. 'In the cold, shadowy interior I could sense something of the ice queen's personality.'

Here was a church that was clearly floundering in the direction of an honourable grave, one which, despite its abundant beauty, had not escaped the sickness of the modern church. In the mad days of the Reformation people cared enough about these places to knock them down. Now they were being killed by the even deadlier attack of spiritual syphilis, and were fast becoming crumbling tourist shrines, bowed down by cobwebs of penury; huge monuments to the death of holiness.

The quest for the purpose and meaning of holiness was at the heart of my journeys that year. I wanted to find out what it meant and if it still existed in a modern world. I wanted to define its characteristics and establish the dispositions of this word from the Anglo-Saxon *halig*: something which must be kept complete or inviolable; something which was one or whole; something which was of high moral excellence, spiritually perfect, of God.

This building had clearly grown out of a sense of holiness; out of something spiritually perfect which had once existed in the soul of man who then created it to mirror that something. It had been built on that which was complete, inviolate, one or whole. Yet the noticeboard alone told you that it was far from complete now. It was incomplete, violated. Could God still reside in this house where cameras flashed and damp winds blew around urgent appeals for yet more cash?

The Lady Chapel was a bright exception to the rest of the building, however: a warm building, generous in its proportions and glimmering with lots of cheerful windows. It was in there that I bumped into a man with the beefy arms of a labourer but who turned out to be a musician. He was blowing down a large tin funnel and listening to the sound. 'An organ would sound lovely in this chapel,' he said.

'So what does it sound like in the cathedral?' I asked.

'It sounds lovely in there too. It's the way you play it, you know,' he added after a pause. 'You can make almost anything sound lovely if you know how to play it. Most musicians are bombastic. That's the trouble these days. Bombasticism. That's why so many organs sound awful.'

He piped on his tin funnel a few more times, nodded to himself and left.

It is not at all easy to get Fen men talking, as I discovered that night at dinner in the hotel when I tried to raise some response from two men sitting at the table next to me. It was only later that I noticed they did not talk to one another either, both just sitting there keeping their own counsel as they munched their way through their food. One picked up a slice of cucumber and held it up to the light as the other just stared into the middle-distance munching quietly. One put down his knife and fork and grunted. The other dabbed the sides of his mouth with a paper napkin and belched. The Fen skies had clearly given them bursting ruddy features with the clearest complexions. They were both built like Sherman tanks and ate every single morsel on their plates, still not talking to one another even during their coffee.

The next day, Good Friday, I went to the morning service in the cathedral. It was the coldest service I have ever attended. At first I found only one lady sitting in front of the altar and asked her if it was just she and me but she said that she thought that there was a service going on somewhere in the choir stalls.

I picked my way around scaffolding draped in polythene sheets and found about a hundred and fifty people shivering in the choir stalls. Staccato gusts of wind jabbed about in the roof and thumped against the polythene. The badly adjusted microphone made the disembodied voice echo like announcements in a railway station: 'We nowowow turnturnturn . . .' All the choirboys were wearing gloves. Most of the congregation resembled dummies in the window of an Oxfam shop with their scarves, grey overcoats and odd glimpses of thick flannelled ankles.

Even that great hymn 'When I Survey the Wondrous Cross' failed to lift the cold. I was shivering so much I could not later understand much of my notes on Canon McDonald's sermon. I think it went something like this:

'At the heart of the gospel there is not a dream but an event, an act that took place in the world. When Jesus shouted that it was finished it was the act of a man who had climbed a mountain and cried in delight that he had made it. The goal has been reached. Nothing more can be done. No more can be added. His death is perfect. There is no more you can say. Here you see God's word for man. The height and the depth. The dreadful evil that is man also. The truth about ourselves. He bowed his head and gave up his spirit. Part of that perfection is faith and trust. In death, Jesus surrenders himself to God and gives himself to you. This is the mystery that Paul so often leads us to. We come not to mourn the passing of the Lord but to receive life. We come to catch the meaning of life. So this is an event in which we are baptised in Christ Jesus.'

The canon's bleak, pithy sentences seemed of a piece with the place; of a piece with the scaffolding and the polythene; of a piece with the bone-crushing cold and the way that the normal ornate silver cross on the altar had been replaced by a wooden cross so that we could remember the original one, rough-hewn and full of splinters. Everything about the service had been so taut and so shorn of anything that might cheer and comfort us that it might even have pleased old Etheldreda herself, might even have put a smile on the beautiful serious lips of that ice queen whose cold, autocratic eye clearly still reigns over her building.

No one greeted the members of the congregation on their way out, though there was a man collecting money.

In a state approaching despair, I jumped on my bike and cycled down to the river where two swans, their necks like great white question marks, were swimming together near a marina called Babylon. A man poked his head out of a hatch and shouted something at me. Later I was nosing around a cemetery where I found a huge mountain of flowers, all dead and rotten except for the giant white lilies. So what was the secret of the lilies? The secret of the lilies, it turned out on closer inspection, was that they were all plastic.

The rain was sheeting down in rods as I struggled against the icy shotgun blasts of the Fen blows along the road to Downham Market and, in time, to Walsingham. Pylons trooped through the rain mists and, in the ditches, pampas grass with forlorn black beards whipped the winds. I picked up that mysterious trail of carrots again and came across numerous corpses of flattened frogs. It was still spring. It was still the time of mass migrations and the endless fornication of frogs.

It was this steady northerly wind that was the greatest cause of my misery and I recalled that old Gaelic blessing:

May the roads rise with you
And the winds be always at your back
And may the Lord hold you in the hollow of his
  hand.

No winds at my back out here. Just a steady pounding against my face and chest like some enraged boxer ready and willing to flail away forever. Just a recurring sense of misery that I was away from my home and new baby, out in the freezing rain, depressed with the sheer unendurable effort of starting a new book, hardly able to understand what I was up to, as usual, again.

Yet Ely Cathedral was still haunting parts of my mind, still rearing up and over me like some enfolding nightmare from which there was no escape. The pillars and shimmering tower of light had come back to me in a series of dissolving dreams, almost as if Etheldreda was trying to say something about herself as I turned my back on her, almost as if she was pointing out that I had made a very big mistake indeed in writing off her house as a cobwebbed tourist shrine.

You do not understand the allure of the ice queen of the Fens then? You do not understand that there is life as well as death in my house? Never forget that like the scorpion I can still lash out and sting you dead. Never forget that I reign over ice.

These mute naggings came to me in wordless, slightly corrosive questions. Was Etheldreda out there in those great billowing rain clouds? Was it her power over ice that was making my hands turn red-raw and my face sting with the cold? Was it her hands that were clutching at my throat and making my chest ache with the pain of her frost? Two lorries roared past, sending buckets of rain over me and making me stop and get off my bike, head bowed low and bones frozen to the marrow, crying out loud for her to stop tormenting me.

The rain stopped for a while and I got back on my bike. Occasionally I spotted the odd farmer going about his work, his farmyard jobs as hard and elemental as the land itself which, together with all these swirling skies, shaped the very rhythm of the Fen days.

The road was curiously empty for this time of year – just the odd car and certainly no one on foot or bicycle. In medieval times, Easter on the road to Walsingham would have presented a very different picture: gripped by fantastic religious spasms, whole armies of people would have been moving along this road at this, the beginning of the pilgrimage season.

The scene is easy to imagine. There would be pilgrims living by alms, mendicants and friars, labourers revolting against the soil and minstrels out to soothe the blistered and weary with their songs. There would be quacks telling of cures from the kiss of vipers and drug-sellers with balms for piles and worms. Peasants out of bond would be scurrying along with falcons and mummers. Tumblers would mix with pardoners selling indulgences which gave time off in hell. And sprinkled through all this would be a whole rabble of clippers of coin, robbers crouching in ditch or coppice, bear-baiters, shipmen pretending losses at sea and singers of bawdy songs.

They would have been on a ceaseless ramble with their screaming children and creaking carts; some seeking to honour vows made in illness and others seeking to square the debt of a terrible sin; some enjoying the merriment of the road and others merely wanting to get up the nose of the king. But whatever their individual motives they all, in their own ways, were brought together in the one common act of pilgrimage insofar as they were all seeking out the guiding, healing, protecting powers of God.

But this morning, with the land all around waiting for the first reviving kiss of summer, no one was going anywhere. Down on the junction to the road to Downham Market a gypsy caravan stood on a grass verge surrounded by a couple of clapped-out cars and a small mountain of decrepit washing machines.

I took lunch in Downham Market. There was a time when the place's only claim to fame was when a local boy came second in the world stock car championships but all that changed in a great explosion of trouble and publicity back in 1975, when Father Oswald Baker of St Dominic's Church rejected all moves to reform in the Catholic Church and insisted that his flock was going to say Mass the way they had alway said it – the Tridentine way, in Latin.

News of this tiny enclave of ecclesiastical discontent echoed around the world. As a writer for the *Sunday Telegraph*, I was sent down here to interview Father Oswald. I found a burly, shy man with a head as bald as a billiard ball and much surprised by all this global fuss. Thousands of letters of support had poured in from all parts of the world and people were travelling up to seventy miles on a Sunday to attend his services. Surprised he may have been but contrite he wasn't in his defence of the traditional liturgy. 'The emphasis of the old Mass was always on sacrifice but, in the new, there is a shift of emphasis and it is more man-centred,' he told me at the time. 'We are in danger of losing the dignity, mystery and relevance of the traditional liturgy.'

He wasn't at home when I called to see him but one of the neighbours said he was still to be seen ghosting around the pavements, reading his Bible and never needing to look up as his feet negotiated the kerbs or corners.

The Church won the fight in the end by booting out Father Oswald but this splendid iconoclast, who rightly wanted nothing to do with the twentieth century and her habits, has now got his own little church just around the corner from the pub where, every Sunday, they still say Mass as they have always said it – the Tridentine way, in Latin.

My left knee was beginning to swell up and give me a lot of pain that afternoon as I cycled past black empty fields towards King's Lynn. Everything seemed banged down by a great fist of grey; rain clouds were piling up on the horizon again. I passed a bricked-up chapel. Was Etheldreda still around and personally escorting me off her property?

Just then something huge and flashily bright began twisting around the middle of the rain clouds. It turned those banked masses from black to grey to yellow and then the winds began shunting them around. Lo and behold there suddenly appeared a massive shimmer of sun; a sort of golden downpour came swarming through a big blue gap in the lightening clouds, singing a hymn of renewal as it drenched everything with a brilliant warmth.

I freewheeled down a hill and, as I passed under the archway of the old walled ramparts of King's Lynn, the sunshine was rolling fantastic golden hoops along the curving streets, dancing up against the shop windows and leaping from rooftop to rooftop, making the whole town glitter like something magical as promises of the coming summer were whispered loud down every lane and around every corner.

King's Lynn is an important centre for pilgrimage since it was here, on the mouth of the river Ouse, that many thousands of pilgrims from overseas embarked *en route* to Walsingham. It still has its own wayside chapel where pilgrims would stop to offer up prayers for a safe journey, and it was also the home of one Margery Kempe, a nutty mystic whose extraordinary life, back in the fourteenth century, was in itself one long pilgrimage which she wrote about in *The Book of Margery Kempe*. She visited Canterbury and Compostela and even accomplished the Holy Grail of every pilgrim: a visit to the Holy Land itself at a time when it was an extremely arduous journey involving taking a ship from Italy to Damietta in Egypt then travelling by camel across the Sinai desert to Jerusalem before coming back by way of Crete, Cyprus or Rome.

A proto-feminist who frequently made life very difficult for any men in her vicinity, Margery Kempe had one great shout of Franciscan joy in her personality. She could also be a pain in the neck. One contemporary wrote: 'A prolonged and violent shriek broke from her lips at the sight of anything holy.'

I passed her birthplace, gulls wheeling overhead, laughing their thin rackety cries as I pedalled painfully along in search of a bed. A lot is made of the beauty of King's Lynn – usually by those from King's Lynn – but I could not see it. Some of the streets, it is true, drip with a medieval charm but there is too much of the new piled cheek by jowl with the old. Warehouses rub shoulders with old churches. Factory buildings brush up against cobbled squares. Indeed the place does not seem to have a coherent personality at all, a little like Margery Kempe, perhaps.

Two pilgrims, come to pay homage to Our Lady of Walsingham, take a rest.

The next morning I cycled out past the wire fences of an industrial estate on the outskirts of the town and, quite soon, picked up that mysterious orange trail of half-eaten carrots again. After the ironed flatness of the Fens, the land out here rolled and sloped in an emphatic way, the fields dotted with cows and fenced around by meandering hawthorn hedgerows which rattled in the breeze.

The swelling in my knee had gone down and, for the first time since I had left home, I was beginning to feel a little chirpy. Old Celtic beliefs taught that, on Easter Day, the sun always danced for joy. Well, the sun was not dancing for joy, but she was certainly winking down through the clouds in great good humour as I bowled along towards Walsingham.

Out in the stubble, pheasants – so common here they are known as Norfolk sparrows – ducked their heads when they heard the thin squeaks of my bike. When I stopped to look at them their heads disappeared altogether, doubtless prompted by some primordial memory of once having them blown off by a shotgun. Later I saw a fox feathering across a field and a meadow choked with daffodils, their trumpets golden blazes in their avid embrace with the sun.

Gardens too were beginning to burst with the first emblems of spring – the delicate yellow avalanches of forsythia, the perfumed curls of the hyacinth and the first pink shivers of blossom on the trees. Clearly Spring was winding herself up to begin striding down over the land – what better time to travel to Walsingham, one of the greatest shrines in all Christendom, to celebrate the death and resurrection of the Lord?

Walsingham attracts two hundred and fifty thousand pilgrims a year, with thirty thousand of them staying overnight. My first impression, when I finally coasted down into the village square, was that they had all decided to pitch up on the same day. The tiny streets were absolutely jam-packed with pilgrims, all wearing their widest smiles and promenading around arm in arm. They gathered on every corner and hung around every lamp-post while nuns skittered through them with their elbows flashing and shoulders jerking back and forth in the I've-got-work-to-do-even-if-you-haven't way that nuns often have.

I signed into the Pilgrim Centre – a positive beehive of fire-doors and spartan dormitories – and soon discovered that the main cause of my impression of a place about to burst under the weight of its own jollity was Student Cross:

a crowd of more than two hundred students of doubtful sanity who, as part of the Easter celebration, had formed into groups from Nottingham, Leicester, Kettering, Oxford, Colchester and London and *walked* to Walsingham on a journey lasting seven days, each group carrying a life-size wooden cross.

It appeared that the people of Norfolk always knew that Easter had begun when they spotted such hymn-singing gangs stumbling past their doors as they shouldered their great crosses over the landscape. Even in the pouring rain it was said to be an extraordinarily uplifting sight as they trooped down into Walsingham, sodden and yet still singing, taking it in turns to carry the cross a few more yards towards their goal.

I located some of these modern pilgrims in a cafe where they were all sprawled around a single cup of tea, many with their arms around one another. They treated their journey, they explained, as a sort of walking retreat, a period of suffering and denial, a sharing of insights and bidding prayers, ending up in a time of joyful celebration here in Walsingham.

After a service in the morning they set off to cover some twenty miles each day, resting at various stations when they might hear a talk from the local vicar or, as on last Maundy Thursday, have their feet washed by chaplains. After a few hours in a pub they slept – died? – on the floors of church halls. 'We like to get through about eight pints a day or else a firkin a week,' one offered. 'Beer keeps you going.'

Pilgrimage being a sort of communal activity, they often flung their arms around one another for a huge cuddle or a lot of shouting. They might massage one another's feet or legs or merely sit around fondling one another's knees. This was called a grundle. 'Grundles were of great help in keeping us on the road,' said Marion Taylor, black-eyed student from London. 'They're just marvellous when you're feeling achey and there's nothing at all sexual about them.'

When they finally made it to Walsingham – this year in a week of continual rain – they were all, according to one, singing joyful hymns and weeping more than the rain clouds. The whole operation had a quality of beautiful madness about it which, I said, rather made my own bicycle pilgrimage, sans cross, seem very puny indeed.

Bicycles, said one cross-bearer. Now that was interesting. Did I know that the local Catholic priest in charge of the Slipper Chapel, Father Clive Birch, had one which, incredibly, had been personally blessed by the Pope? I couldn't believe it but, bad knee or not, in a flash I was up and hobbling off after Father Birch to check this extraordinary story.

I finally tracked him down in the refectory of the Pilgrim Centre. He was an ample, bearded man who seemed to be suffering from some sort of enfeebling wound. I could not quite decide why I thought this, since he did sometimes suffer from outbreaks of mirth. But even when chuckling, his aura of melancholy still did not seem to go away. Perhaps it was the strain of dealing with the thousands of pilgrims who flock here each year looking for their spiritual highs or perhaps it was something else altogether but, in any event, as he sipped his tea with great care, he sketched out the history of Walsingham and how he had ended up the custodian of a bicycle which had been personally blessed by the Pope.

The history of the village, he said, went back to 1061 when a Lady Racheldis had a vision in which the Virgin Mary asked that a shrine should be built here which would be a replica of the holy house in Nazareth. After much meditation and prayer a simple wooden house was built and, later, a priory which, for popularity and importance with pilgrims, soon took over from Canterbury. The shrine was destroyed by Henry VIII, who took away the statue of Our Lady and had it publicly burned in London. The priory was also pulled down and, for several centuries, any devotion to Mary was outlawed and nothing happened here.

The Oxford Movement led to an upsurge of interest in the village and the tiny Slipper Chapel – where pilgrims took off their shoes to walk the last mile barefoot into Walsingham and which had thankfully been left intact – fell into Catholic hands. In 1934 it was declared the national shrine of Our Lady. The Anglicans established their own shrine too and, each year now, the number of visitors is rising so much, and interest in the shrines is such, that the place was booked solid every weekend for the next two years.

What about the bicycle? I asked him. It turned out that one of the Pope's mates ran a cycling club in Rome. One year, he suggested that they both send off a bike to Fatimah. Quite why they decided this is unclear but, nevertheless, a bike was despatched to Fatimah and, the next year, it was suggested that they send another to Walsingham. Sure enough, John-Paul II duly blessed the bike in St Peter's Square and it was ridden to Walsingham where it remained while all scratched their heads about what to do with it. 'Just what do you do with a bike blessed by the Pope?' asked Father Birch. It puzzled me. 'We finally decided to put it up for raffle to raise funds for the Slipper Chapel,' he went on.

When I began showing what might have been construed as an absurdly inflated interest in what was, after all, only a bike I noticed that Father Birch began dissembling and getting very protective, even secretive about his sacred two-wheeler. And when I asked if I could possibly have a ride on the thing he became even more protective and secretive and gave vent to a fair bit of umming and aahing.

It would be no trouble, I said. I'd just call on him wherever he kept the Pope's bike, at any time of his choosing.

Ah no, he said, relenting a bit. He would bring it here to the refectory, first thing in the morning. After all, if I knew where it was stored, I might try and pinch it.

I was sure I would not endanger my immortal soul by

trying to pinch the Pope's bike but I was later to learn that someone had already risked his by pinching the leather saddle and replacing it with a plastic one; a crime which, I guessed, warranted a very long time indeed in the burning pit.

That evening a gang of us trooped out of Walsingham for a communion service in the Chapel of Reconciliation, the new Catholic church built next to the old Slipper Chapel. It was a warm, dark night, full with the sounds of a chuckling river and creaking tree trunks. Bare branches waved over our heads like poised whips and something small, black and squealing with fright dashed across the road in front of us.

Appropriately millions of stars were smashed all across the sky, like vast scatterings of powdered glass. The Milky Way was once known as the Walsingham Way – partly because it became associated with Our Lady's milk and also because, at night, it illuminated the lanes and directed the pilgrims who were journeying to this blessed spot.

I left the group and went into the Slipper Chapel alone, finding it to be a sort of stone-built crypt with a few pews and a prayer on the altar: 'That we may be one.' Just next to the altar was a glimmering bank of votive candles, shivering bright in the draught and with curling wisps of black smoke. I find flickering flames of candles are very evocative. They continue our prayers even after we have finished them and there is something deeply pure in the tiny heart of those yellow flames; something which draws your face into them, like a moth bent on self-immolation perhaps, as their warmth strokes your cheeks and you ponder on the souls of all those millions of pilgrims who have come and gone; those who also lit candles here before taking off their shoes and walking the last mile to the village, heady with things felt but not seen, beautiful with

Once Walsingham's priory exceeded Canterbury in its popularity with pilgrims. Now its landlord does not always care to open the ruins to the public.

a prayerful heart as they held out their hands to receive the blessings of Our Ladye of Walsingham.

A German choir, dressed in smart blue coats and dicky bows, had joined us for the communion service in the Chapel of Reconciliation, with its modern circular structure designed of red brick and polished wood. It turned out to be one of those very beautiful services that makes your heart go hang-gliding and you wish would go on forever. Their guide, a Welshman, read from St Paul's letter to the Colossians. Then the German choir sang their hymns of love with a blissful relish and, clearly inspired by their carolling ease, the congregation followed their lead, weaving harmonies with their harmonies until one suspected the very walls might collapse before the swelling beauty of the hymns.

Thine be the glory, risen, conquering Son,
Endless is the victory Thou o'er death hast won;
Angels in bright raiment rolled the stone away,
Kept the folded grave-clothes, where Thy body lay.

'One of the most telling evidences of the truth of the resurrection is the change of attitude of the apostles,' Father Birch said in his sermon. 'They went from gloom to despair to overwhelming hope. The resurrection of Jesus brings us living hope. The Lord has risen and lives forever. The Lord came to bring us life. Christians ought to be the most joyful as we live in the hope of resurrection.'

Everyone was invited to embrace and shake hands before taking communion. 'It is a matter of regret,' said one priest, 'that we are forbidden by law to give communion to any other than Catholics.'

It was the one sour note in an otherwise fine evening. Here we all were, at a time when unity was at the heart of most prayers, in a village where Anglican and Catholic leaders had taken thousands of their followers to each other's shrines, in a building where a congregation had worshipped, beautifully, together and still the black lunatic hand of a centuries-old schism was hanging over us like some dark demon that had managed to wriggle out of Martin Luther's grave.

All any sane Christian wants is to kneel together before one God but still there are Church leaders, with their doctrinal blinkers and tupenny ha'penny visions, determined that we should stay apart and suspicious of one another. Even those glorious students who had spent a week shouldering their crosses together all those hundreds of miles could not now take communion together in Walsingham. How this separation must cause grief to a God who has already suffered much. A church at war with itself is a church at war with God. A church which fails to live together will die apart – as it is doing now, little by little, throughout the land.

It was not long, however, before I resolved the problem about communion by taking it wherever it became available on my pilgrimages. No one was, after all, going to produce a lie detector before giving me the wafer and the wine and I anyway resolved to enjoy the different denominations wherever I found them. I was going to be my own tiny instrument of the Church's healing.

And so it turned out as I bumbled around the country taking communion from hands young and hands gnarled; sipping wine sweet and wine sour; listening to benedictions soft and benedictions harsh; enjoying my own prayer life without getting angry and bogged down in the dog days of some old bishop's bigotry.

Later that night the pubs in Walsingham were full to bursting as the more secular songs of the German choir competed with the clink of beer glasses and the buzz of bar talk. Priests in habits sat supping with the local workmen; students laughed the froth off their pints among fat old ladies with ruddy faces and flabby Guinness muscles.

The demon drink has clearly found a leading role for itself in the pilgrimage play. Indeed, the landlord of the Pilgrim Bar told me that he even had to ban one visiting priest after he persistently became drunk and disorderly. 'I warned him again and again,' he explained. 'Then I banned him.'

There is nothing wrong with a Christian taking a drink, of course. Nowhere in the Bible does Jesus ask for a cup of tea or a can of Coca-Cola. His very first miracle was to change water into wine and, when the wine ran out, he made some more.

The next morning I went down to the refectory for a ride on the Pope's bike. It turned out to be a super lightweight Dezzi with racing handlebars, Columbus tubing and Zeus brakes. Father Birch allowed me to ride on it, too, and it was stupendous – as light as a leaf and as finely tuned in all her parts as an athlete in the peak of fitness. You hardly had to pedal it, unlike my rumbling warhorse, sold to me by someone who said he was a friend and which I was planning to abandon as soon as possible before it finished me off.

I noticed Father Birch's hands twirling with anxiety as I circled around and around the refectory. He was clearly not going to let me take it out on the road or, miracle of miracles, let me finish my Easter pilgrimage on it. But there was still some, if tiny, hope, and I bought a big pile of raffle tickets for the bike. With some luck, I might even have got to do chapter seven on it.

I spent the next few days wandering around Walsingham, learning much of its past and present while finding it a most agreeable hotch-potch of a place, populated by people both prayerful and eccentric. It has three pubs in which it is easy to get involved in wonderful rambling conversations about God. It has cafes for sipping tea and eating cream

*The very stuff of a
modern pilgrimage – along
with beer.*

cakes; a ruined priory owned by a reclusive landlord who
does not like to open it to the public; a batch of women
who pray for the sick of the world on a regular basis; several
shops selling gaudy devotional items and smack in the
middle of all this, at odds with everything, an Indonesian
restaurant selling sateh and rice wine.

There is a saying that when England returns to Walsingham, Our Lady will come back to England. Soon,
though, there will be no room for anyone; the Brotherhood
of the Russian Church in Exile has taken over the railway
station and the Sisters of Jesus have their own tiny church
in a flag-stoned cottage just up the hill.

One of my favourite places was the old court room
which had been turned into a museum. It is a small wooden
room with severe benches and a prisoner's lock-up complete with barred window and a grille. In the cell itself there
is a pallet of bull-rushes which served as a mattress and
must have been murder to sleep on. There was something
quite shivery about the whole place, evocative as it was of
the Georgian era – not of its elegance, but of its vigour,
discomfort and harshness. Records on the walls showed
that, in 1833, a man was sentenced to seven years transpor-
tation for stealing six hens. A five-year-old boy was given
seven days in prison for stealing a box.

Again and again I returned to the Anglican shrine which
surrounds a replica of the original holy house seen in the
vision of Racheldis. The irony here is that the Anglican
clergy are far more Catholic than the Catholics themselves
with their smells and bells, crossings and kissings, chasubles
and surplices. The atmosphere of the shrine is somehow
more medieval too in its shadowy smallness, in its baroque
ornamentation and drifting aroma of incense, in the
shadows of a hundred flickering candles.

It is built over a well with a small iron gate and stone
stairs leading down to the water. Outside in the garden,
the Way of the Cross has been set up along with replicas
of the hill of Calvary and of the Holy Sepulchre. But it is

to the holy well that the sick and the lame come with the one prayer on their lips: 'Lord, they whom thou lovest are sick.'

Here I saw an old lady with parchment skin, her trembling fingers twisted by arthritis, kneel by the well whence water was taken out by a long silver spoon. Her forehead was marked with a cross and she drank the water which was then poured over her hands. Just behind me there were small wooden plaques thanking Our Lady of Walsingham for help with matters as diverse as the solving of money problems, the restoration of sight, the cure of throat cancer and the treatment of brain damage.

The restoration of health has always been central to the notion of pilgrimage and, ever since this wooden shrine was first built, there have been records of many miraculous cures and remarkable answers to prayer. Contemporary chroniclers have told of the lame being made whole, the blind being able to see again and, according to one ballad, even the dead being brought back to life:

Many seke ben here cured by our laye's myghte
Dede agayne revyved of this no dought . . .

There is a story of how one Norfolk knight, Sir Ralph Boutefourt, was being pursued on horseback by his many enemies. Invoking the name of Our Lady of Walsingham, he found himself transported miraculously to the priory grounds and safety. That ironic scholar, Erasmus, visited Walsingham in 1511, just before Dissolution, and in his *Colloquy* was very sceptical of this story. He goes on to describe how the sick came here seeking the chapel where they could kiss the finger bone of St Peter – *for a fee*. He also found that the custodians of the shrine were boasting that they had a crystal containing Our Lady's milk. 'As soon as the Canon in attendance saw us he rose, put on his surplice, added the stole to his neck, prostrated himself with due ceremony, and worshipped: anon he stretched forth the thrice Holy Milk to be kissed by us. On this we also, on the lowest step of the altar, religiously fell prostrate . . .'

Seeing that old lady, with her arthritic hands and mumbling prayers, I thought of beady old Erasmus standing here with a smile curling on the corners of his lips. I thought of others too who, like Erasmus, came to mock and stayed to pray. I thought of the thousands and thousands who had come to this well muttering the same prayer: 'Lord, they whom thou lovest are sick.' Kings and queens, beggars and saints, housewives and vicars, seamen and soldiers – all of them coming to this strange little village and falling 'religiously prostrate'; all stretching out their hands and looking for healing from Our Lady of Walsingham.

Something had gone badly wrong with my own pilgrimage, however, since I had set out from London in perfectly good health and had now got a very bad cold and was hobbling around the place with a swollen knee. It reminded me of the mordant story of those two pilgrims who set out for Canterbury in good health and then returned with incurable diseases.

On my last evening in Walsingham a tiny group of us went to the small cottage of the Sisters of Jesus for communion, and a wonderfully pleasant evening it was with one of the sisters playing a guitar and singing as sweetly as a dozen nightingales. The trouble was that all of us, without exception, were snuffling and sneezing with colds. 'Here we are at the time of the resurrection and here we all are full up with germs,' said Father Birch, reaching for a tissue.

Afterwards the sisters treated us to tea and crumbly chocolate cake and the one with the nightingale voice said that, during the week, she packed carrots for Tesco's.

'Did you know that there is an Our Lady of Tesco's?' asked Father Birch.

I did not.

He explained that they were building a supermarket in

'In medieval times, whole armies of people would move along the road to Walsingham – mendicants and minstrels, clippers of coin, tumblers and pardoners.'

Ipswich and found the remains of some holy shrine. 'They preserved what they could and it's now called Our Lady of Tesco's.'

It was a lovely little story, I thought. Perhaps I had better make a special pilgrimage to Ipswich to find out what it was all about. Was it a little grotto surrounded by special offers?

Next morning, and it was time for me to go. Charabancs were disgorging more pilgrims on to the grey damp streets. This lot gloried in the title of the Twelve Apostles of Leigh which, one explained, was a Catholic club from just outside Manchester. 'We've come 'ere for week so it's services in t'morning then back 'ere for a bit of jugging,' he explained. 'Off to t'beaches wi' t'kids in t'afternoon an' back 'ere for a bit more jugging.'

They clearly set about this splendid mixture of prayer, fun and drink with great flair, too. No sooner had they got off their charabancs than they were forming up into a huge crocodile in the middle of the road with four men carrying a monstrance, the others holding their rosaries, a man chanting the Aves: *Hail Mary full of grace for the Lord is with thee* . . .

Then with a stumbling lurch they moved off for the mile walk to the Slipper Chapel. *Blessed art thou amongst women and blessed is* . . .

With my knee still badly swollen I was forced to leave my bike behind, and carried on to Norwich by bus. *Welcome to Norwich, a fine city*, is the self-confident boast on the sign on the city boundary. I soon saw that this was not an empty slogan drummed up by the local tourist office. Here was a very fine city indeed, with its higgledy-piggledy streets and twisting alleyways, its waterways with launches chugging slowly around the bends, its sleek leggy girls and crusty colonels in tweeds with angry bulging eyes and that sprawling market place where the stalls are scattered beneath multi-coloured canvases like a medieval tent city.

It was the sight of a red bus going to somewhere with the enchanting name of Heartsease that immediately won me over to Norwich's side. This affection grew deeper as I meandered around the streets, sitting on stone walls and listening to its sounds, poking my head down lanes and sniffing its smells, finding the place bursting with old churches and lively shops.

The cathedral now attracts half a million visitors a year and I understood the pull of the place as soon as I stepped inside; the building, with its lightly coloured stone, is one ravishing bouquet of happiness and light. Everywhere the air was as clean and pure as a peal of bells. Where Ely Cathedral was a chilling tribute to a dark God of infinite mystery, Norwich was the scrubbed, flower-filled home of the patriarchal God of the Sunday School who chortles a lot and hands out sweets as he watches the children go off on a horse-drawn cart for their Whitsun treat.

It had magnificent cloisters for lounging around and dreaming in. The huge vaulted roof of the nave carried some two thousand gold bosses – some describing incidents in the Book of Revelation – which I studied with the aid of mirrors mounted on wheeled trolleys. Coloured shafts of light shivered radiantly in the great stained glass wheel of a window and an organ sent out notes fat and sweet enough to make an angel weep.

As I wandered around I suppose it was the sheer love and care that had been poured into the place that captured me. Everywhere there were sprays of daffodils and forsythia and, just near the altar, a magnolia tree. The golden organ, which sat in the middle of the nave, looked as if it had just been buffed with a thousand tins of Brasso. I could have unwrapped my sandwiches and eaten them off the floor and there would not have been a speck of dirt on them.

Yet the real enchantment of such a place is being able to nose around for hours and even days and still not understand it all; still be left with the suspicion that you have missed something vitally important in the flamboyant tapestry of the cathedral's personality. But in such a place you do not set out to understand or even see everything; you just sort of mooch about quietly, now and then stopping to marvel at those great soaring arches built with not a care to cost or practicality; at the cascading stone walls and the distant secret galleries; at the delicate painted reredos and the large Easter banners hanging off the pillars. *Unto Us A Child Is Born. Peace With Love.*

Dotted among a lot of tombs on the floor near the altar I spotted the burial place of Herbert de Losiega, the founder of the cathedral. *You may not stand on this*, said a notice, though you did have to stand on the tomb of Mary, the wife of an ex-Dean, to read it, which seemed a bit tough on the memory of Mary.

Further on I found the Jesus Chapel, which formed a shrine to St William, a boy said to have been a victim of a Jewish ritual murder in the twelfth century. He is felt by many historians to occupy a key place in the rise of antisemitism. Young William was alleged to have been tortured, murdered and hung on a cross in 1144 by Jews in Thorpe Wood. The boy had done nothing noteworthy in his life but a cult grew up around him after his death. He was finally put under that glistening polished tombstone and many stories of miracles and visions subsequently ensued. People were said to have abandoned their crutches here while the mad became sane and monks threw holy water into the faces of the blind enabling them to see again. William was later canonised and his life was recorded in *The Life and Miracles of St William*.

The story of his murder, however, is rotten and improbable, and very likely fabricated – as were many yarns – for financial gain. Norwich never had a saint of its own and as saints meant pilgrims and pilgrims meant money

and money meant bigger buildings, then someone with a thing about the Jews and an eye on building a new chapel or two must have decided that such a legend was just the thing they needed.

In the treasury there was a lovely collection of communion chalices: it seemed it was once the practice to bring one's own glass for communion, at which vast amounts of wine were quaffed. I read how 'Bishop Wren ordered that, in future, no bottles or taverne pottes be brought to the communion rail.' I could not but smile at the thought of all those farmers and drovers coming here in happy anticipation of one big thrash of a communion. They are, after all, a singular bunch in this city. They had a quarrel with the Pope himself back in 1274 and that was only settled after they promised to build him a big stone gate, the Ethelbert Gate, as a token of contrition. Charles Wesley once complained that Norwich gave him more trouble than all the rest of England put together.

Out in the cathedral cloisters I found two punks sharing a cigarette. The boy had a lavatory brush hairstyle with a huge skull emblazoned on the back of his torn leather jacket though it was the girl who was the real harpy; she could easily have been stuck on the cathedral wall to double up as a gargoyle. Her fishnet stockings had large holes in them; her short leather skirt had a broken zip and her ragged jacket was daubed with swastikas. Some sort of studded bondage collar was wrapped around her throat too and her green and crimson hair stuck straight up as if she had just seen the ghost of Sid Vicious. The boy seemed quite taken with her though, perhaps proving that love really is blind, since they were sort of sniffing one another like a couple of dogs investigating each other's organs as well as taking it in turns to have a puff on the cigarette.

In the cathedral shop one of the assistants told me that the cathedral had been plagued by a string of thefts. They had even had the microphone stolen off the altar the other week. 'It goes in waves in the shop here,' she explained.

Norwich Cathedral: 'a ravishing bouquet of happiness and light.'

'One might chat you up while the other steals. It's the parents I blame.'

It was a sad yet recurring story. I was to find again and again on my modern pilgrimage that the authentic sound of holy shrines was no longer that of bells but of clanking locks. I was also to find that the thefts were a lot more serious than the loss of a microphone on the altar and that the dark hand of lawlessness was reaching into unimaginable areas.

Vandalism, I came to learn, is now affecting one building out of four in the Church of England alone. With three thousand insurance claims lodged each year with the Ecclesiastical Insurance Office, incidents range from alms boxes being broken open to serious cases of looting. At one ordination service in Chelmsford a missile came through a stained glass window while in St David's Cathedral, an old and valuable door stone – which might have been used by St David himself – had been stolen.

Lunch in Norwich was a despondent, lonely affair. I should have seen that there was something wrong with the Chinese restaurant by the way there was no one else sitting in it. The soup was so foul I half expected a monster with two big eyes to raise its head and look around, the tepid chop suey smelled much like my eldest son's socks. Resolving never to patronise a Chinese restaurant again, I left feeling as hungry as when I arrived and went off down the hill in search of the ghost of one of the greatest of all English mystics, Juliana of Norwich, who has also now become the patron saint of women in the Church of England.

Her visions of the revelation of Divine Love in Christ (1373) contain marvellous insights into the way the universe finds its unity in the love of God. In a vision God showed her a 'little thing, the size of a hazelnut, on the palm of my hand, round like a ball. I looked at it thoughtfully and wondered "What is this?" And the answer came, "It is all that is made." I marvelled that it continued to exist . . . It was so small . . .'

Juliana spent her life meditating on the meaning of her visions and became an anchorite in a cell next to the church of St Julian. Pilgrims could get indulgences just by looking her out but there were no indulgences to be had that afternoon; when I called, all the doors were locked and a ginger cat was snoozing peaceably in a warm splash of sun in the porch.

I went around the building, trying a few more doors and peering through windows. Then I noticed that a police patrol car had stopped in the road and a set of eyes beneath a peaked cap were staring at me. I smiled stupidly and hurried away, blushing.

At the railway station I checked out the time of the next train to London and, with an hour or so to spare, had a cup of tea and a bun in a converted Portakabin overlooking the river. The sun danced a magical gavotte on the foaming wakes of the launches; swans moved to one side as they swept past. Later I was crossing the station forecourt when something scrunched underfoot. I looked down; it was a half-eaten carrot.

TWO
'HALF CHURCH OF GOD,
HALF CASTLE 'GAINST THE SCOTS'

ESCOMB·DURHAM·BAMBURGH·LINDISFARNE

It was still early in the morning but already the sun was boiling the brains out of the land as our coach swept through the Durham countryside. Bright red puffs of poppies stood in the young silky green corn, the massed trumpets of the giant hogweed standing on the bank of a burn. Bits of gravel pinged on the metal underbelly of the coach and its engine roared lustily as the driver changed down before turning corner after corner.

We swept through yet another of those perfect Durhamshire stone villages where some children were playing hopscotch near an old church and a pair of naked feet were poking out of a window. What magical places these villages were with names that tugged at the heart like Spennymoor, Seldom Seen and Pity Me.

All week we had raced over sprawling moors and past pigeon lofts and allotments; we had climbed over ruined castles and been told tales of the giant Lambton worm; we had 'click' stops to photograph mournful Gothic ruins and coffee stops in strange villages where fluorescent bingo halls sat next to gilded curry palaces.

Everywhere the summer had begun to burst up out of the land, making the weeds and nettles come charging up out of the industrial litter of abandoned factories, sending warm cartwheels of sunshine rolling over the stepped mounds of the open-cast mines, dragging out the first of the leaves on the trees, energising the very soil and making everything as lusty as a new-born baby.

Today, on the sixth day of our pilgrimage around the holy spots of the North of England, we were going to Lindisfarne, Holy Island, tucked right up in the north-east corner. The gears growled low and loud again as the coach toiled up a savage slope.

We had all gathered the previous Sunday at Durham University, an unlikely collection of pilgrims for the most part. There were touches of the shires, the odd whiff of the holiday camp. We were not too poor and not too rich but mostly we seemed reasonably well educated. For the most part we had silver hair, thick legs and varicose veins. We wore sensible clothes with flat leather shoes. Now that we had lost the self-absorbed vanity of youth, we understood that beauty was a purely temporary gift. There was the odd gash of lipstick and the perfume was dabbed on the neck, more to create a noise than an alluring scent. We had put all that aside now.

We took lots of photographs with cheap cameras and were for ever telling little stories and laughing a lot unless someone tried to pinch our allotted seat on the coach when icicles froze our laughter and we stamped our feet and got very serious indeed.

We had a fair bit of religious conviction too and lots of us whiled away happy moments studying the shape of the church rafters or going down on our knees in prayer at the altar of some small Saxon church, mindful of the continuity of prayer of many thousands of people over the centuries. We were a mellow bunch, not given to postures, calm as people often are in the autumn of their lives, ready now for what was to come, a lot of us hopeful that we would soon be returning into the arms of husbands and wives we had buried years earlier.

Yes, that was about the way we were on that bus. We were happy and easy in our stained glass hours. We wanted to go, if that was all right, but we would stay if it wasn't. We just didn't want to make any sort of fuss.

We were not all pensioners on the bus, of course – or senior citizens, as horrid modern argot has it – even if we were claiming their financial advantages. One of our group was a tender twenty-six, an odd little fellow with thick black glasses and an upper lip which turned into a slight snarl, showing the joins on his false teeth. Somehow it all reminded you of a hungry rabbit about to demolish a giant lettuce. He was Geoffrey, and quite why Geoffrey had joined us was never quite clear. He evinced no spiritual interests; he saw such preoccupations as a definite sign of insanity. When we took off looking for churches, Geoffrey went collecting pub signs.

He had visited some two thousand differently named pubs by public transport; already that day he had bagged The Shepherd and Shepherdess. He had an almost encyclo-paedic knowledge of pubs which he was all too ready to ventilate before anyone foolish enough to ask.

The smallest pub in the land was The Nutshell in Suffolk; the pub with the longest name is The Thirteenth Mounted Cheshire Rifleman Inn and the shortest is C.B. in North Yorkshire. The commonest name is The Red Lion. People began to avoid Geoffrey very early on.

Our first stop of the week had been at Escomb to visit the Saxon church there, one of the oldest in Britain. Sunshine streamed through the yew leaves in the graveyard and the air was abuzz with midges and the thwack of tennis balls. Just near the porch I found a gravestone with a carving of a man smiling his head off on it. I told Jenny that I liked that very much and rather hoped to have something like it on mine. 'All things duly considered,' I wanted written on my tombstone, 'I would rather be down here than watching television.'

We also found gravestones with the skull and crossbones on them. Knowledgeable Jo explained that the skull and crossbones were traditionally supposed to show that death had been by plague or even that they had been robbers or pirates. This was not so. The skull and crossbones, she said, were thought to be the minimum that Gabriel needed to fix up our resurrection; they were the very symbol of hope to medieval people and were only later taken up by pirates. Jo knew everything and it was to her that we all scuttled when we needed something explained.

It was in that graveyard that I first noticed Walter examin-ing the trees. He had been levered out of his own garden to come on this trip so, while others looked at old things, Walter mooched about examining trees and shrubs, pulling them to one side and feeling their stems before nodding, satisfied, and, more often than not, taking his pipe out of his mouth and letting fall a long stream of spit.

The church itself was a sparse, witty structure in mismatching stones taken from the ruins of a local Roman fort. Outside there was a sundial on the wall with just three lines on it suggesting, thought Jo, that the monks were more concerned with the times of prayer than the exact hour of the day. Inside the church really did have the shorn piety of the age of Bede: simple whitewashed elegance, a spray of lilies next to the font. A New Testament was open at Romans 12: 'Adapt yourselves no longer to the pattern of the present world but let your minds be remade and your whole nature thus transformed.'

There were no windows on the north wall, the devil's wall, and, during christenings, the door was always left open to let the devil out. You could tell that the church was still deeply cherished from the polished pews and spotless stone floors. 'I love things that have been looked after,' said Pat. 'To me that's lovely.'

Today, on our journey to Lindisfarne, the sun was still climbing steadily up the back of the bluest sky. Gaudy lines of shivering lupins were marching down through the gardens of the old cottages, some smothered with roses and clematis. Everyone was chattering away happily with only the occasional interruption from the guide. 'We're just passing through Newcastle. This bypass was built by John Poulson.'

The chatter continued and I noticed, not for the first time, how incredibly well-travelled we all were; of how the conversation swung easily from the tulip fields of Holland to package tours of the Rhine; of how Venice was full of rip-off merchants and how they often charged an extra pound just to sit outside and drink a cup of coffee. One spoke of the incredible cost of toilets in Capri and how her husband had always promised to buy her a black frock and a toilet in Capri for her retirement. Madge recalled how difficult it was to climb the spire of Canterbury Cathedral while Jo had even been to Egypt but had found it 'hot and tiring' so she was going to stick to good old England from now on.

They were great travellers in the Middle Ages, of course, and coming along this road we would probably have been complaining of the high entry fees at Fontainebleau, the way they had let the abbey go at Maubuisson and the terrible state of the roads to Santiago de Compostela. We would have been travelling on horseback along a gravel track yet still wearing our finest clothes in all that heat with flies whizzing around the horses' rumps. We would have been covering about fifteen miles a day with a string of pack horses following behind with two iron-bound chariots which contained our personal effects, our food and beer. The house servants would have been whipping along the pack horses, mingling with the archers and savage watchdogs provided for our security. The uncouth archers would, as usual, be complaining of hangovers. I pictured myself as a rich and restless merchant, dogged by guilt and worried about the future of my soul. I would have been wearing a long tapestried cloak with a saint's tooth on a leather thong around my neck 'to protect me from thunder and lightning'.

As it was we were on a coach out of Durham, on a charter to Tate's Travel, twenty-nine of us – nineteen women and ten men – going at fifty miles an hour up a tarmacadam road with everyone laughing their socks off and coming now to the village of Felton. 'The sweet william flower came from here,' the guide said on the microphone. 'It was here that William gathered forces against the Scots under Bonnie Prince Charlie. Thereafter, in Scotland, the same flower was called the stinking billy.'

Everywhere we travelled we heard of the centuries-old

The River Wear at Durham, where a friend of Canon Smith fell out of his boat and was drowned. 'Had I not had the presence of mind to hit him on the head with my oar when he tried to climb back in he would have capsized us,' the canon told the coroner.

quarrel between the English and the Scots. The tartan terrors had spread such fear they even prompted the Romans to build Hadrian's Wall to keep them out; in later years, an order came down that 'all havens should be fenced with bulwarkes and bloke houses against the Scots'. Churches had to double up as fortresses in which the women and cattle could be hidden when the boys came down intent on a spot of looting and raping. Some of them still had their arrow slits.

In Chester-le-Street, we were told that, until recently, there had been a ball game in which the whole village had taken part, kicking one ball around, stemming from the time when knights had kicked around the heads of Scottish invaders. Sir Walter Scott had described Durham as 'Half church of God, half castle 'gainst the Scots'.

One night in Durham our group was lectured by a splendid old Welshman, C. W. Gibby, a retired professor of history with silver hair and steely blue eyes. He had left West Wales many years ago in search of work and ended up here. He told us of the warring factions of the Saxons, Angles, Jutes, Danes and Norwegians who had all come here to see what they could rob after the Romans packed up; of how Durham became a base for operations against the Scots and the rules of the old Prince Bishops, with their awesome concentrations of military and ecclesiastical power.

He also told some lovely stories about the local characters, too. Of Canon Samuel Smith – otherwise known as 'Peace of Mind Smith' – who, when in a boat, saw a friend of his fall into the water. 'Had I not had the presence of mind to hit him on the head with my oar when he tried to climb back into the boat he would have capsized us,' he later told the coroner.

He also told us of the local preacher who was so boring he fell asleep in the middle of his own sermon.

We had a 'click' stop at Walworth Castle – 'painted by Turner and written about by Shakespeare,' said our guide – before driving on past sloping fields and a languid sea. Just off the coast sat the Farne Islands, dull brown in drifting white, immobile in the plashy waves, as mysterious as the sea mists that drifted over them. A flock of oyster-catchers wheeled overhead, their beaks shrieking with bad news as their bellies glinted as if on fire in the still rising sun. A water tower sat on the horizon like a giant black mushroom. It was going to be a boiler for certain, though way out on the horizon, some grey-black clouds were piling up with the promise of a few cooling spits.

The lunch stop was at Bamburgh. Even before the driver had switched off the ignition, many of us were already

*Three by three on
Lindisfarne.*

Even as we alighted I noticed again that we did not
cohere as a group; that no one stood around waiting for
someone else to take the lead. The whole lot split up
immediately like a school class dismissed at the end of the
day, with each person chasing off after whatever pleased
them. This decisive independence had been born out of
long periods of loneliness, perhaps, since I was certain that
a lot of us were lonely. The young cover up their loneliness
with endless chatter and jungle music but, sometimes, I
caught one of our lot standing in the corner of a graveyard,
dusting an invisible tear away from the corner of her eye
with her fingertip as her body was mauled by a lovely
memory, perhaps, of a time hand in hand with a loved one.

There were couples, of course, like Danny and Anne or
Walter and Pat. I must say that I know of nothing more
fabulous – in an age when relationships everywhere are
fracturing – than following Walter and Pat, with some
160 years between the two of them, as I did that day in
Bamburgh, as they tootled along the pavement, arm in
arm, quietly fussing over one another.

'Ee Walter I do hope they've got real milk with the tea
in this cafe.'

'They'll have some, lass. Stop worrying will you?'

'It's daft, I know, but I just can't drink tea without real
milk.'

Some went straight into the cafe but most of us wandered
on up the road to St Aidan's Church, the site of the
death of Aidan, the stag, the first apostle of Christianity in
England. The shadows of those great saints of old fell across
my path again and again that year. In Aidan's story, we
have the perfect example of one such man, ushered into a
confused age by God to set up a communion of saints and
an age of scholarship, and, in so doing, to save the world
at a time when Rome had fallen and all certainties had
broken apart.

Aidan was first sent here from the island of Iona by St
Columba, and the Northumbrian king, King Oswald,

standing up in the aisle wanting to stomp up the hill 'to do'
the castle before eating. It was extraordinary, I thought,
the way some so old became young again; the way they
were happy to tackle the biggest slopes while the rest of us
were rather more content to stick to the flatlands and quiet
little hobbles, sucking a lollipop. We weren't all bursting
with energy. The hardcore always waited for the rest to
get off the bus before they stood up.

'What I've always said is never stand up when you can
sit down,' said Stan. 'And never sit down when you can
lie down.'

made him the first bishop of Lindisfarne. From this island retreat he journeyed on foot, far and wide through Northumbria, across marsh and meadow, often through thorns and stones, everywhere reciting psalms, reading the Bible and preaching the wild word of God.

A model of moral probity, his method (and that of his followers) was to teach by the example of their goodness and gentleness; by the sacrifice of all luxury. They preached into the teeth of a hurricane of violence and their mission was to heal. Their prayers were to quench the fires of the repeated Danish invasions.

King Oswald died and the next king, King Oswin, gave Aidan a fine horse on which to make his travels. Aidan immediately gave it to a beggar. The infuriated king asked him if he could not find a less valuable horse to give away but Aidan replied merely by asking the king whether the child of a mare was more important than a child of God. Nevertheless the two became great friends and, when the king was murdered, Aidan was shattered with grief and died of a broken heart, here in Bamburgh, twelve days later.

It had been a glorious summer day, just like this, when he died but that night the sky turned black at the edges and there was a fury in it. A great beam of light shone down through the fury and a crowd of angels climbed down it, as if it were a ladder. At the foot of the ladder the angels picked up Aidan's soul and carried it up to heaven. This great metaphysical retrieval was witnessed, in a vision, by a seventeen-year-old boy who had been out looking after his sheep on those low hills that night. He went straight to the nearest monastery at Melrose – a sister house of Lindisfarne – and became a monk. Which was how, in 651, St Cuthbert entered our journey.

On one side of St Aidan's Church was the rolling moorland of the Budle Hills, with the waves of the sea swelling lazily on the other. The church itself was captivating in its spacious simplicity. Down near the altar, a group of us

The causeway at Lindisfarne: 'a clear promise of holiness.'

fussed around looking for the squint through which lepers were once allowed to watch the services. Here, though, the squint was merely for members of the congregation sitting on the sides.

There were ornate screens on the altar. 'Typical bit of late Victorian that,' said Jo. 'They had such a high opinion of themselves.' A sundial was carved on the north wall of the southern chamber of the crypt, where St Aidan was buried, supposedly recording the hour of his death at 3 p.m. on August 31. Barbara spotted the lancet window which could have supplied the sunshine. Also in the crypt was a suspended lantern containing a silver cross and a shining light, serving as a memorial shrine to St Aidan. As we were walking away I noticed Madge slip back to the shrine where, alone, she went down on her knees at the prayer stall to say a few words to the old apostle.

After Bamburgh the land became flatter with sparse lonely trees, hunched down against the bitter North Sea winds, when I caught sight of Lindisfarne castle, vivid and alluring, poking up above the sunken contours. It disappeared and came back again, a big and bold sort of fairy castle with sharp black lines which sprang out of the rock in such a way that the castle and rock seemed one and the same.

We turned off the main road and down a cow parsleyed lane where there were curling trails of tractors in the young green corn. A chattering helicopter was swooping back and forth spraying the crops.

Big black-faced gulls swooped overhead when we came down to the causeway and the road which was to take us to the island. This causeway always has an enchantment about it – especially when you are part of a group of fellow pilgrims. I had gone back to this spot three times that year and the aspect had never ceased to amaze, not because of

its spectacular view but because of its clear promise of holiness. It was here that I made my first real discovery about holiness since such islands have it in abundance, which was why those saints of old sought out such places.

Islands mediate the concept of holiness to us. They are one, whole, apart. They are places of pure solitude where man alone may seek out and attempt to understand the nature of the mystery. The sea all around is the very material of God – the way of baptism, regeneration and faith; the waters in which we must be born again. To such islands the soul might return at the end of life.

Yes, there's a powerful, dreaming holiness around Lindisfarne. It drifts through the great sea winds, through those wide stretches of sand dotted by pools and the curling mounds of the lugworm. You can hear it even in the fluting calls of the sandpipers, in the flapping wings of the stork pinning a beautiful arc of flight against the clear sky and the low distant roar of the incoming tide.

But, most of all, holiness is not suggested by a great edifice which had taken hundreds of years and thousands of lives to build. Here, on Lindisfarne, it is etched across our minds by the line of old, broken sticks stretching across the sands to mark out Pilgrim's Way. Holiness is always best expressed by the simple, the humble and the poor. And here those sticks sing a song of holiness to the sea winds; they surround the journeying pilgrim with the very music of the Cross as he makes his way across the softly sinking sand to Holy Island itself.

Even in the pouring rain the island can look ravishing though, that day, it looked particularly magical. The sun burnished the huge pools dotted around the causeway, goslings moved through fiery yellow pools as children on the other side tumbled down the slopes of the sand dunes. About a dozen people were following the broken sticks of Pilgrim's Way.

'We are staying here for three hours,' said the guide. 'First the bad news – the car park is a mile away from the

'Over sands dotted by pools and the curling mounds of the lugworm they tramp towards Holy Island.'

village. The good news is we can stop in the car park of St Aidan's winery where they make Lindisfarne mead.'

We all climbed out of the bus in the village and crowded into the winery where they still make the same mead as that once made by the island monks. It was a pleasant little shop which also sold honey, lemon curd and marmalade. I found some of the old factory rules of the Lindisfarne Liquer Company pinned to the wall:

*Godliness, cleanliness and punctuality
are the necessities of good business.*

*Daily prayers will be held each morning in the main office.
The clerical staff will be present.
Clothing must be of a sober nature. The clerical staff will
not disport themselves in raiment of bright colours,
nor will they wear hose, unless in good repair.
The craving for tobacco, wines or spirits
is a human weakness and as such is forbidden
to all members of the clerical staff.
Members of the clerical staff will provide their own pens.
A new sharpener is available, on application to Mr Rogers.*

Lots of other visitors had jammed into the shop and it was while still studying the old rules that I heard this deathless line: 'Mrs Macgregor said that I could have tasted some of her mead but then she went and finished the bottle.'

The village was a sprawling stone jumble, gathered around post office and pub, pegged out between the priory ruins on one side and the bay road to the castle on the other. There was a large stone cross in the square where a pack of clean and scrubbed cub scouts were sitting together eating their sandwiches on the grass. By contrast four skinheads, tattooed with swastikas and with shaven bonces, were considerably enjoying themselves by shaking up their beer cans and spraying the passers-by.

In the priory grounds a centuries-old rubble, with a few walls and one big arch still intact, stood around in elegant retirement. A few of us tagged along behind a guide who said that the local people were so keen on honouring the saints of old they bought all the red sandstone and built this priory for nothing. 'Up here is what's left of a flying buttress.'

'What's that? Some sort of butterfly is it?'

We saw the dining area where the old monks would have eaten. We know that they ate no meat, drank no ale and refused anything with dripping or seasoning. The remains of another room showed a stone-lined pit where they salted food. It must have been a life shorn of any shred of comfort, maintaining the rounds of work and worship, conducting the long night vigils, teaching by their perfect example, exalting Christ and crucifying selves.

A young girl was breastfeeding a baby on the steps of the statue of St Aidan in the graveyard. On the other side of the statue three of our lot were eating their packed lunches. Somehow St Aidan had an exquisite look of holy hauteur as he held onto his crook. He had high hollow cheekbones, a ski-slope nose and eyes which turned upwards, distant, a bit aloof from the little cameos of feeding that were going on around his feet. His cloak was stained brown and green by the weather.

But, of all the saints, it was Cuthbert who was the most vivid. His silver tongue could wreak havoc, even in the imaginations of birds. In common with many other saints, Cuthbert had a marvellous relationship with the animal kingdom, once reprimanding a flock of crows who kept pinching the priory's barley and even telling off some others for taking the thatch from his house. When they still did it he banished them from the island until they came sneaking back, muttering apologies.

Once, when hungry in the wilderness, an eagle dropped a fish for Cuthbert to eat. He was particularly fond of the eider duck – still known as St Cuthbert's ducklings. It was sometimes his practice to stand in the sea all night praising God and, often in the mornings when he had finished his prayers, seals would come out of the water to dry his feet and breathe on them to restore the warmth.

A specialist in personal holiness, he was also a terrific preacher with the gift of healing. Bede, the chronicler of those times, repeatedly referred to him as the 'child of God' and, once, Cuthbert healed a woman's dying baby with a kiss. When he became prior of Lindisfarne he had to wean the monks off ancient forms of Druidism, instituting prayer as the main weapon against evil. But he always longed for the solitary life and, after twelve years on Lindisfarne, he went to live as a hermit in a small rough cell on the Farne Islands. He died in prayer at his remote church on March 20, 687. Lighted flares told of his death and monks brought his body back here to rest.

The main church on Lindisfarne is the parish church of St Mary, a fine mish-mash of the original and the restored. It has a beautiful carpet on the altar which reproduces a page of the famous Lindisfarne Gospels, now in the British Museum, which were written with quills, soot, glue and water. The church had a fine, cosy porch too – most important in any church since it was here that all services

Lindisfarne Castle sits brooding darkly over the North Sea.

Later a few of us walked out past the bay down to the castle. The bay itself had the confident sweep of a tropical lagoon, dotted with strange upturned fishing boats now used as sheds. Lots of kids were messing about in the rock pools. Some of our group had gone straight to the bay-front benches to sit, legs apart and hands dangling between knees, and gaze out at the riffling waves. Is there something primordial about gazing at the sea? A fascination with the movements of the sea is, of course, something of a habit with the old. Perhaps the ceaseless movements of the waves speak to the unconscious about renewal; perhaps they spoke to them of their lives, soon to be taken away from them, which in their turn would then be given back. Perhaps they too sensed that there was a deep holiness in the sea and that, to those mysterious moving arms, they would soon be returned.

The castle itself – now owned by the National Trust – was an enchanting place with small cosy rooms and long galleries, all largely built from stone from the priory when it was knocked down in the Dissolution, as yet another fortification against the marauding Scots. Out on the battery there was a breathtaking view from Berwick-on-Tweed in the North to Bamburgh in the South. Islands were scattered haphazardly over the sea; Lindisfarne was spread out at my feet, as bright and glittery as a sparkler in all that sunlight, a magical little kingdom of criss-crossing dry-stone walls, ruined priory and petrel-haunted crags. Just across a channel was a bank of sandbanks and mudflats with two strange obelisks on one island, put there as navigational aids for ships at the turn of the century coming in to pick up consignments of lime.

Today it was quiet with just the noise of its visitors, amplified by the warm sunshine, drifting up towards me. How different it must have been when the Vikings arrived. Symon of Durham's prose captures, with a racy vivacity, the atmosphere of one raid here on June 7, 793:

'They came like stinging hornets, like ravening wolves,

began; here that we are supposed to begin our communion with God and his angels. Or so Jo said.

It was in this porch that I met the curate of the church, Reverend Dennis Bill, a man of grey hair and porcelain piety, who told me that some hundred thousand pilgrims a year were now coming to Lindisfarne – some ten thousand alone the previous Saturday, when they had all walked out over the sands. He said it was a vital part of his work to encourage such pilgrims and let them know something about the island's past. 'It would be a very sad place without pilgrims,' he added.

Buffeted by stormy seas, lashed by salty winds, Lindisfarne is no cosy place for pilgrimage.

Northumberland: the story of the long and exhausting journey of a group of terrified, faithful monks looking for somewhere safe to lay the body of their beloved Cuthbert.

Even on his death-bed the saint told his monks that they should remember that, if forced to choose between two evils, it would be better that they lift his bones from the tomb and take them to wherever God decreed. 'Better that than you consent to evil and put your necks under the yokes of schismatics.'

So when the Vikings came the frightened monks gathered together the body of St Cuthbert, the skull of King Oswald, some of St Aidan's bones and the Lindisfarne Gospels and set out on an epic journey which took them the length and breadth of the land. They travelled carrying the coffin on a bier; only seven of their number were allowed to touch it. They took refuge in eight places in all, and their flight took them via Chester-le-Street, Ripon and Durham before they returned to Lindisfarne. Yet even there there was no rest. Harried again, they even tried to cross over to Ireland but were caught in a fearful storm in which the treasured gospels were lost. And yet, incredibly, this priceless relic was found on the Galway coast.

Visions and miracles surrounded the whole journey; even nine hundred years after his death, Cuthbert's body was found to be 'sound, sweet, odiferous and flexible'. The coffin was opened twice – in 1104 and 1537 – when rude fingers even twisted his ears backwards and forwards and found them, and indeed the whole of the body, quite uncorrupted.

In the final stages of this long journey the bier's wheels became stuck in a bog. The monks responded by fasting and creative prayer, asking God for advice. A voice said 'Dunholme', so they took off to this place on a loop in the River Wear and finally laid the saint's body to rest at the spot where now stands Durham Cathedral.

When we returned to the winery car park at the appointed

they made raids on all sides, slaying not only cattle but priests and monks. They came to the church at Lindisfarne and laid all waste, trampled the Holy places with polluted feet, dug down the altars and bore away the treasure of the church. Some of the brethren they slew, some they carried away captive, some they drove out naked after mocking and vexing them. Some they drowned at sea.'

Among those broken-jawed ruins, then, began one of the most fabulous stories I know. A story which was to survive for several hundred years and which was to come back to me again and again on my travels through

The cloisters of Durham Cathedral, 'whose great shadow had fallen over us like a blessing from the angel Gabriel himself.'

battlements of the castle, later slowing to walking pace to drive through the stone arch on the main street. 'I've been through this from the other side but never this,' said the driver. 'So tuck your elbows in. Better still close your eyes, 'cos that's what I'll be doing.'

This was to be the last day of our pilgrimage together and as we roared southwards I closed my eyes and thought of the week and its shifts in mood; of those who had been travelling with us; of the quiet and noisy; of the deaf and ebullient; of the prayerful and atheistic; of the lonely and merely pathetic. We had explored some glorious ruins together and seen some enchanting churches but, of all that we had heard about and seen that week, there was little that matched up to the magnificence of Durham Cathedral whose great shadow had fallen right over us like a blessing from the angel Gabriel himself.

We had gathered inside the cathedral early one morning to be shown around by one of the vergers. It would be good to get there early in the morning, we'd been warned, because the guides were still fresh. I suspected that this one was still fresh when he went to bed since he was the sort of man Augustine might have described as a hallelujah on two legs, clearly mad about the place and lifting the enthusiastic level of his words way above the normal turgid trudge of guide books as he waved his finger here and there, pointing out the massive stone pillars, the ribbed vaults and the great crowning glory of the nave. 'The rock of faith stands here at Durham,' he said at the outset. 'Stand still and look and study. Ask yourself how it has come to survive in a modern world. Remember that architecture is but history written in stone.'

We shuffled after this font of odd facts and learned that the bishop's throne here was the highest in Christendom; that the organist had a closed-circuit television to see what

time, a few of us had gone missing yet again and the driver was worried that we would be stranded on the island by the incoming tide. 'These old 'uns can be reet pain in the neck they can,' he moaned. 'They go off into fields and have a snooze and it takes ages to find them. No idea of time they've got.'

We drove off the island with the sun dipping down towards the trees and throwing long shadows over the road. A man was out in his garden with a hose spraying a lot of tiny rainbows into his plants. Down in Alnwick we paused to admire the strange mock figures on the was going on in the services and that there were twenty boys in the choir. Some sixty people were employed to work here and, since the building cost half a million pounds a year in maintenance – with one hundred and eighty pounds a day to heat the place – they had to treat the cathedral as something of a business, making money where they could.

If I ever wanted to make money I can't say I would think of running a cathedral but, just nosing around on my own, I found all manner of little avenues of income: fifty pence for the use of camera (one pound with tripod); ten pence to see the library; twenty pence for most leaflets; twenty-five pence for postcards (fifty pence for colour); forty pence for Coca-Cola; thirty-five pence for squash; forty pence to see the treasury. This was the only English cathedral in the *Good Food Guide* while, of course, there were collection boxes placed strategically on every door with the usual notices outlining the cathedral's problems. Terrible.

In a year they could get upwards of a million visitors; only last week, the guide said, eight hundred pilgrims came from Sheffield on a chartered train. 'The best time to be here is during the Durham Miners' Gala,' he explained, 'even if there are a lot of wonky notes and the smell of beer coming out of their brass instruments.'

Even as he spoke, you could almost hear the noises of the Scottish rabble Cromwell locked up here back in 1650. A lot of them died, and they burned the furniture to keep warm. They also ripped the nose off the bishop's recumbent form on his tomb. 'Curiously they did not burn the lovely clock,' he noted. 'Perhaps because they wanted to know the time.'

Just near the altar he pointed out a carving of the devil. 'We are quite sure that the devil gets in here from time to time.' He did not say as much but I knew that some months earlier a man had cut his throat on this altar; they had to close the cathedral down until it could be re-consecrated.

And then as we wandered around listening to him talk I thought again of how cathedrals can be formed within the character and ideas of their founding saint. There was much here that owed itself to Cuthbert. The old saint's hospitality to strangers was legendary – he once really did look after an angel he found in the snow – so it was fitting that this building became a famous place of sanctuary where criminals could seek the asylum of his spirit. Until 1540, when Henry VIII did away with it, some six men a year found their way here and knocked on the sanctuary knocker which is still there as it was – a huge knocker built out of the motif of a lion's head with flowing mane, huge eyes and the knocker itself running through his mouth. Such men had to wear black gowns with a yellow cross on the shoulder, and during their stay here had to decide if they would stand trial, leave the country from Hartlepool or else be bundled over the border into Scotland. If they decided to go into exile they carried a white wooden cross signifying that they were still under the protection of St Cuthbert.

Yet here again we find evidence of one of the more baffling characteristics of the old saints. Most of them seemed to hate women and, in this respect, Cuthbert seemed to be no different. We know of no woman in his life and, in the whole history of sanctuary, it was only ever extended to one woman. Anything of a sexual nature was strictly taboo and when Queen Philippa was caught sleeping with Edward III in the priory she was thrown out in the middle of the night. Also, more tellingly still, the guide showed us a line of black Purbeck marble just near the font at the rear of the nave over which no woman had ever been allowed to step.

In the Galilee Chapel we were taken to the tomb of the Venerable Bede, the monk of Jarrow and the father of English history, to whom we owe so much for our knowledge of such as Cuthbert. His most famous work was the *Ecclesiastical History of the English People* which now is probably one of the best-selling paperbacks in the history of the world. He also translated part of the Bible into Anglo Saxon. 'Bede thought that the world was round long before anyone else had thought it,' our guide told us.

Just near the tomb was a prayer stall with the prayer of the Venerable Bede: 'I implore you good Jesus that as in your good mercy you have given me to drink in with delight the words of your knowledge so of your loving kindness you will also grant me one day to come to you, the fountain of all wisdom and to stand for ever before your face. Amen.'

The greatest scholar of his day, however, would have been mightily displeased with the way, after his death in 735, his bones kept on being stolen and shifted about as different groups argued about who was going to look after them. Indeed the travels of his bones further remind us of how the history of reliquary was so often the history of theft. Even the extraordinary collection of relics said to be in St Cuthbert's tomb must have been collected by foul means rather than fair: all in all, we had here the elbow of St Christopher, a finger of St Lawrence, some hair of St Ambrose, a bit of St John the Baptist's shirt, a piece of St Andrew's cross and, yet again, another alleged bit of the True Cross. (Around this period there were enough bits of the True Cross to build a dozen ships.)

Nevertheless it was quite moving finally going to the tomb of Cuthbert himself at the other end of the cathedral; a long plain slab surrounded by high candles and with just the name CUTHBERTUS on it. We all stood around silently and looked down at the simple slab as our guide reminded us of the hundreds and thousands of pilgrims who had been here before us, of how bishops had issued indulgences from this spot releasing people from the fear of their sins or penances imposed by a confessor. Here was the fountainhead of our English faith.

'Why is a woman stronger than a man? When he dies it

takes six men to carry the coffin. But it takes just one woman to put him there.'

The driver was telling another of his excruciating jokes and, perhaps because this was our last hour together, he began telling a whole series of them which made the heart weary and the toes curl up inside the shoes. Then he sent around little paper towels for freshening us up which, we somehow learned, he had bought at his own expense. It was clearly softening-up time and, sure enough, a large brown envelope for the guide and driver was passed to my seat at the back. I had a look in it and found it jam-packed with pound notes and fivers; his jokes couldn't have upset too many.

After dinner in the university hall of residence that night I walked back into the old town of Durham, taking a steep path down to the road which took me through a wood to the eighteenth century Prebend's Bridge, a stumpy stone bridge over the river where I lingered awhile as the sun turned the night into a pink bonfire. Even so late the air was still as warm as toast with lovers walking arm in arm along the river banks. Over in the tree-tops on one side was a clamorous row of rooks having a huge bedtime argument, and on the other side of a hurrying weir was a precipitous bank of elm, poplar and beech. Right on top of it all, as thrilling as a cavalry charge, rose the gloaming spires of Durham Cathedral, turning from gold to pink to dark brown as the sun bowed out of the day. Just under my feet was the gentle plash of oars, the boat gone from view leaving just the footprints of some giant sculling insect in its wake. Further away again the noises of rugby from the public school tangled up with the frantic midges. The distant roar of traffic on the next bridge mingled with the strident barking of a dog.

Tired though I was after a long day it was all so perfect; the soaring music of a vivid English summer all being orchestrated in the twilight above a moving river and below a gorgeous cathedral built in the love of the Lord who first built the gorgeous cathedral of the world.

At 9 p.m. the curfew bells began duelling over the grey slate rooftops of the old city just as they have here every night – except Saturday – since 1068. I continued on up the cobbled slopes, past old iron boot-scrapers, until I came to the Shakespeare pub. Here I discovered that what is sweet to the ear of a visitor can be a ball of pain to the local ear.

At the bar I met a man doing the Australian pools. I asked him what he was going to do with all that money if he won and he said that his dearest ambition was to fix all those damned bells. Wilf Ridley was his name and the curse of his life was those bells; he lived just over the road from the cathedral. He said that he had visions of all those bell-ringers out every night, eyes bulging and mouths slavering, bouncing up and down on their ropes and shouting, 'Right. It's time to fix Wilf Ridley.'

He wouldn't mind if it was a simple peal. He wouldn't mind if they had a bit of melody about them. But most of the time they just went *bing bong bing bong bing bong bing bong*. On Monday nights they began bing bonging at 5.45. Tuesday night was bell practice when the noise was simply awful – just continual acid in the ears. Thursday was bedlam too and Friday was so bad he left town for a drink.

Just lately he had been sending anonymous pen letters to the cathedral authorities complaining bitterly. 'But they know who's sending them.' Every now and then he went out on his doorstep and glared at the bell-ringers when they came out. 'But they don't take much notice.'

Sometimes if it got really unbearable he would get ready to go and punch someone. But as soon as he put on his coat, they would stop. They knew, see? He wouldn't have minded so much if he was working or doing something around the house but there was this man with a telescope up in the cathedral tower who kept continual watch on his kitchen. He waited until Wilf had sat down comfortably in an armchair and lifted up a newspaper when he immediately

'Right on top of the old town, as thrilling as a cavalry charge, rose the spires of Durham Cathedral.'

signalled for the bell-ringers to get going. 'It wouldn't be so bad if I was religious or something. But I don't go in for all these banging doors and flinging holy water everywhere.'

We left the subject of bells and it turned out that Wilf's job was delivering books to prison – 'they like cowboys, gardening and do-it-yourself books' – and he'd got a very soft heart which had once been broken by a girl. 'I became a tramp for a bit but gave it up because it was just too much like hard work.' He also told me of such legendary local characters as Johnny Sixpence and Major Flynn. 'Major Flynn was small like a rugby ball on two legs. He would spend his life going around pubs selling racing tips and stealing people's drinks when they weren't looking. If you bought one of his tips he wrote it on the floor with chalk between your feet. When you had read it you were supposed to rub it out with your shoes.'

I promised to exchange Christmas cards with him as I left. It was late and dark as I made my way back to the hall of residence. Arc lamps powered over the tombstones and smashed up against the cascading walls and spiky turrets. Millions of moths and insects danced in the fluorescent-flashed night, somehow adding to the vibrance of that majestic shape. In the square behind me a man in a car was kissing a woman, his hand holding a cigarette as it rested on the steering wheel. As I walked back down towards the bridge the jubilant sounds of rock 'n' roll were coming from somewhere and a woman was drawing her curtains, pausing first to glare at me for looking at her.

Back down on the stone bridge the dark deep river was still going on its way, glazed orange in parts from the city lights. The floodlit cathedral was still towering over all and demanding obeisance from all. A sense of a beautiful past came seeping out of the night sounds, transforming a tired loneliness into a meditative and peaceful solitude which provided its own dislocation.

We came down that very lane, you know, when I was on that trip. There were fifty of us that night, all carrying torches as the wheels of the bier came squeaking and clanking over the broken road. It had been a rough few days too and I had been feeling low in those long cold nights. Even my eyebrows kept freezing over. It was all this travelling in the darkness to keep away from prying eyes and brigands that was the worst. We wanted to put away the things of the night and become sons of the morning again, proud in the sacred custody of our beloved saint. But it was not to be. Everyone was hungry these days – even the wolves. Only the night before we had to fight off yet another wolf attack with our staves.

We stopped to rest and drink from our leather bottles on a wooden bridge just there. I was dragging behind the rest of them, as usual, and by now all but crying with hunger and exhaustion. I could never remember a trip so bad. It wouldn't have mattered so much if I could have got warm. I've always hated feeling the cold. A lot of us were suffering from dysentery and sores too. To make matters worse, the thong of one of my sandals had broken. One of the wheels of the bier would soon need repairing, too. I certainly understood that prophet of old who wondered how long he could keep putting up with all these blows from God.

But at least the others were in much the same state, too, all of us weary now after years of wandering, looking for safe shelter from the storms of men. There was no merriment with us as there used to be; just heads bowed silently deep within our cowls. I took another swig of the water and was gazing at the red cloth draped over the coffin when some voices ahead began singing one of those new canticles of praise. How could they be singing at such a time? Others took it up and a few were dancing around the bier and hugging one another. 'What is it?' I shouted out to them. There were further outbreaks of singing and dancing with everyone getting more and more excited. 'What is it?'

Now they were all bunched on the other side of the bridge and looking up at the trees on the hill. I shuffled through the darkness to join them, cursing softly as my sandal fell off yet again. But then I stood with the rest of them and a bright fire of gladness erupted in my belly. Our three generations of restless travel had come to an end. We had arrived at the end of our pilgrimage and our sooty faces were stained with tears. Dunholme.

I lurched off the bridge and, just by a lamp-post in a splash of orange phosphorescence, I spotted a scrunched-up beer can. I kicked out at it, making it scream with tinny laughter, as it bounced across the lane and jumped into the darkness of the wood.

THREE

CHILD OF THE HEBRIDEAN WINDS

GLASGOW·IONA·ST ANDREWS·CARFIN

Deep in the bawling streets of Glasgow where, at midday, there is a bustling pandemonium of shoppers, buskers and cars screaming around corners; where black-eyed girls dolled up like Sheena Easton mingle with punks with green and pink hair-dos; where skinny dogs piddle on milk bottles outside grey tenement blocks; where students, who know their Plato from their Aristotle, skirt around dried pizzas of vomit on the pavements; where tiny brown gospel halls are lodged between newsagents and launderettes and where small, bandy-legged men, who seem mounted on invisible elastic and always look drunk – even when sober – bounce their way to seedy pubs . . . deep in all the vivacious shunts of a great city going about its business is the Necropolis, a quiet and still cemetery on a hill just next to the cathedral. It was there, one rainy day in June, that I began the Scottish leg of my modern pilgrimage.

Even in the silence of the Necropolis you could learn a lot about Glasgow; of its secret lusts in the used contraceptives scattered inside some of the brooding Gothic tombs; of its problems in the way that many of the tombs had been vandalised; of its weakness for drink in the empty whisky bottles discreetly sitting in the bushes; of its energy and contradictions by looking all around at the city at your feet – the factories and motorways, hospitals and shipyards all jumbled, cheek by jowl together in one sprawling Hell's Angel of a city who will show you anything but the basic softness of her heart.

I was sitting in the speckling rain, munching a pear at the base of a stone column with a statue of that great holy ranter, John Knox, atop it. 'To the memory of John Knox,' it had carved on the base of the pillar. 'The chief instrument under God of the Reformation of Scotland, died 1572.'

Knox had a natural feeling for the iconoclasm of the Scots and found something deep in their bruising psyche which he could shape and form into the instrument of

Glasgow's Necropolis: vandalised tombs and empty whisky bottles, cheek by jowl with factories and motorways, tiny brown gospel halls and bustling shoppers.

But, most importantly of all, this Lutheran avenger insisted that the people themselves should become the orderers of things. People, he came to believe, could resist, if necessary, by force. By 1560 his people had control of Edinburgh and this fiery man engaged in a battle with Mary Queen of Scots in which he came to triumph. The people did indeed become the orderers of things and Knox had laid down the Calvinist basis of Scottish spiritual life. It was men like Knox and Luther who had become the architects of schism and their ideas still live out there in those streets.

And there he was, standing on his column, his ferocious tongue now frozen in stone but with his fist held high in angry wrath at the continuing venality of this tough, uncompromising city as it brawls its way through the twentieth century, crucifix in one hand and broken bottle in the other, possibly the ugliest and yet most energetic city in Europe.

I threw away my pear stump and it was still spitting with rain as I gazed out over the city and the distant traffic roar. Somehow light grey rain seemed to suit Glasgow. The thin drizzle was in keeping with the monochrome streets and the high exposed yellow sweeps of the motorways. The damp blended nicely with the ugly high-rise flats, long abandoned by real families and given over to students who did not like them either. Out on the horizon the cranes of the Clyde shipyards poked into the swirling rain mists and, just to my left, was a factory making beer, its pungent smell damped down by the rain. But what could ever look worse than that cathedral just down there with her walls blackened by the city's smoke and her roof a horrible green colour? Green!

St Mungo, the patron saint of Glasgow, can hardly have had this sprawling mess in mind when, all those years ago, he came to a lonely spot called Glasghu in search of peace and quiet. A community soon formed around this austere man – who used to stand in a stream of ice-cold water

furious rebellion. He presented the people with ringing truths wrenched out of the Gospels and brought them together in a tremendous destructive stand against the authority of Royal London and Catholic Rome. His was the doctrine of personal responsibility: that, in the end, the individual was alone and answerable to God. His was the belief that truth could only be found in scripture: *verbum Dei* – the word of God. His was the affirmation of the simplicity and puritanism of Calvinism, turning to simplicity in worship and away from the stately masked ball of Roman Catholicism.

when he went through his daily offices – until he finally died in 603 from, it was thought, the shock of sitting in a hot bath.

A middle-aged woman walked past me, her hands pulling on a handkerchief and her eyes red and puffy through too many tears. I offered her a pear; she gave a quick shake of her head and continued walking. Her shoulders were slumped low and a good three inches of her slip hung below the hem of her brown coat.

St Mungo actually founded that black and green cathedral, described by some as the finest medieval building in Europe, but, shown around by a kindly Flora Smith, I thought it rather narrow and crabbed with lots of nasty pockmarks on the pillars. In the Reformation these pillars had been bashed about as 'monuments to idolatry' – Knox and his boys again. The place was also excessively gloomy. In one corner I found a well full of litter and, on the other side, a door riddled with holes.

The crypt where Mungo lies buried has clearly been abandoned by daylight forever. Thick stone pillars stand around in cold, damp shadows; just being there makes you shiver. But Flora did show me a rather lovely modern tapestry, full of life and colour, which depicted the life and miracles of the old saint. Flora used this tapestry to explain the various symbols on Glasgow's coat of arms: the tree being the frozen branch with which Mungo kindled a monastery fire; the bird the dead robin he brought back to life; the bell he brought back from Rome and the salmon, with the lost ring in its belly, whose miraculous capture saved the honour of a princess.

'Ye see Mungo was guid in all matters,' said Flora. 'And he protected a guid princess from a jealous king. She'd given a ring to a knight and, when the king found out, he snatched it off the knight and flung it into the sea. He asked the princess aboot the ring an' she could nae find it, of course, so Mungo sent one o' his monks in a boat to bring back ye first fish he caught. A salmon it were and, when

Glasgow Cathedral, 'described by some as the finest medieval building in Europe. I thought it narrow and crabbed, with nasty pockmarks on the pillars.'

they cut it open, they found the ring which ye fish had swallowed. Guid story eh?'

Very guid. Flora also pointed out a high wooden gallery in the roof of the cathedral where the tax-collectors went to worship for fear of having the congregation throw missiles at them.

As she was talking one of the cathedral guides went scooting past, angrily berating a man for wearing a hat in the church. Later I went over and had a chat with him. He was one of those mystifying Glaswegian midgets with black brilliantined hair, a ramrod-straight back, bandy legs and shining black eyes which always seemed to be brimming with alcohol. The thing about such men, I have long decided, is that it is almost impossible to guess their age; this one turned out to be an astonishing sixty-one, when he could so easily have been twenty-one.

The following Sunday morning I came back with my friend Anne Johnstone for the morning communion service. We were met by long rows of serious-looking ushers, dressed in the white tie and tails more befitting a posh restaurant in London's West End than a cathedral with a green roof in Glasgow.

We were guided to our seats on the far side of the aisle to discover that the service was specifically for nurses from the local hospital who were all sitting in the front rows in great phalanxes of starched hats. Suitably enough the sermon was about Florence Nightingale who in the words of the preacher:

'. . . brought hope to people who had no hope. Hope is something of the heart, something which gives people the glimpse of the possibility of something more. She brought the flame of passionate concern. With the fire of her spirit she broke through red tape and inertia, carrying the lamp of high standards. The spirit descends and rests on individuals. The lamp is handed on. The spirit is the fire within; the light, heat and power of your spirit. The spirit sets people an example of devotion; handing on these tongues of flames of fire . . .'

What began as a strong direct sermon then began unwinding and curling about like a slow-moving stream on a lazy hot summer's day and I found my attention wandering, first to the plump generosity of Anne's hands then to the faces of the nurses; one in particular, with green eyes which were also looking around for something interesting to focus on. If only I had a penny for every hour I had daydreamed during a sermon, thinking of friends past and present, a scene from a film, a line from a book, a little worry about whether I had enough money on me to buy lunch . . .

The sermon ended; I began studying again those burnished and best-suited ushers as they moved around preparing to serve communion. These were the honest burghers of Glasgow, weaned on fat cigars and the finest port. I noticed the cold reptilian eye of a banker. There was the adding machine face of an accountant. The pursed lips of the publisher of academic books. A small cold mouth here – of an undertaker, perhaps, trained for a lifetime never to show sadness or mirth. Light blue veins wriggled around beneath the polished forehead of the insurance broker. None seemed to have ravaged whisky noses or faces torn down by a passionate woman. All were perfectly shaved with skin the colour of old piano keys. The suits fitted like old gloves and the shoes were polished. You had to shield your eyes from the dazzle of their respectability. These were the professionals of Glaswegian commercial life with their exquisite hands and carefully manicured fingernails; men who would make it such a pleasure when they took your money off you. They served communion with all the restraint and quiet grace of a four-star hotel, cloth over arm and waiting with infinite patience as you sipped your wine and passed on the chalice. Then came the wafers. By now, the sacred significance of the occasion had been lost on me altogether as I regarded them moving around me with all the precision of a drill square.

But those faces! They were such a collection of fine faces – each brilliant with the impress of their professional individuality – they might just have been waiting all their lives for Rembrandt to come and immortalise them.

They would not have liked the painting in the end. They could not have borne the old master's truth. They would probably have done to him what the honest burghers of Amsterdam had once done – suppress it.

The service ended and, as the ushers trooped out, I was still smitten by the aroma of their relentless respectability. I wondered aloud to Anne if she thought they sinned much and, in that laughing cynical way of hers, she decided that they were probably at it all the time. At what though? What were the dark secrets inside those polished and burnished souls?

Had any of the ushers of Glasgow Cathedral ever taken drugs and danced the night away on heart attack rock 'n' roll? Had they ever known what it was like to be broken on the anvil of a sexual passion? Had they ever been forced to steal bread for a hungry babe? Could any of these men have ever *known* – really known – what it could possibly have been like to lie broken in the gutter with newspapers wrapped around their bodies, looking at an empty sherry bottle and choking with humiliating despair?

The ferry went pounding out of the grey granite fishing town of Oban with sleek white gulls swooping down over the aft deck. Some hovered uncertainly, gabbling their fury as the bolder ones snatched bread out of the trippers' hands. All around us, in the great shivering lagoons, were tiny islands dotted with ruined crofts. Way out in the distance a cormorant was busily diving in the hope of food, and further out again was the snow-capped peak of Ben Nevis. 'It never gets above nought degrees on the top,' said a man leaning against the ship's rail.

But that day it was far above nought degrees. After days of rain, with everyone wondering if they should build their own Ark, sunshine was striding down over the mountain, beaming happily and very full of himself, like an American missionary in a white linen suit and with a huge black Bible under his arm, come to polish up your rusty soul. Behind me a baby was grizzling thinly above the rumbling of the ship's engine.

Early that morning I had driven out of Glasgow and along the dreaming banks of Loch Lomond on my way to the isle of Iona, the most holy place in Scotland; a lovely, enchanted place – or so I had been told – which had once been colonised by Druids and where, later, the Celtic Church had been born, a child of the purest innocence, conceived out of holy wedlock between the sea mists and the great Hebridean winds. Bag on shoulder, I was travelling to pray to St Columba, 'tender in every adversity'.

But first after the ferry there was the island of Mull to cross, some thirty miles of single track road which meandered over gorse hills and swooped down the deepest valleys. Even as I sat in the bus I could see that Mull was a hymn to desolation where nothing moved except wind on stone. Looking out over the rubbled moors, I thought that, perhaps, I could just as well have been travelling across a lunar landscape. There was nowhere to run or hide or even weep. There was barely any colour in the land either – just light greys and faint greens with the odd smudge of crimson. We passed a herd of shaggy Highland cattle with their huge, ferocious horns and, later, a working peat bog with whole fields set out like line upon line of massive brown Swiss rolls.

At the bus stop in Fionnphort was a sign saying that all cars were banned on Iona – a promising start to any journey which had the effect of making me as absurdly happy as a baby with his first toffee apple. The island really did look like something from the pages of myth: shell beaches whiter than the whitest detergent, grey crofts dotted around the harbour, stone crosses and cairns, the ruins of the nunnery and the object of my pilgrimage: the great abbey itself where white doves fluttered around the slate roof.

Even as we crossed the causeway on the Iona ferry, with the sun blazing down like a savage wound and a foaming trail of spume in our wake, I knew then that I would fall madly in love with the place; that I would leave a bit of myself behind me on those white sandy shores. Emotions soar and plummet when on the move but, on that short ferry ride of just a mile, I stood there bursting with soaring gratitude that, at a time when many people had unpleasant jobs, I could make a living of sorts doing this.

The sea all around heaved with belches of brilliance. I had been told that Scottish painters had been obsessed by that Hebridean play of light on water; by the dark greens and purples of the sea bed and the awesome brilliance of that white sand. In all this we could see the colours of holiness again – in the tumbling waves on an isolated is-land; in the calls of birds in a wing-flashed sky. It is the elemental speech of a loving God communing with the simple, faithful heart. I looked up and, suitably enough, saw that the trails of two jets had emblazoned a huge fluffy white cross right across the blue sky.

The ferry's metal ramp clanked down on to the small concrete quay and I walked up past the crofts to the abbey. An elderly woman was out sunning herself on her doorstep, her hair in tight curls and her stockings rolled down below her knees. Tiny midges flashed across the lane and, just by a small stone kirk, there was a furious babble of rooks in a tree, all squawks and shrill screams.

'Och, they're nesting just now so they're that noisy,' a man said. 'In some ways they're useful ye know. They keep all other birds from the vegetable garden and dinna touch them themselves. My theory is they keep their own vegetables in case of emergency.'

I came across the ruins of the nunnery – piles of rubble made to look tidy by the straight borders of closely cut grass. I could just about make out the nave and an aisle, and the ruins of the Lady Chapel. There really was some-thing serene about those old stones and I felt that sense of continuity; that feeling of human depth that you often feel, alone, near something very old and sacred. It was to these same ruins that the great English moralist, Dr Johnson, came with his fawning sidekick, Boswell, back in 1773. 'That man is little to be envied whose piety would not grow warmer among the ruins of Iona,' Johnson wrote. Boswell was so moved he resolved there and then, for the umpteenth time, to change the course of his life.

The air was a bucket of warm sunshine and the warbling of doves when I approached the abbey. It is not one of those great churches with a splendid ecclesiastical flourish, though there is a certain fitness about the stone cloisters and the granite church itself. On one of the walls was written:

If any pilgrim from distant parts, if with wish, as a guest to dwell in the monastery and will be content with the customs of the place and does not perchance by his lavishness disturb the monastery but is simply content with what he finds he shall be received as long as he desires. If, indeed, he find fault with anything or expose it reasonably and with humanity the Abbott shall discuss it prudently lest perchance God had sent him for this very thing. But if he have been found gossipy and contu-macious in the time of his sojourn as a guest not only be he not joined to the body of the monastery but also it shall be said to him that he depart. If he goes not go let two stout monks, in the name of God, explain the matter to him.

The trouble was that these days the abbey liked you to

book. They weren't at all keen on people just coming and knocking on the door; there was one man in particular who had just one leg and was always turning up and making a nuisance of himself. You just can't boot out a man with one leg, it seems. It's very bad for the image of the place.

It turned out that a German party from Munich had taken over the abbey that week. They all arrived an hour later – a jolly lot they were too – a beefy and well-fed bunch of pastors, office workers, soldiers, engineers and retired people. Even though much of what they were saying was unintelligible to my Welsh ears, the individuals soon began emerging over our first meal together that night in the dining room. There was Fritz Eisman, who had escaped from the East to the West and now had the novel ambition of wanting to escape back again. Fritz's other problem was that he was as blind as Mr Magoo. On the journey to Iona, he had got on the wrong ferry out of Oban but had thankfully been spotted actually standing on the bridge when the ferry was only a few hundred yards out to sea. Then there was Gunter Gruner who specialised in asking very long questions about very obscure spiritual problems and Barbara Schuett – 'I am coming from Munich. I am dreaming of coming to Iona for a long while. I am very happy to peel potatoes.'

Peeling potatoes! Hah! I hadn't know about that one. St Columba, who first founded a community here, was a many-sided figure – politician and patriarch, soldier and saint, animal-lover and also a bit of a big mouth. He was also a great ascetic with a weakness for the rough things of life which included the laying off of alcohol, working the land along with the rest of the monks and sleeping on a stone pillow.

Clearly the abbey had been built on the foundation of his hair-shirt, since hardly had our first meal together finished than I was out in the kitchen, rushing about and washing up hundreds of dishes with the others in a clatter and bang reminiscent of the Parisian plangeurs in George

Orwell's *Down and Out in Paris and London*. Neither did it end there. Guests were also expected to lay fires, clean the toilets, wash the floors and prepare the food, and were organised into tightly regimented groups accordingly. The Germans accepted this quasi-military regime with fair good grace but I suspected that, had it been an English party in Germany, everyone would have risen in armed revolt.

Added to this the water system worked haphazardly, if at all. The rooms with rickety bunk beds were extremely small. And all night long, you could hear the swish and trickle of water going along a large pipe at the end of the room, all rather like a gang of demented fairies rolling home after the office party. The metered heater had a mind of its own too; when mere money failed to get it going, I found you could just pick it up and drop it and that sometimes did the trick. If it didn't, the only way to keep warm was to get into bed, but the pillow was so hard it might even have been modelled on St Columba's original stone one.

That night, after the evening service, I went with warden Ian Galloway for a pint in the newly opened pub on the island. He is a bearded man with the laughingest eyes and the strong nose of a prize fighter; though I did find it rather difficult to disentangle his ideas: they might best be described as something that Tony Benn might come up with after a conference with St Peter during a CND march. The community of Iona – which is seen in Scotland as something to do with the Labour Party in prayer – is founded on the four principles of peace, new social order, community work and youth, he explained. The abbey had been rebuilt in 1938, following a vision of one George Macleod, and was now supported by groups throughout Scotland. Only a few days later Ian was off to help in yet another demonstration against the bomb.

I suppose what made me rather uneasy was the way that politics – which are largely about the material claims of people – had here been interwoven with religion – which

is largely about the spiritual claims of God. The community's newspaper too was little more than a CND tract and in other ways there was the smell of pulpit politics: yet another disease in the body of our fallen and largely moribund church.

It was dark when we returned to the abbey with the moon sorrowing over it all, mad and accusing much like the eye of a dead fish you are about to eat. 'Look at it all. It's so nice now,' enthused Ian. 'It's been the best day of the year so far.' A night wind scampered around the ruins with dance music coming from the church hall.

I left Ian at his house and walked back along the Street of the Dead to the graveyard where sixty-four kings, from Macbeth to King Duncan, lie buried. Throughout the Middle Ages this was also the burial ground of the great West Highland chiefs. Tonight as I stood there nothing stirred in the mind but the dark and the cool. 'Do not ask questions here,' said Dr Johnson. 'Let him hide in submissive silence if he loves to soothe his imagination with thoughts that naturally are where the great and powerful lie mingled with the dust. If he asks any questions his delight is at an end.'

I looked out over the moon-glazed water to Mull and did ask one question. How did they come here?

They came at night, when there was a great meteor shower over the Hebrides. Spurting stars flashed across the sky and the very darkness was broken up by the dancing shimmering visions of the Northern Lights. I was the watchman that night and saw them coming around the headland . . . six, seven, nine . . . twelve coracles bobbing along, black on brilliant yellow. They were all shouting at one another with their monks' cowls quite visible as they passed by. I waved and shouted at them. But they neither saw nor heard so I ran home to tell the family that all those prophecies on the winds had been fulfilled. God has finally made His move, my child. He's sent those thirteen men to talk about His son, that pale and broken redeemer of the world.

The music from the church hall drifted back on the wind

Iona, the most holy place in Scotland. 'There was something serene about those old ruins, a certain fitness in the stone cloisters and the granite church itself.'

A pilgrimage around Iona: 'We made our way up a rubbled stone track, tip-toeing around cow-pats and across fields drowsy with daisies.'

and the blazing green eyes of a cat regarded me angrily before they disappeared into deep shadow.

The next morning we all gathered around the stone cross of St John for a pilgrimage around the island. A very strange gang of pilgrims it was too: around sixty Germans in their Bavarian hats and lederhosen, accompanied by some greying elders of the Church of Scotland in their walking boots and about twenty kids from Glasgow over for a week on holiday in the abbey's community centre: dirty wee sparrows with bruises all over their thin white legs, ill-fitting T-shirts streaked with stains and thick brown coatings of nicotine on their fingers. They had no fancy leather bags or binoculars. They had what they stood up in.

'This is not a race,' said a girl from the abbey who was leading the pilgrimage. 'It's walking together, talking together and sharing the island together. This stone cross has been here since 1200. Please shut all the gates behind you. Please leave no litter. Only those over seventy-five can drop out.'

We made our way up a rubbled stone track, tiptoeing around cow pats and across fields drowsy with daisies. Tiny hanks of sheep's wool hung on the barbed wire fences. Even with flies dive-bombing all around, everyone was cheerful and chattery as the Glasgow kids each took it in turns to dump a fat girl on her backside. But she always seemed to be able to bounce straight back up, waving her beefy arms about and smiling in a way which suggested she too thought it was all a lot of fun.

'Ah, zis is a lousewourt,' said a German lady, falling on her knees and shoving her nose right up against a tiny blue flower. 'You see. It insect-eating. Vunderbar.'

We squelched down through a ravine that was half bog and half rock until we came to an old marble quarry, its machinery eaten away by rust since its closure in 1914. Here the leader asked us all to take a piece of marble in our hand and beat time to a hymn – 'Christ the Worker'.

You who labour,
You who labour,
Listen to his call,
He will make that heavy burden light.

Boswell thought that Iona was a fertile island; Sir Walter Scott found it desolate and unbearable. But, just walking over those dung-dotted slopes, you could see that this small island of some three thousand acres was barely generous with itself. The tiny reservoir was hardly enough for the island's population of eighty in the winter – let alone in the summer when this number went up by four hundred per cent – and even then the brown water looked more like whisky. The soil itself was thin and sandy, whipped by centuries of salt winds. Where there was no soil there was muddy bog with small black slugs roving about and yellow irises so bitter not even the sheep would eat them. For weeks during the winter months the wind blows with such destructive violence that some abbey workers moved around with large rocks in their pockets to stop them from being blown over. Even the huge stone cross of St John has been blown down twice.

But today the sun had got its hat on and we all streamed over the golf course to St Columba's Bay. The waves were collapsing and wheezing into the shingle; a group of brown cows sat at one end of the beach like a small picnic party of fat, horned day-trippers. It was here, in 563, that Columba and his twelve disciples finally landed after a battle in Ireland when three thousand had been killed. He came, he said, determined to convert as many to Christ as had died in the battle, and the cairn just next to the beach marked the spot where Columba's beloved Ireland finally vanished from view. 'It became the cairn that turned its back on Ireland,' said our guide. I picked up a shell and listened to the winds howling inside it.

The day sounded much like that when I was standing holding my baby watching them pulling their coracles up over the rocks. Their robes were sodden but they were happy enough as they gathered around Columba who had the loudest voice of any that I had ever heard. His eyes had a great soft look about them and the very pebbles rang as he prayed to God aloud, thanking Him for the safe passage and asking Him to bless their work on Iona.

We helped them as they worked over the next few months, showing them where they could get the most suitable rocks to build their beehive huts and how to make flint axe-heads to shape them.

Later they built a tiny church out of wattle and daub with a thatched roof and surrounded by an earth fortification. In the mornings I would come over with the baby and watch them sing psalms and sacred hymns to one another as they worked. More visitors came: strange men speaking in strange tongues and travelling in stranger boats. That winter stables went up . . . cowsheds, a mill, a dairy and guest quarters. There was a service every midnight and, when the men were not working the fields, they were engaged in the copying of books and manuscripts, which were one of Columba's main loves.

Soon he began sending his men out on journeys, telling them to concentrate on converting the chieftains and kings of the tribes. They went to all parts of the world: to the Orkneys, Lindisfarne and Iceland, many never coming back again. But there was one who was so arrogant and haughty he soon returned and then they sent dear Aidan. I was sorry to see him go. You know, the strange thing was that almost as soon as those men came here the island seemed to get less windy, warmer and, somehow, more comfortable to live in. The baby began walking that winter as well.

Some mornings I would sit on that cairn and watch Columba going about his work. He was quite tall and his voice was so loud they could hear him over in Mull. He could analyse strangers with just one look, they said, while he was also a man of singular beauty with the strongest will, swift in anger and quite merciless in the exercise of discipline. Some spoke of him as being the most perfect marriage between Old Testament prophet and New Testament saint.

My greatest joy, though, was to watch him working in the fields, talking to the birds. On some days he would have whole flocks of them around him, he speaking to them and they singing back to him. He once took a weary crane to his quarters and made him 'a pilgrim guest'. He also completely cured a sick swan. 'No harm shall touch thee, whole be thy wounds.'

He even, one morning after a conversation with a robin, went back and told the men how the bird had come to have a red breast. The robin was in a nest near Calvary, the bird had told him in a song. Jesus saw the robin flying near and there was such a look of searing agony in the saviour's eyes the robin flew and pulled out one of the thorns that was causing Jesus such great pain. As he pulled out the thorn the bird pressed its light brown chest against Jesus' brow and a spurt of blood swarmed over it. 'My breast is red because I was there when he died.'

A mini-van from the abbey came bumping across the field and we all queued up for our lunch: a plastic cup of tea from a silver urn, a package of spam sandwiches and an apple. I have always hated spam and apples but was so hungry I all but ate the wrapping as well. We threw the apple stumps out for the sheep.

During the break I spent a happy half an hour sitting on a rock chatting with Tom, an East End social worker, who had come with his wife to the island for a break since he had a serious chest complaint. He told me that a bull had got loose on Iona the day before and, as it came down the lane, everyone was leaping and diving over the nearest fences and hedgerows. Even poorly Tom had got over the hedge like he had suddenly become Superman. 'The only time I ever want to see a bull is inside a hamburger,' he added with a shiver.

After lunch we trooped across more dung-littered fields and came to a ruined hermit's cell where the monks had once come to be silent with God. The guide asked us all to be silent for three minutes and we sat around the rubble just listening to the sounds as the monks would once have heard them: to that skylark who seemed to have been busy whistling his brains out all day long; to the conversation between wave and beach; to the thin beleaguered cries of the sheep and the wind quivering in grass like tension. To the medieval mind all such sounds had meaning.

It was to the accompaniment of just such music that Columba himself came to this secret hut in the wilderness. In fervent prayer, he sought to clad himself in the whole armour of the apostle Paul, so he could fight off the repeated attacks of wicked spiritual forces. He had already seen in a vision, he said, a huge host of black demons massing to attack his work here on the island. He had already engaged in metaphysical duels with his arch-enemies, the Druids. But he was now so worried by this massing array of demons that he came here to bargain with God for the assistance of angels in enabling him to drive them off.

By late afternoon many of the pilgrims had fallen away as we toiled up the final – and highest – hill on the island. There was a fabulous view of the one-hundred-and-ten-mile sweep of the Inner Hebrides; of the rugged outline of Jura where Orwell wrote *Nineteen Eighty-Four*; of the innumerable caves of Staffa, including Fingal's Cave, immortalised by Mendelssohn; of the wild torn slopes of Skye with its whisky stills . . . all dotted over the glittering blue waters like great grey battleships moving in for battle.

Here the guide read us the passage from the Bible where Jesus took Peter, James and John up the mountain. 'This is my own dear son,' said God. 'Listen to him.'

By now our faces were as pink as prawns from being out all day in the sun. We were quite tired too; not much chatter was left in us. Only the Glaswegian children were still leaping around as if they had just got up though the fat girl, clearly fed up with her role as their ball, had gone missing. A few of us went off to a nearby well in which, according to pagan rite, if you washed your face you could stay young forever, before tumbling down the iris-spattered slope and back to the abbey for a shower and snooze before dinner.

That night bells sounded in the glimmer din – as they charmingly call twilight here – and, dinner over, we all crowded into the church for a healing service. Healing, in the spirit of Columba, is central to the abbey's work and has been going on here since 1939. There is a monthly intercession whereby people can write in asking for prayers for someone. Lists of names are then sent to one hundred and thirty intercessors scattered over the country and the sick are all then prayed for on a regular basis.

But tonight was to be a laying on of hands service. 'We

see this as the very work of the church,' said the speaker. 'We are his hands and feet. We do this because we have been commanded to do this. Mark said that believers will put their hands on the sick and they will be healed. Touch shows sympathy and empathy. It shows Christ's love and compassion for every person.'

A group of people filed up to the altar with the rest of the congregation coming up from behind, all placing their hands on one another and on their sick brothers and sisters. *Lord, they whom thou lovest are sick.* It was a tender moment in the flickering half-light, some ministering to others in faith.

It was heartbreaking for us all when the great healer Columba himself became too senile to walk around the island and had to be carried everywhere in a cart. Nonetheless he was more than happy that the best was yet to be and continued writing and translating the psalms until, on his last day, a white horse came to him and let his grieving tears fall freely on the old saint's body. 'Let him that loves me,' said Columba, 'pour out the tears of his most bitter grief here on my bosom.'

In his last hours he went to the altar of his beloved church which became suffused with such an unusual light it could be seen all over the Hebrides. It was June, 597 and angels had come to collect his soul.

Columba, the dove, had died with his tiny prayer for the world on his lips:

May the wisdom of God guide you,
May the strength of God uphold you,
May the peace of God possess you,
May the love of God enfold you,
Now and to the end of your days.

God's grief was great that day and, at midnight, a huge pillar of spurting fire rose up from Iona which even lit up Columba's Donegal and Londonderry. Tempests came ripping and howling in from the Atlantic and, for three days, the waves were so high mourners could not cross from Mull to attend the funeral.

Adonman, Columba's biographer, wrote: 'As soon as interment had taken place, the tempest fell, the wind ceased and the whole ocean became calm.'

I crossed back to Oban, on the ferry, sitting on the aft deck, chatting with a wonderful old man, Harvey Dunlop, a former colonel, who told me that he had worked with George McLeod on the rebuilding of the abbey. Harvey had now retired and, as his wife was buried on Iona, he had gone back there for a week to be near her. I remembered that I had often spotted his silvery round head bent in prayer in the corner of the church. 'I pray just that I will be reunited with her soon,' he chortled, with not a trace of sadness or morbidity.

He added that, just lately, McLeod had been developing some rather outré ideas like the abolition of money and had been corresponding with Tony Benn about them. He and McLeod had both once been social workers in Glasgow together and, of course, their greatest problem had been wrestling with the city's humiliating poverty. 'Sometimes the men would be so poor and desperate for a drink they would buy lemonade and run the gas taps through it. That was guaranteed to produce a semi-comatose state.'

The weather was still acting as if it had taken a permanent lease on the sun when I got back to Oban but it was spitting with cold rain when, a day or so later, I drove into St Andrews, a salt-blown, grey granite town of great age and no small loveliness. It overlooks a wild, wild sea with the ruins of a cathedral at one end and the famous golf courses on the other, all built around the oldest university in Scotland. Row upon row of students' bicycles were locked to the railings in the streets and I was half in love with the place at first sight until I went in search of a bed, being told again and again that there were none since I had arrived on a popular golfing weekend. 'Ye'll nae get a single anywhere.

Ye might get a family room but ye'll be paying family prices.'

And so it turned out: one old curmudgeon, clearly sensing my anxiety and offering me a room with three beds at three times the single rate. Had I been a bit sharper I would have paid up and gone out to find two of the smelliest tramps in St Andrews to sleep in the other two beds. On second thoughts though I could not imagine that St Andrews had such things as smelly tramps. The place was clearly a snob of the first water and had abolished tramps long ago.

I finally did find a room in a ruinously expensive hotel and, after a snooze, I went for a walk on the seafront. I stopped in at one of the many pubs. It was there, sitting at a table with a group of teenagers, that I discovered that the next generation had forgotten how to talk. They could, it is true, mime to pop songs on the jukebox, but mostly the whole lot of them sat there staring blankly into space. When one looked at his watch, the others looked at theirs. Only very rarely did they sip their drinks – lager for the boys and weird luminous cocktails for the girls. Little wonder the whisky industry was on the skids. Their fashions were about a year behind London's and a few direct questions revealed that they were suffering from that universal malaise of the teenager – boredom.

There is little more deadly and lacking in fun than the educated Scottish middle class and here, of course, we were sitting in its very temple. The only cinema in St Andrews had long closed and the council had refused to let it be turned into a disco. The nearest disco was about five miles away but they stayed away from that because of the fights. The churches provided no social entertainment worth speaking of. The students were also extremely stuffy and kept to themselves; all in all, growing up here was the most boring occupation imaginable. 'I'm an artist,' said one. 'I draw the dole.'

It is always sad listening to kids who have dropped out

of the race even before they have got to the starting line. Later, I walked around the dark cobbled streets again with the sheer emptiness of them rewinding through my mind. Even worse than having nothing to do, they had nothing to say either.

I walked down near the ruins of the cathedral where the steady splashing of the waves mingled in the broken-jawed silhouettes. All the rain clouds had cleared up by now; from somewhere in the town there came the bright music of breaking glass. Patches of phosphorescent light broke up on the cobbles when a seagull came twirling around in the brightness, its long yellow beak screaming as if in pain before it flew away again. Stars glinted in the sky like crushed white jewels scattered over a field of velvet when, out of the corner of my eye, something moved and there was one of those beautiful, long, silent, enchanting slides of a shooting star falling through galaxy after galaxy.

Shooting stars always remind me of angelic activity: of some great angel going about its business from one end of the universe to another, possibly carrying some momentous news about developments in God's kingdom. I have been something of a student of angelology – the orderly statement of biblical truths about angels – and if you want to know what an angel is like I will tell you.

Your average angel is generally invisible, always unapproachable and does not suffer from human needs. They have their own distinct personalities, are mainly based in Israel but have each been assigned to certain territories which they have been told to look after. They cannot be in more than one place at a time and, contrary to popular belief, we only know of one with wings who can fly. An angel never ages or falls sick or feels randy. They do experience joy, particularly when a sinner repents. They do not marry, nor can they be given in marriage though

they do make an awful lot of music. They play harps continually and their language is Welsh.

As agents of God's will they are constantly active throughout the world, helping people, saving them from danger, delivering messages or even being instruments of revenge, sometimes carrying flaming swords. They are stronger than humans since it was they who rolled back the stone. In appearance, they might be swathed in radiant light, occasionally representing themselves in visions, burning bushes, dreams or even as humans.

Angels are capable of sin and it was because of Lucifer's sins of covetousness and pride that Michael booted him out of heaven after a momentous fight. It was then that Lucifer – the most beautiful son of the morning who had once walked proud on the holy mountain – came down among us where he has been causing us nothing but trouble ever since.

The next morning I went back to explore the cathedral ruins properly. It is a total ruin, with just one high wall intact, yet the outline of the original church – built as the longest in Britain after Norwich – is easily discernible, the thin nave leading down to the twin turreted east gable. The west front archway is half missing, as though chopped right down the middle by a giant cleaver. The grass lawns – at odds with the fragmented ruins and stone arches leading nowhere – are perfectly kept, the tombstones are set out in regular marching lines. Just here was the worn head of a mitred churchman; over there the broken remains of the sanctuary wall.

There was a definite whiff of holiness here and no mistake. In spite of the ruin you can feel the strength of the old faith that built the place. Even in what is left you can see that it was built with care as a beautiful argument for God and the assembly of His people.

The ferry to Iona: 'Scottish colourist painters were obsessed by the Hebridean play of light on water.'

Yet such ruins also tell us something of man broken to pieces after the Fall. Just moving around them enables you to meditate on the ruin of man himself – to see clear traces of his original glory but now to recognise the patterns of rupture, the way in which the temple of his body has become broken and ruined. Yes, you can really hear the chants, the prayers, the bells of the faithful of old. But if you listen really hard in such ruins you can also hear something louder. You can hear something terrible and achingly painful. You can hear the crumbling music of the breaking heart of God.

The history of this cathedral is as vague as a ghost at dawn. According to legend Regulus, a Greek monk, was warned in a vision in 345 that the Emperor was about to remove the holy relics of Andrew, one of the twelve disciples and the first to be called to the work by Jesus. Regulus hurriedly went to the shrine in Patras where the relics were kept and took the three fingers of the Apostle's right hand, his tooth, a kneecap and an arm-bone then set out with a group on a journey to 'a region towards the west, situate in the utmost part of the world'. After a long and hazardous voyage they made landfall here, in St Andrews, building a church in thanksgiving for their survival.

The actual foundations of the present cathedral were dug in 1160, the building later surviving a great fire, until the Reformation in June 1559 when John Knox preached for four consecutive days on the subject of 'The Cleansing of the Temple'. Soon afterwards the local townsfolk rose up, 'burning the images and mass-books and breaking of altars'. Lots of the sacred stones were carted off to build houses and walls.

After walking around the ruins I climbed the hundred-and-eight-feet-high stone circular staircase of St Regulus' tower. The view over the spired town was terrific; the riffling white horses of the waves galloping in on the wide curving beach and the outline of the old cathedral itself. Alongside me, four rowdy teenagers were clutching giant plastic litre bottles of Coca-Cola to their chests. One of them kicked another and they all ran off back down the staircase screaming joyfully.

It was only just becoming clear to me how and why the church had fallen apart throughout the land; how what was once one, holy, and inviolable, how what had been set up by scholars and saints in age of darkness had now become divided, at loose ends, at war with itself. When Jesus wept when he foresaw the destruction of Jerusalem he was weeping because he was foreseeing the destruction of his church. When you hear the crumbling music of a breaking heart in these 'Reformed' ruins you are listening to the sound of a great universal anguish that His church has been corrupted by schism, hate and divisive tongues.

Anxious to learn a little more of John Knox I later went down into the bustling town, finding my way through the narrow lanes and past the busy shops where red-gowned students brushed past a man shouting to himself on the pavement.

The Parish Church of the Holy Trinity in South Street, where Knox preached his first sermon in 1547, was a surprisingly spacious place, full of warm brightness and seductive shadow. There was a lovely stained glass work on the subject of Woman; a pulpit with an incandescent base made out of orange-veined Iona marble and the chancel itself was also paved with Iona marble. It was while sitting in a pew next to the altar that I first spotted the redoubtable Harry Eagle smoothing his hand over the altar cloth and examining his palm for dust.

I approached him and he turned out to be a man of fine, determined moves and the radiant manner of someone who makes his faith beautiful, attracts people to it and provides an inescapable argument for it – just by being what he is. He was balding but burly with a rude good health. Even before he opened his mouth you knew that he would never tell you a lie. You also knew that he would continue living in your mind long after he had gone away.

He was now sixty-six and had resigned from looking after the church, he explained, but those who came after him 'would'nae do the job proper'. In the end he went back but there were lots of problems. A brass vase had been stolen off the altar and three times now the collection boxes had been burst open. No, there was nothing of the original church as John Knox knew it. 'The university took his pulpit and we could'nae get it back. We asked but they would'nae give it.'

He took me into the Session House and unlocked the vault where they now keep all the church silver. And a fabulous collection of the finest silverware it was too; one chalice had been given by an Archbishop Sharp, who was later murdered five miles outside of St Andrews.

I asked if anyone had ever complained about using the same cup for communion.

'People say it's nae hygienic but no one's come back here with foot an' mouth.'

He also showed me an old weather vane and a scold's bridle once used by a bishop on a woman who kept interrupting his sermons. Most chilling of all was the coat of sackcloth and the old black bench with REPENTANCE on it. A sinner had to wear the sackcloth and sit on the bench in front of the congregation on Sunday mornings.

'What sort of crimes would that be for?'

'Fornication, I suppose.'

'Adultery you mean?'

'No. Any sort of fornication.'

Harry later took me out to see the John Knox porch. 'In this town and church began God first to call me to the dignity of preachour,' read the letters carved on the wall. It was also doubtless in this church that Knox preached those momentous sermons on 'The Cleansing of the Temple'.

Not a lot has changed, it seems. 'We still dinna get on with the Catholics,' said Harry. 'But, there again, we dinna really get on with one another. Not that many of our side comes these days. The church could seat two thousand but, if I told you that two hundred come here on Sundays, I'd be exaggerating.'

The sky was gunmetal grey going on for stormy black when I arrived at Carfin, a scruffy, litter-blown mining village just outside Motherwell. It was almost as if the colour of the sky had seeped into the very council houses as they stood, back to concolorous back, in curving dejected lines, as dogs sniffed around for any interesting smells on the dandelion lawns. A milk van pulled up and a hooter sounded. A gang of kids came marauding down the pavement on chopper bikes, whizzing past the rubble and twisted iron of an old factory site. Just over the road was a mini-market run by Rashid and Bari – the windows heavily grilled – and, way out in the distance, white and black pillars of smoke curled above the steelworks.

In many ways the estate reminded me of the Falls Road in Belfast or the sprawling council estates of the Creggan in Londonderry. Not only because of its sense of grey desolation and the 'Smash H-Block' graffiti daubed on the walls, it was also the determined lack of any exuberance or colour in such places that got right to you. Everything was so drab you wanted to run amok and paint a house canary yellow or scatter crimson paint over the tired privet hedges or even grab one of those manky dogs and dye him a bright forget-me-not blue.

Such greyness often goes hand in hand with unemployment, of course, and here one in five were 'on the broo'. Yet not all is as it seems, since right smack in the middle of this industrial backwater – as unlikely and incongruous as a pork chop at a bar-mitzvah – is a huge and splendid

grotto; a collection of glass chapel, shrine and statue, centred around a small lake and sprawling over some twenty acres of avenue, path, hedgerow and tree. There is a statue of St Francis atop a large knoll known as Mount Assisi and just nearby a domed replica of the house in Nazareth.

This grotto is also known as the Lourdes of Scotland. The next day, thousands of pilgrims were due to come from all over the land to honour that great Catholic matriarch, St Margaret, one-time Queen of Scotland.

Hoping to make contact with someone who would tell me about the place, I went up to the new red-brick church of St Francis of Xavier, just next to the grotto. It was another of those modern jobs, clearly put together with an eye on cost; instead of lighting a votive candle, you pressed a button and got a horrid red candle-light run by electricity. ONE DONATION = ONE CANDLE, said a sign.

It was a Saturday afternoon, yet the church was packed; a mixed wedding was in progress. 'Such weddings are fairly new around here,' the official photographer explained to me in the vestry. 'They didn't used to allow it but now one side gets communion and the other doesn't.' It's a start, I guess.

The photographer added that the man in charge of the shrine was notoriously difficult but she would try and get him to see me. He did come out and see me in the end but with the greatest reluctance and only after telling the photographer that I could learn all I wanted to know about Carfin by buying a book in the grotto shop.

This priest could have been one of the most obnoxious and unhelpful men that I have ever met – in or out of the cloth. Unlike St Margaret, who was a great example of kindness, goodness and the finest spirituality, this sucked and spat-out cough drop was a pillar of crabbiness.

When he did finally come out he had a fag dangling from his fat lower lip, his shoulders were hunched down, his nose was full and veined and he kept repeatedly examining

Above: Among Carfin's vast collection of statues and assorted reliquary.

Left: Carfin, 'a huge and splendid grotto smack in the middle of an industrial backwater, as unlikely and incongruous as a pork chop at a bar-mitzvah.'

I asked him how the church rebuilding fund was coming along and he said they still needed to raise about six thousand pounds, then lapsed into another sighing silence. I was at a total loss by now so, in desperation and in the obsequious way that sometimes bucks people up, I took out my notebook with a big flourish and held out my pen, carefully writing down the figure. It was my way of telling him that I really was concerned about his shortage of funds but all it did with him was make him worse. He pointed his finger at the page and told me to cross it out. 'I don't want to talk about that. I don't want to talk about anything.'

Clearly defeated I put away my notebook and asked him if he minded if I came to the grotto the next day for the pilgrimage. He thought about that for a while then said 'That's all right. But don't go lifting your eyes in the air when the collection plate comes around.' He did give me the name and address of the woman who had written the book on Carfin which, as it turned out, was the wrong address.

When I did leave him to watch his all-in wrestling he suddenly got very animated and shouted across the courtyard to me: 'Listen. Don't use my name in connection with anything at all you hear. Nothing. Nothing at all.'

The next day, before the pilgrimage proper began, I went to look around the grotto and found a shed with dozens of relics on display. It was the first real collection I had seen, relevant as it was to any work on pilgrimage. The first thing I saw was a letter written in the hand of St Therese, 'The Little Flower', who was a French Carmelite nun and co-patroness of the grotto. She had once seen a vision of the Virgin Mary. Just next to the letter was one of the lilies that she had worn in a crown on her head and a brick from the infirmary in which she had died. I also bought a card containing her definition of holiness: 'Holiness is not a matter of this or that pious practice: it consists of a disposition of the heart which makes us small and humble in the arms of God, aware of our weakness, yet

his watch since, he said, he had managed to get out of going to the wedding reception that afternoon since he did not want to miss the all-in wrestling on television. I explained that I had no desire to interfere with his enjoyment of all-in wrestling and just wanted to have a short chat with him about the grotto. He took his fag out of his mouth, looked at it with a long sigh and again repeated that there was this perfectly good book down in the shop which would tell me all I wanted to know about the place.

Another long sigh followed and he lit another cigarette.

confident, boldly confident – in the goodness of our Father.'

There was also an artificial rose which cured a child of heart disease; some charred bones of the Boxer uprising in 1909 together with some bones of St Gregory, St Osmund and other medieval saints; a carved wooden crucifix from an olive tree in the Garden of Gethsemane and some stones from Calvary and the Church of the Holy Sepulchre. 'It's the largest and rarest collection in Europe,' a lady told me. 'Where they are not authenticated they are hallowed by centuries of prayer.'

It seemed ironic that Martin Luther had forged a Reformation largely on the basis of an objection to such reliquary and all these years later they were here with us still. At least there were none of the more ludicrous items that we had heard about over the years: Gabriel's feather left behind after the Annunciation; Christ's breath in a bottle; countless girdles of the Virgin Mary; ten heads of John the Baptist and enough nails and bits of the True Cross to build a fleet of ships.

Indeed it was because of the relic of St Therese that Carfin's most famous healing was recorded. On July 29, 1934, Miss Mary Traynor from Chapelhall came here, according to the records, suffering from rheumatoid arthritis and a stomach disorder which had reduced her weight to under six stones. She had been vomiting constantly and, after several visits to hospital, had been pronounced incurable. On her first visit to Carfin she drank the water from the grotto and her vomiting ceased immediately. The next Sunday she returned and, at the end of the main service, went to the lower grotto for an individual blessing by a Father Taylor with the relic of St Therese.

'When Father Taylor clasped Mary's hands to touch the relic the seemingly impossible happened,' said a witness. 'The clenched fingers of the invalid's hands slowly uncurled in the priest's hands, allowing the cotton wool with which they had been packed to fall away. The stiffened hands became supple and flexible. While the relic was being applied to her legs, the trembling in her limbs became so severe it was with difficulty that the relic was kept in place. Mary's prayer of thanksgiving "My God and my all" warned those who were waiting in turn that something was happening. Her next words, "I can walk", raised a paean of thanksgiving from those present.'

After leaving the collection of reliquary I had a chat with one of the grotto workers who took me to look at a heli-pad at the other end of the grotto. A heli-pad in a grotto? It seemed that they had been given the word that the Pope had intended to visit Carfin the previous year by helicopter. A huge panic ensued, since His Holiness would have nowhere to land, so they duly moved a statue of St Andrew and built the thing. Sadly, the Pope had no intention whatsoever of visiting Carfin. Then, with the bricks left over from the heli-pad, they built a wee bridge over the lake which was another mistake since those in wheelchairs could not now get to their normal places for the services.

The grotto was actually dug out by miners, I was later to discover. It seemed that a Father Taylor had been much impressed by a visit to Lourdes and, when he returned, was lucky enough to find that all the local miners were out on strike. 'The Catholic miner possessed the combination of qualities required for the task,' he wrote in his diary. 'Faith, endurance and faith profound. He lacked only the leisure. However the strike proved extraordinarily propitious; a strike of almost a year's duration afforded him the long hours necessary to realise his dream. Summer came again and the autumn and the making of the grotto embankment proceeded. The enclosure was levelled and the banks began to take shape. It was a difficult and arduous work.'

I went ferreting around some more and found a shrine given by the Catholics of Quebec and another to St Joseph, which had been donated by a woman who said that she wanted St Joseph waiting for her at the head of the ladder

Carfin, 'the Lourdes of Scotland', boasts twenty acres of grounds, a sparkling glass chapel and a heli-pad built for a pope who never came.

on her last journey into eternity. Other small shrines had been set up by Polish miners, Goanese sailors and the Ancient Order of Hibernia. The lake itself was the shape of a shamrock; one section was dedicated to St Patrick, the second to the Venerable Margaret Sinclair, who came as a poor pilgrim to the grotto, and the third to John Ogilvie, the Scottish Jesuit martyr who had been canonised in recent years. The water was very cold to put the hand in.

Soon afterwards the pilgrims began streaming in for the afternoon service, mostly by chartered coach from such places as Calderbank, Cumberland and Newcastle. And a great motley crowd they were too: the women with vari-cose veins and hobbling walks carrying bags from the Costa Brava; the grey old men with their flat caps and folding chairs; the cub scouts with their faces as shining and scrubbed as little pickles; the wheelchair pilgrims whose wheels scrunched through the gravel; the young girls in their frothy white lace confirmation frocks, all as pretty and as perfect as morning daisies. They brought with them a rising buzz of cheerful excitement as the green-sashed stewards directed them to places around the lake. The voices of the huge choir seeped through the damp trees: 'Christ has died. Christ has risen. Christ will come again.'

'Eight hundred years ago Margaret came to be queen of our nation,' said a priest. 'We are here to proclaim the truths of Catholic faith just as she once did in our country. She saw Catholicism as providing a unity for Scotland. Here we are gathering from the four corners of Scotland for that unity.'

Another man spoke about the Pope's unforgettable visit to Scotland the year before, bringing with him an atmos-phere of peace, prayer and love: 'a new Pentecost indeed'. He also spoke of the awful consequences of hate in Northern Ireland and asked that God would heal us from a thirst for blood.

A light rain began spitting during the communion hymn. Most were standing but one man was kneeling on his own.

Way out over the fields, waving pillars of grey and white smoke belched up out of the Ravenscraig steelworks. A burst of distorting static whined in the loudspeakers set up in the branches of the trees.

It was both good and moving to be a part of that worshipping family that rainy afternoon with the phrases of the hymns sweeping around and around. They had all come together because they had been motivated by faith and mere rain was not going to dampen their ardour. If the truth be known they did not even seem to notice it, singing lustily from their hymn sheets.

Afterwards we all formed into crocodile queues around the grounds to take the communion wafers. In such queues everyone was as silent and imperturbable as a man surveying his cabbages on an allotment. You neither spoke to nor looked at one another. What, one always wondered, was going through their minds as they waited to be fed with the body of Christ? I recalled that scene in Graham Greene's *The Heart of the Matter* when Scobey, in a state of sin because of his adultery, was kneeling at the altar rail full of guilt while listening to the rustling of the priest's robes. There was always something, wasn't there, that you remembered at the last moment? The hymn again:

In bread we bring you, Lord,
    our bodies' labour.
In wine we offer you
    our spirits' grief.
We do not ask you, Lord,
    who is my neighbour?
But stand united now in one belief.

When the service ended the people dispersed, some filling their bottles with holy water from the tap near the entrance or queuing to buy a souvenir in the grotto shop. It was only then, as I was walking around, that I noticed the many women sitting around on the benches under the trees, chortling merrily and producing vast piles of sandwiches and thermos flasks full of steaming tea which they then distributed to the equally vast numbers of their families.

Many of them were beefy baby machines, disdainful of birth control, as strong as oxes and as durable as the plastic flowers and gilded polythene statues for which they seemed to have such a weakness. These women were the very engines of the huge and inviolable families which were the peculiar if unfashionable triumph of Catholicism. I looked at them, not so much one woman as a whole procession of them, with great bosoms for the broken hearted to sob on and broad backs to shoulder the greatest burdens. Most of all you noticed their hands, some as big as shovels, abrim with the maternal love that heals all hurts; that sustains through illness and poverty; that succours all, particularly the rejected and the handicapped; that takes the effort to turn out the little girls in such wonderful dresses for their confirmation; that, over the years, has peeled a million tons of potatoes, washed a cathedral of windows and scrubbed a whole planet of floors.

These are the great sturdy oaks of motherhood, all come to give tribute to that perfect flower of motherhood, St Margaret – herself a mother of six sons and two daughters – and, also, of course, to that most venerated mother of them all, Holy Mary, mother of God.

FOUR
ST PATRICK'S DEMONS RETURN

SLEMISH·DOWNPATRICK·SAUL·BELFAST·DERRY

It was 7.30 p.m. and I was sitting jotting down notes in the shelter lounge on the aft deck of a Sealink ferry, the M.V. *Galloway Princess*. It was a grey summer evening in July and we were all waiting to leave Stranraer to cross the Irish Sea – the ancient lake of the saints – to the port of Larne in Northern Ireland. Two boys were flinging chips at hovering gulls. Tired parents were walking around with tired children, trying to soothe them after a long and napless day.

Bored and fractious myself, I queued up for a cup of tea. It was served up in a cardboard cup by a spotty callow youth with dirty hands who seemed to have no skill at all in shortchanging his customers.

Almost the second we stepped off the train at Stranraer and crossed the quayside there was evidence of the tightest security. Men from the Special Branch watched you searchingly. You could tell they were Special Branch since they still had the unfashionably bright clothes and long hair of the Sixties: a style once used by the FBI to infiltrate student bombers on the campus and one now long since abandoned by both sides. Their mouths might never have been disfigured by a smile. They would shoot your spleen out sooner than look at you, you guessed. There was a tiny bulge just below their left shoulder-pad.

Just behind them were warnings of another kind. *Kindly note that passengers will not be permitted to take alcoholic drink aboard Sealink vessels and no person under the influence of alcohol will be allowed on board . . . Football supporters will not be allowed to embark if displaying their club 'favours' in any shape or form.* Tickets were checked and re-checked. The silhouettes of the webbed feet of gulls could clearly be seen through the polythene cover over the gangplank. Everywhere on the ship, in the lavatories, the lounges and the decks, hung the faint but unmistakable smell of vomit.

Tonight I was off on the Irish leg of my pilgrimage. I

felt gloomy and doomy, particularly as I would be passing through Belfast, my least favourite city in the world. The place has always frightened the wits out of me; it often features in my nightmares. I could not even think about the place without the pit of my belly heaving around. It was a thick lump in my throat, a kick in the head, a hole in the ground into which I kept falling. Perhaps I could avoid the city; it had no special significance in my modern pilgrimage. Or had it?

We rumbled slowly out of Stranraer as it settled down for the evening with a fun-fair in full scream. A large, wan, silvery cloud passed through the blackening sky overhead. A few beer cans and jellyfish bobbed just beneath the brown, brackish surface of the sea as we steamed out of a broad inlet.

I walked around the ship wondering what Columba, in his coracle, would have made of all this convivial vulgarity – of the crowds in the casino gathering around the croupier flinging his dice; of the Vincent Price bingo tickets with the prizes of up to a thousand pounds; of the queues in the duty-free shops for cheap cigarettes and whisky. These were T. S. Eliot's broken finger-nails of dirty hands; the decent godless people who expected nothing. A man was reading a paperback while listening to headphones, reminding me of an old flatmate of mine who liked to read a book, listen to music, watch television with the sound turned down, smoke a roll-up and drink a pint of beer – all at the same time. It was his idea of heaven.

As darkness came on I stayed out on the deck to get my first sight of Larne. It looked magical and almost ghostly, set next to a power station swathed in a great pool of yellow phosphorescent light. We were pounding towards the dock when the ship's engines stopped and we turned back; an abandoned boat had been spotted from the bridge. It turned out to be an empty, listing row-boat half-filled with water and we circled it with the ship's lights sweeping over and around it before we got on our way again.

The fields around Slemish where, some fifteen centuries ago, the youthful St Patrick tended his flocks of sheep.

It was a strange moment, as the passengers crowded on the ship's port side to look down on this half-sunken row-boat. Columba, the dove, would have made a roughly similar crossing in a roughly similar vessel. Now, all these centuries later, we were moving along in his wake with our dice and bingo tickets and duty-free Scotch. All these centuries later we had learned nothing and progressed nowhere and it was as if Columba had called us back to look at that humble, empty craft to remind us that we had been given everything and had got nothing.

It was, as they say here, a moisty morning on the farm and I was standing outside a shed watching piglets being born. One by one they fell out – slimy pink sausages, looking as though they were without life or animation, until Tom Hoey, the farmer, picked them up, peeled the mucus off their little snouts, picked off the umbilical cord and put them to fight it out with all their other brothers and sisters already chomping greedily on the two rows of mother's teats. He threw the umbilical cord to his dog who snaffled it up in two slavering chomps. 'The old dog loves that stuff he does,' said Tom.

We had been up early to keep an eye on the pigs and, out in the fields, the grass was bejewelled with silver drops of dew. A fat spider was twisting around inside its web in a hedgerow throbbing with the life of the rain. Out on the horizon sat a giant plug of volcanic rock known as the Mountain of Miss or Slemish, its gaunt fist sticking up out of the Antrim plateau. It drew all eyes to its barren, black-eyed majesty did Slemish and I was anxious to get there since it was the first stop in my search for Magonus Succatus Patricius, otherwise known as the patron saint of Ireland, St Patrick. It was around the base of that uncompromising thrust of rock that he spent many years of his youth looking after sheep.

The farmstead that Patrick had stayed on was the basic economic unit of fifth-century Ireland – raising cattle, sheep and pigs – so it was somehow appropriate that I had begun my Irish pilgrimage staying with my friends Letitia and Tom Hoey on their own farmstead in the sight of Slemish. Here they have done it just as they must have always done it since Patrick's time; drawing the water up from a well in the yard, milking the cow by hand, picking up the chickens' eggs out in the field and burning peat which has always been the authentic, if acrid, smell of feudal Ireland.

I was standing there daydreaming and gazing at Slemish when Tom walked past holding out a jam-jar containing a pair of pliers. 'Time for the dentist,' he said, picking up each piglet and snipping its teeth with a loud, wince-making snap on either side of its mouth. Most of the piglets put up with this horrifying operation with an heroic good grace until one began wriggling its legs, opening its mouth and emitting a furious protest of high-pitched squealing pain. I could never remember hearing a sound so nightmarish – this little sausage but minutes out of the comfort and security of the womb and now wailing like a drug-crazed banshee as its teeth were being snipped with a pair of pliers.

I just had to walk away from the shed when Tom shouted after me: 'You be sure to be around next week now. That's when I'll be castrating them.'

I went over to Slemish that afternoon with John Hoey, home on vacation from Oxford University. We stood watching the bees buzzing in and out of a clump of fox-gloves. John said that when he was a kid they always used to take the flowers off the foxgloves and put them over their fingertips to make a glove.

With an Oxford blue for rowing, John found the scramble up the steeply rising black jagged rock of Slemish an easy one but I huffed and puffed a fair bit. Occasionally the rocks powdered and fell away under my feet while many more were just too jagged to hold with your hands. A large black slug went elasticating over some moss and, all around, the plaintive cries of the sheep rode the winds.

The sky still spat biliousness now and then, with dark masses of black cloud sweeping in over Belfast, invisible in the rain mists. Miniaturised fields with curling hedgerows were scattered everywhere with two men out working in the long chocolate wheels of the peat bogs. Even as I stood on the peak of Slemish looking out on to this kingdom of green grass and grey rain I could hear nothing except the blood moving around in my ears. I asked John if he ever heard that. He said that he did, often, particularly when he was lying with his head on his hands in bed. Sometimes he heard the blood moving in his hands, too. More great slivers of mist came curling past us.

So this was the mountain home of the boy Patrick, where he spent six years tending flocks for his master, Milcho, after being captured as a slave at the age of sixteen. It was during those years of bondage that the youth underwent his conversion to the Lord. 'I used to pray many times a day,' he wrote in his *Confessio*. 'More and more did the love of God and my fear of him and faith increase and my spirit was moved so that in a day [I said] from one up to a hundred prayers, and in the night a like number, besides I used to stay out in the forests and on the mountain and I would wake up before daylight to pray in the snow, in icy coldness, in rain . . .'

Indeed it was on these very slopes that Patrick learned the exacting spiritual disciplines – solitude, repetitive prayer, vigil and fasting – which would one day give him the strength to rout the fearsome Druids and, in so doing, free the Irish from the sin and superstition that held them so tightly.

We walked across the top of Slemish and found a small, man-made, concrete pillar whose technical name is a Triangulation Pillar. This was one of the fixed points in the mountains used by the Ordnance Survey people to produce their highly detailed maps of every slope and cranny in the country. Some Republican had climbed the mountain and painted it white, green and orange.

'Last time I was up here it was the colours of the Union Jack,' said John. 'Who would want to climb all the way up here just to paint that thing?'

I swallowed and looked at the pillar silently. I had so far managed to avoid this wretched sectarian war which was so befouling the province, but the signs were all there nonetheless. They were there all right.

I was soaking up a beautiful, balmy summer evening in the graveyard of Down Cathedral in Downpatrick. Behind me a man, stripped to the waist, was cutting a hedge with electric clippers. A dog began barking and a woman's voice shouted for it to be quiet. I had heard a lot of barking dogs around the town. Weeds and nettles were springing up among the grey crosses and small ashen statues on the tombstones. Vivid red puffs of poppies were scattered around the graves, some but pods waiting to burst and spread their seed. Graveyards are excellent places for meditating on the cycles of life and death. Nettles grow particularly well in graveyards, a man once told me, because they thrive on the sulphates in human bones.

The sun slanted away behind me sending long thin shadows stretching down the slopes. Gnats danced around my legs. The dog began barking again. Directly below me was a wooded valley with the thin whine of passing traffic coming from out of it. Just over on my right were the mountains of Mourne; one great etching in purple, humped with great age and suffused with the golden glow of a withdrawing sun. The song of a bird began duelling with the bark of the dog. A leaf fell into the grass with the softest splash of noise. Then another leaf fell.

Now the mountains were actually changing colour in the sunset, going from purple to misty black and lightening in part to brown. The drifting white smoke of three wood fires, soft white on hard black, was dotted along the length of the mountains. A huge bird glided on unseen thermals overhead. The serenity of it all was quite magical: a perfect moment in a perfect creation just sitting there waiting for a great painter to come and capture all this sorrowing grandeur in oils. For the mountains were sorrowing – of that I had no doubt.

I had come to Downpatrick, the county town of Down, by bus, first signing into Denvir's Hotel in English Street. The hotel is said to be more than three hundred years old and, to be fair, looked every second of it. There did not seem to be any other occupants either. In all the time I was there, I only ever spoke to the affable lady who, with her sister, owned the place. She was hoping to sell it soon.

That afternoon I had gone to see Colin Crichton, the owner of a local newspaper, the *Down Recorder*. He is a man of exquisite grooming and a silky voice who kept putting me in mind of the perfect creamy froth on the top of a pint of Guinness. He was also, it emerged, something of an amateur historian and archaeologist, telling me much about how St Patrick came to nearby Strangford Loch – 'the fastest tidal movement in Britain' – before putting up his first church in neighbouring Saul.

With a population of nine thousand, Downpatrick was overwhelmingly Catholic, he explained. In spite of sectarian strife, both sides often came together to worship in the cathedral. Inevitably the conversation drifted to the Troubles; indeed, almost every conversation I had in Ulster drifted into the same wretched terminus. 'It's the media always talking of violence, it is,' said Colin. 'There's lovely colourful wee things out here. Why don't you people from London come over and write about them?'

I couldn't agree more, and said so. Yet it was not to talk of the Troubles that I had come to Downpatrick, but for the cathedral. Just over the other side of the graveyard where I was sitting was the burial place of Patrick, marked

with a Celtic cross and a large grey stone slab in the shadow of a yew tree. The name PADRAIG was just discernible amidst the pinky white patches of lichen. Columba and Bridget were also said to be buried in this grave: 'In Down three saints one grave do fill, Brigid, Patrick and Columcille.'

Still glorying in the voluptuous twilight I walked around the graveyard and into the cathedral. The sun was sending long golden bars across the nave. I was immediately confronted by the organ erected on the choir screen. It resides in a huge Gothic case and is an instrument so perfect and so complete and so original that, it says in the guide book, it is the most broadcast organ in Ireland.

There was no one around as I walked down the aisle – and no sound either, just the sad and pungent smell of damp. Much of the plasterwork was clearly spalling and falling away with enough damp seeping out of those walls to give a dozen snails rheumatism. They say it will take a quarter of a million pounds to fix it.

A beautiful gold cross sat on the altar beneath a stained glass work featuring many of the saints. The pews were brown and polished with a rude granite christening font and a bishop's throne set in the middle of the congregation. This, according to the guide book, symbolises the Shepherd with his flock around him. Most interesting of all were the cornices on the tops of the pillars, all of them different. One showed the tonsured head of a cleric with, on each side, two villains attacking him with ravenous, evil jaws.

The ubiquitous John Wesley came here in 1778 when the cathedral was a ruin. 'At the head of English Street stands the Abbey on the hill,' he wrote in his journal. 'It is a noble ruin, the largest building I have seen in the kingdom. Adjoining it is one of the most beautiful groves covering the side of the sloping hill.' Wesley preached in that grove though there were, of course, few places he had not spoken in. Travelling a hundred miles a week, five thousand miles a year, his Call took him the equivalent of nine times around the world. He preached forty thousand sermons.

'Downpatrick was
overwhelmingly
Catholic.'

When I asked a lady by the cathedral door to show me the grove where Wesley spoke, she pointed down through some trees. These days, she said, the police went down there every night. It was where the local teenagers gathered to sniff glue.

The sun had dipped over the mountains but there was still plenty of light in the sky. I followed a wooded lane down to a meadow where there was a lovely, still lake which erupted in a flapping gale of ducks and moorhens when I walked up to the bank. It might have been on this very bank that Patrick knelt with a prayer of thanks after he had been returned to Ireland. It might have been an unreal radiance, such as this night's, that spread over the land for the twelve days after his burial when there was no darkness at all and hymns and canticles were sung for his soul throughout Ireland.

Patrick had spent six years on Slemish when, one day in 421, he was vouchsafed a prophecy that there was a ship in Drogheda which would enable him to escape from his serfdom. After a storm-tossed voyage they finally landed in Gaul where he stayed for eight years. It was after a brief spell in Britain that he returned here in 432 to evangelise the Irish. He sailed first into Strangford Loch; I could just see it in a low dip of the darkening hills.

'We beg you holy youth, that you shall come and
   walk again among us.'
And I was stung intensely in my heart.

Patrick built his first church in Ireland at Saul, just a few miles down the road. The original church has long gone but, when I went there, I found a powerful wee church built out of light-grey Mourne granite. Its design, with its pointy, pencil-shaped tower, is based on that of the early Christian church. Inside there are some stones thought to come from Patrick's original abbey, though all that remains of the abbey today is one powdering wall with ivy lapping around it and two small corbelled cells, which may have been used by anchorites but are now overgrown by every weed that ever enjoyed a picnic in a graveyard.

It was in the nave that I met an old man and asked him how many people came along to worship here these days.

'Let me see now. On the last count there was twenty-four families and, the way it's going, soon there'll be no more.'

'You've been getting no converts then?'

'None. When we die the church dies.'

'God not doing too well here then?'

'Not in this country he's not.'

Something dark and fleeting darted in his eyes like a trout diving deep for cover and he turned his shoulders to cough into his hand. I recognised that dart in his eyes. It was the sudden realisation that an old and faithful Christian had lost his faith too; that he shouldn't have said that but now it was said anyway.

So the cycle of belief and disbelief had swung its full course. Even in this very church, where Patrick had first brought news of God's love to the Irish, there were those who had been sustained and nourished by that news all their lives but who had now lost it; those who had cast out certainty for doubt; those who believed that all those hours of worship had been in vain.

It was only that momentary look in the old man's eyes that made me realise the full and awesome extent of the Troubles in Ulster; that, in this country, the fear and hatred had become so pervasive that they had not only destroyed families and homes but attacked the very mind and thought of God too.

After completing his work in Saul, Patrick embarked on a magical, mystical tour throughout Ireland, baptising thousands of converts, getting clapped in irons, laying curses of unceasing persecution on those who opposed him, turning poisoned cheeses into stones, blessing rivers and making them fertile with abundant fish, resurrecting a man who had been dead for twenty-seven years and, most exquisite of all, breathing on children's teardrops and turning them into gems.

But his greatest battle was with the wizards, sorcerors, soothsayers and witches who had gathered in the court of High King Laoghaire.

It was the Druidic custom that, on the approach of an important heathen festival at the time of Easter, all lights in the land were supposed to be extinguished until a burning brand was carried from the king's hall. But Patrick, on the hill of Slane, broke with tradition and lit a Paschal (Easter) fire, proclaiming the death and eternal resurrection of Jesus Christ. This was Patrick's notice on a reign of evil that it had come to an end; it was his great act of shining defiance; his incandescent announcement that God's Kingdom had come to Ireland and was going to last for ever and ever.

Even when the enraged king ordered his soldiers to kill Patrick he remained magnificently defiant, shouting, 'Let God arise and scatter his enemies and let those who hate him flee from his sight.'

Later Patrick engaged in great magical duels with the Druids, causing snowstorms to come and disappear, lifting the very darkness and creating miracles with water and fire. A terrified and very impressed king soon bowed his head before the true God.

But what is the true God? Where is God? And of whom is God? And where is God's dwelling place?

'Our God is the God of all men,' said Patrick, his mind deep in the Holy Spirit. 'He is the God of Heaven and Earth, of seas and rivers, of Sun and Moon and stars, of high mountains and deep valleys, the God over Heaven and in Heaven and beneath Heaven. He has his dwelling place in Heaven and on Earth, and in the sea and in all that is therein. He informs all things, he brings life to all things, he surpasses all things, he sustains all things. He gives light to the Sun and the Moon by night. He makes fountains in

Belfast, its streets scarred by years of sectarian violence: 'A high-tech war had ripped the heart out of the city.'

the dry land and islands in the seas and he sets the stars in their places. He has a Son, co-eternal with himself and in his own likeness. Neither is the son younger than the Father, nor the Father older than the Son. And the Holy Spirit breathes in them. The Father and the Son and the Holy Spirit cannot be divided. Believe.'

I walked back over the meadow and climbed a fence, stumbling into a school playing-field where a young boy on a motor-bike was whizzing back and forth over the grass slopes, doing a fair imitation of Steve McQueen in *The Great Escape*. He was mad about motor-bikes, his father said as he stood with a few others watching him. He was just getting in a bit of practice for now before being allowed out on the streets.

'I wouldn't let any son of mine ride a motor-bike,' I said.

'I don't like it myself but he's crazy for the things. What can you do?'

I walked with them back up into the town. Darkness came and all was quiet, the townsfolk indoors and nothing stirring in the sloping streets. Signs announced that this was a Control Zone. I walked past the police station; with all the wire mesh around it, it looked like a fully armoured tennis court about to move into battle. Down on the next terrace I saw a gang of youths watching me. I turned around sharply and went back to the town – the dry ice of fear again. On the main street the broken rafters of the gutted town hall stood black against the dark blue night. The phosphorescence of the street lamps gleamed on a forest of metal grilles and locks. A car drove past me, slowly at first, its headlamps sending my shadow dancing all around me. Then it accelerated away fast. The flickering grey lights of the television sets shone in many windows.

In that thick sense of lurking evil, I understood, that night in Downpatrick, why holiness had been swept out

ARTILLERY STREET

of Ulster. Holiness had died since the demons, which Patrick fought with such energy and faith, had returned to the land. The spirit of the Druids was again abroad in the streets and fields. Oh, to be sure, they had come back in a different form and by different means but they were there alive and well in every home in this long season of black rain.

The most surprising feature of Belfast is the magnificence of its setting. It is ringed by high hills and sits on a misty sea lough overhung by the giant crucifix shapes of the Harland and Wolff shipyard. The suburbs could be the suburbs of any European city but, as you travel on down towards the city centre, certain things begin lodging in your mind: the wire grilles on the shop windows, the swathes of barbed wire atop the garden walls, the mirrors to see around corners and the closed circuit television cameras. You also begin to notice lots of empty houses with the windows blocked up by breeze blocks.

This was my first visit to the city in nearly a decade. For a time I had come to know the place well as a reporter for the *Sunday Times*, scampering around these streets in the explosive early days after internment. Then I had walked unbelievingly around the hate-filled pavements with the colours of the Union Jack painted on one kerb and the colours of the Tricolour on the opposite side. I had heard shots ring out in the darkness, seen homes ransacked and burned, even stood consoling a woman one afternoon as she sobbed pitifully while neighbours swarmed into her house and pulled all her furniture out into the front garden.

I had been to clandestine meetings with members of the Irish Republican Army, even once sat in a barber's shop in Hooker Street and had the most severe haircut of my life as I interviewed the barber about the riot outside his shop the night before. I had watched the blazing fires from the petrol bombs, smelled the rancid smell of CS gas and even bought rubber bullets off the children who scavenged for them in the wake of the riots. During those days I had stared squarely into the face of terrifying hate.

I had seen all this and done all these things but, even so, nothing could have prepared me for my return to Belfast. Where once the troubles were largely confined to working-class areas like the Falls or the Divis Flats, they had now clearly moved right into the city centre. What I saw that afternoon was no longer the evidence of a suburban working-class punch-up but the result of a high-tech war waged by terrorists which had ripped the very heart out of the city.

It was shocking to look around and see the way that whole blocks had been razed to jagged piles of rubble, with old prams and shards of coloured glass scattered all around. Some of the rubble had been there for so long that tiny, scrubby saplings were growing out of the broken bricks. Even such buildings as had been left intact had been attacked again and again. I grew to recognise the sooty whorls left on the walls from the petrol bombs.

A further shock came on approaching the shopping centre. The streets had been sealed off by a high red metal fence, and everyone entering had to be searched. Policemen in green uniforms and flak jackets stood around holding sten guns as hands searched your body, running up and down inside your legs before giving you a quick tap on the behind telling you to get on your way. All pretty useless, it seemed to me, though it did apparently help the unemployment problem.

'They make bombs so small there's no chance of finding them,' a policeman told me. 'At best these gates keep out the big car bomb. It's propoganda, showing the boys we are doing something. Aye. Propoganda. That's what it is.'

The worst part of moving around those streets was all those suspicious eyes, fastening on you like radar. Wherever you walked you could touch the fear. For fear is the most destructive emotion of them all and no mistake; that feeling of impending danger which paralyses the will to the good; this feeling which is the implacable enemy of trusting love; this feeling which opposes life itself.

But this fear was not only in all the eyes watching you since it quickly seeped into your own body too and, again and again, you felt that dry cold feeling in the mouth, the faint shrinking of the heart, a sense of hollowness in your belly – all the characteristics of fear.

I wandered out of the shopping centre and went down to the Forum Hotel – formerly the Europa – in which I had once spent so much of my time with the rest of the international media circus. It was eerie and even a little chilling wandering around those lobbies and through those bars. We all of us had played our own significant part in the Ulster murders. We had inflamed and encouraged the dragons' teeth of violence that had been sown throughout history. We too had set up fatal mirrors of distortion. We had been the cloud from which the black rain had poured in and, in so doing, had helped reap this dead harvest.

St Patrick fought and conquered the demons of the court of the High King Laoghaire. The same demons are back now but in a different form. The demons of today are technological and the children of corrupt thought. These demons come in flashing, elusive images and are pulling this society apart just as surely as the Druidic demons of old. The very fabric of Christian love has been eaten away by these demons. These demons have divided the community into armed and hating camps. They are the spiders who nest in the cave of the media, seizing on the wicked and odious imagery of the knee-cappings, the tar and featherings, the riots, the disfigured corpses, the shattered glass and spattering of blood on the roads, the burned-out houses, the para-military funerals . . . then transforming them into bustling, savage agents of hatred – the same evil children of the Druids who were once routed by Patrick's

Paschal fire on the hill of Slane. They are back with us and more destructive than ever.

It is not the events that are important but the mind which gathers them up and rams them down the throat of the community. It is this mind which is the mother and father of the Ulster demons and, if the mind was removed from the community, this strife would be over in a year. Love would be restored and stability returned. The spirit of St Patrick would come back to the land and people would reach across divides again.

Later that afternoon I did find an escape from those demons in Belfast Cathedral where a sense of peace enfolded me almost as soon as I stepped inside. It was as if I had moved from hell to heaven in just one rotation of the revolving door.

The nave had clean straight lines with a dramatic sense of spaciousness and light. An organ was playing as I approached the altar and, almost for the first time since I had arrived in the city, I had no feeling that someone was watching me. I suppose that it was somehow fitting that this house of God should be the one oasis of peace and calm in this bombed-out city with its barbed-wire heart. One of the most persistent lies about this conflict is that it is a religious war when it is in fact a small localised fight between two tiny groups of loonies which, in its turn, has been internationalised, exaggerated and inflamed by a secular media which loves violence more than life itself.

I looked out the verger and had a short, pleasant chat with him. I was becoming something of a connoisseur of vergers that year, often finding them more interesting than bishops or deans. This one was a curious, chortling little character who had been with the cathedral for thirty years. All he believed for certain was that as long as you loved your wife and the Lord then nothing else mattered.

I said that it seemed to me that the cathedral had been left untouched by the Troubles.

'It's true what you say so it is. There was a few windows blown in by bombs but nothing serious. No. Nothing at all serious. At all. Groups meet here to pray for unity so they do. But everyone's too intransigent. Heard on the news just now that another policeman's been shot. On the news.'

So we were straight back to it again. Same route, same terminus.

I took a room in a guest house near the university and went over to the Botanic Gardens later in the afternoon, first looking at the tropical plants in the Palm House then lying down on the grass in the sunshine. A shadow flitted over the yellow blaze in my closed eyes followed by a thump on the grass just next to me. David.

He was a wee scruff of a boy with a T-shirt, on which, suitably enough, was written 'Here Comes Trouble'. We got to chatting; rather he did all the chatting, giving me a lot of information about himself and occasionally allowing me to say yes or no, nothing more.

He was seven. His Ma was going to get him new shoes the next day. His Da had gone to heaven. His Ma was sitting on a bench over there. Would I like to go and meet her? Could he jump over me again?

He jumped over me a few more times then came back with his non-stop chattering. Did I have a big knife at home, did I? Did I have a big knife to stick into someone if they upset me? He wanted a big knife when he grew up. He would like to get a real gun too. Would I like to meet his Ma? Best of all he was good at throwing things. Those flowers over there. Could he go and pull them up? Come over and meet his Ma.

After a while his Ma came over and apologised for him, scooping him under her arm and taking him away. I lay back on the grass, thinking about the child's words, his anxieties and insecurities; his fascination with big knives

and pulling things up and throwing things around. That was the way a whole generation of young minds had been slaughtered.

I walked out of the gardens and cars roared past as I stood next to a lamp-post, marooned in a city afternoon, with a few old newspapers rustling around in the gutter at my feet. Yes, we all had children in Belfast. There was a part of all of us here in this city, in this season of black rain.

> The reason why I love Derry is
> For its quietness, for its purity;
> For 'tis full of angels white
> From one end to the other.
> *Columba*

So it was then that I took off to Derry, again in search of Columba, my dove, who had once founded this city calling it his 'little oakgrove'.

Derry was once one of the main ports of Ireland and the great northern outlet for trade and emigrants to America. No city could have a finer setting, scattered, as it was, over gentle hills and sitting next to a fat, curling river. Sunlight burnished her roof-tops and, as a swarm of starlings bundled over the chimneys, the whole city looking as quiet and perfect as a wild flower.

'Look at her,' said James Doherty, a ruddy-faced butcher who had given me a lift in his car. 'Looks good from out here, doesn't she? Just wait until you get inside.'

James, a father of ten children, had much entertained me with his droll stories of cattle-smuggling into the Republic and of how farmers claimed an export premium before smuggling the beasts back again. But now that we were crossing the bridge into Derry a lot of the humour had dropped out of his words as he pointed, often without comment, at the Republican flags flying over the flatlands of the Bogside; at the Union Jacks flying on the other sections; the burned-out and bricked-up buildings; the miserable monuments of a city at war with itself.

But after Belfast I was going to ignore all that stuff. The purpose of my pilgrimage here was to sniff around in the smoke of Columba's life, to track down his associations with the little oakgrove from where he had first journeyed in that sacred curragh to Iona. After Belfast I was going to seek out what St Paul had called the 'good and deserving of praise: things that are true, noble, right, pure, lovely and honourable'. I wanted to see whether if we pondered on such things we could, indeed, come to know God.

It was impossible, of course. Just impossible. The angels white have long since flown the oakgrove.

Here, if anything, the devastation was more complete than in Belfast. By St Columba's Cathedral way up on a hill inside the walled old city, I was mooching around the graveyard when I bumped into a policeman, his fierce black eyes regarding me with suspicion. He held a rifle at the ready; you somehow don't expect to meet armed men in graveyards. I didn't say anything and withdrew in some confusion. It was only later I learned that the cathedral is just behind the courthouse and, that day, there was a terrorist in the dock.

I decided to walk around the old wall ramparts next to the cathedral, barely a mile long and a pleasant hobble but I might have been walking through a nightmare with all the broken glass and concrete bunkers. Everywhere, on every spare bit of wall, there were coloured swathes of graffiti, those flowery epitaphs that we always find in dying cities. PROVOS OK. STUFF THE FENIANS. U.D.A. FZ.T.R. UP THE BRITISH ARMY. Every hundred yards or so there were giant concrete bunkers smothered with rolls of barbed wire and telescopes with which the Army could keep an eye on the unruly elements of the Bogside. Through a slit I saw a visored face watching me looking at him. This is the dreaded sangar, one of the most punishing and destructive routines for the professional serviceman.

On the inside walls of the sangars they have photographs of wanted men; the soldiers keep a constant watch on the

Derry: 'I might have been walking through a nightmare of broken glass and concrete bunkers.'

streets. All movements – even those of a man delivering milk – are logged and timed. Rifles are always at the ready. In the summer sangars are boiling hot and in the winter freezing cold. All the men ever have to keep them company is their boredom. Even as I lifted my hand and made a little wave at that visored face, I could see the butt of his rifle moving along the slit, ready no doubt in case my friendly gesture turned into a swinging hand about to hurl a petrol bomb.

I came to the Grand Orange Lodge spattered with paint and the black whorls of petrol bombs. The church next to it had been bombed repeatedly; a vast corrugated iron shield had been erected on the wall. How, I asked a passer-by, do those all the way down there manage to throw a bottle all the way up here?

'Oh they use inner-tubes they do. They use them like catapults. They know all the tricks.' He took me to the stump of what was once Patrick Walker's statue. 'That came down in one blast. They say the Welsh did that. Skilled job it was. We couldn't have got it down in one go, that's for sure.' That lovely, crackling Irish humour again. These people spray wit over everything. Sometimes you suspect it's only their sense of humour that keeps them going.

YOU ARE NOW ENTERING FREE DERRY, it had emblazoned on an arch over the road leading into the Bogside. IT'S NOT LONDONDERRY IT'S DERRY, it said on the other side of the arch. I walked with the man awhile and, a little further on down the wall, we found something of a novelty in Derry – a completely new bank built out of chocolate-coloured *ungrilled* panes of glass. We both stood there marvelling at the bank's optimism. Somehow you forget that virgin panes of glass exist in their own right in this city but someone else had spotted the bank's gaffe too and two of the incredibly thick windows had been smashed with bricks.

Here and there red hands (the Protestant resistance logo)

were painted on the pathway. Even the old cannon were daubed with graffiti. Yet just along the wall I caught the authentic smell of every provincial British city – the wafting spicy aroma of chop suey boiling in a Chinese takeaway. Somehow, in the middle of all these gutted ruins, the smell was reassuring. It said something about the abiding need to eat: the persistent and very human quest to survive.

I had a short nap back in my guest house. It was dark when I awoke. I walked back down into the Bogside, finding lots of florid murals depicting Armalite and Thompson guns painted on the street walls. There were faces set in heroic postures and lists of the dead. I was again certain that I was being watched – that hot ice of fear again. Now and then small anoraked figures moved through the splashes of the street lamps on the dark pavements. A dog growled lustily somewhere in the darkness, making me jump.

I went for a drink in the Bogside Inn where I fell to chatting with Mick, an old man who seemed to be on a drip-feed of sorrow. His eyes were of the coldest and hardest blue; his huge hands shook around like a pair of moths fretting indecisively about where to fly next. It was his nerves that had gone, he said. Everything was finished; there was no work to be had since the Troubles began. He was down here for a couple of bottles of Guinness then he was away home to watch TV.

'Derry was a lovely place an' all. Everyone was so friendly but now it's gone to the Divil. I worked on repairing those city walls, you know. We had lovely gardens and flower beds all around them then. We were proud of those walls. Today they're a real disgrace so they are. Now it's just battlefields. We're all divided. It was a great, grand wee city but now we're all divided. We danced and

Bobby Jackson, father of twenty-four and a man of the purest enchantment. The verger of Derry Cathedral, he staked his claim to the job by painting his name on the noticeboard outside.

prayed together, you know. But times is changed. Times is far, far changed. It's terrible awful to think of it. We don't want the Republic. Most of us don't anyway. It's those teenagers causing a lot of the trouble. The parents I blame.'

We gloomed our way through a few drinks as we went over the demise of Derry. Although he was repetitive and sunk in nostalgic sorrow, Mick stayed with me longer and more vividly than most, still coming back to my mind as freshly as a remembered burst of savage criticism. I can still see that hunched broken figure sitting on the bar-stool as he spoke quietly; a man surrounded and tossed about by the tide of events that he barely understood, bemoaning the loss of the past, trying to survive in the bleak present and looking forward to an even bleaker future.

The only time he cheered up at all was when I was leaving. I told him that God's hand was everywhere and I was sure He would sort it out in His own time and way. We should never come to believe that He would ever abandon us.

'If only I could be sure of that,' he murmured as I headed for the door.

The next day I went back to the cathedral and almost immediately bumped into the verger, Bobby Jackson, a man of the purest enchantment who, as soon as I looked at him, told me that my visit to this beleaguered city had not been in vain.

He had a tiny shrunken head mounted on a long neck with big floppy ears, bushy eyebrows and the tightest, smallest mouth. He said he was 'just eighty-three' and the oddness of his appearance was made considerably odder by the fact that he was as bald as a snooker ball with tiny red veins running about his boko like a relief map of the rivers of the world. The whole of this amazing head positively

glistened as if it had been given a tremendous once-over with floor polish.

When I met him in the vestry he was polishing a communion cup and singing to himself: 'Oh to be sure I'm the happiest man that ever walked on two legs. Aye.' And what was the reason for all this romping happiness? Well, he had been having the very divil of trouble with the graveyard gates but now workmen were out there fixing them and that made him happier than ever.

He showed me around the various war mementoes in the museum, together with the bomb mounted on a small plinth in the porch. This bomb was fired into Derry by an invading Irish army on July 10, 1689. It did not explode and instead was found to contain a letter offering the most favourable terms to the besieged loyalists if they would surrender the city. They had been besieged for eighty-five days and a lot of them had died, the survivors living chiefly on starch mixed with tallow. Nonetheless they refused to give in.

We also took a look at the epitaph to Rev. Robert Higginbotham who died of fever in 1857. Penned by Primate Alexander, it is widely thought to be the most beautiful ever:

Down through the crowded lanes, and closer air
Oh friend! How beautiful thy footsteps were,
When through the fever's fire at last they trod,
A form was with thee like the Son of God.
'Twas but one step for those victorious feet
From their day's walk, unto the golden street,
And they who saw that walk so bright and brief
Have marked this marble with their hope and grief.

All his life, Bobby said, he had got up at 5 a.m. and worked through to 6 p.m. for just half a crown a week. No tea-break. Nothing. But look what the workers got these days. 'I was watching this man painting, so I was, and he was painting over some dog mess he was. I said you should clean that, I said. But no. No pride, that's the trouble these days.

'My belief is that plenty of hard work keeps you young. That's my experience too. I raised a big family. I had no broo or assistance. I had to go out for money to feed them. We got nothing from the British Government but now they take seven pounds twenty tax a week off me from what I earn here.' It was then that he told me that he had no less than twenty-four children.

Later that morning there was a tiny communion service with a congregation of ten in the small chapel on one side of the nave. Afterwards, I had a long chat with the Dean, the Very Reverend George Good. I asked him if Bobby really did have twenty-four children. 'He does,' was the reply. 'Twenty-four children and a very tired wife.'

Bobby specialised in the year 1689 and knew everything about it. Even today, he maintained the tradition of ringing the curfew bells at 9 a.m. and 9 p.m. It wasn't true that he was always happy; if he was wearing a cap that meant trouble. People suspected that he was even older than he said he was. 'The locals say that he's really eighty-eight. He decided to leave out the war years.'

It turned out that Bobby had come to them one day to act as a relief verger and the first indication that he was permanent came when he painted his name on the bottom of the church noticeboard. He added that Bobby had lost his hair through shock when he had been upended into the brass funnel of a fire engine during a riot in the Bogside. All his hair fell out in the same night. The astonishing sheen of his head posed problems when the television cameras were here in church. The technicians wanted to powder his head because his boko kept catching the lights and glowing like a great belisha beacon.

The Dean was an affable man with a most engaging sense of humour but with the strange and disconcerting habit when talking of making his eyeballs disappear as his eyelashes fluttered up and down to show a vast expanse of white. He had been here sixteen years – just one and half before the balloon went up – and they were doing what they could to keep the spirit of Columba alive in the wreckage.

'I know all the members of the other churches by their Christian names. We meet a lot and the Catholic clergy come to the services here. The Presbyterians won't mix with the Catholics though. Paisley has caused a lot of trouble out here.'

Television has played its part too. Sometimes they would just have to set up the cameras and a riot followed within minutes. When there were riots, everyone longed for 6 p.m. to come. That was when the mobs went home to watch themselves on the box. Then they'd come pouring back out on to the streets again, added the Dean.

I had been surprised to learn that the Scottish media always ignored any sectarian troubles, I told him. Did he know that? No, he did not.

He said that they tried very hard to keep the notion of pilgrimage alive; indeed, a few years back, to commemorate the fourteen hundred years since Columba sailed from Londonderry, the cathedral had arranged for thirteen people to row a curragh following Columba's original voyage. 'When they arrived in Iona the mist was so thick a bishop got lost in it,' he recalled.

They still celebrated Columba's birthday every year though it had to be remembered that this was not the site of the original church. He unlocked a large vault and showed me some very old and probably very valuable maps, showing the Church of the Long Tower, just a mile or so from the cathedral where the original church had been built.

After I left the Dean I walked down into the Catholic enclave to have a closer look at the Church of the Long Tower. Again, it was one of those horrific walks, looking around at the high fortified corrugated fence – compliments of the Department of the Environment – which divided the communities and the endless vista of grilles over the windows.

One flat had been burned out with just a charred curtain fluttering forlornly in the gutted window frame. 'One of our idjeets did that a week ago,' said a man passing by. 'Right bloody idjeets, ain't we?'

A man was painting a wall with brilliant white emulsion. How long would that last? He tipped the peak of his cap up on to his head and looked at his Omo masterpiece. 'Oh, about ten days, I'd say. Ten days at the most.'

The church was yet another oasis, pleasing to the eye and enlivening to the spirit, where three people were praying amidst lots of polished wood and banks of glimmering devotional candles. Outside I found a stone which said: 'This ground on which you stand is holy. Here Columba said his first Mass in Derry in August 546. Never since has Mass ceased to be offered on this spot. Here he had frequent visions of the angels and at least one apparition of the Lord.'

I was making a note of the inscription when a man came over to me, one Shamus Kavanagh, who took me on a tour around the church, showing me the original marbles and the old graves at the rear. He also showed me Columba's stone built into the wall with two whorled holes in it. 'Some say the holes came because he was kneeling on it all the time. Others because people all over the years kept touching it.' His old fingers reached out and smoothed around inside one of the holes. ''Tis a powerful holy place to be certain.'

'This stone was removed from the street in 1897, near St Columba's Well, where it had lain for centuries,' it said on the inscription. 'In 1898 it was solemnly enshrined on this Calvary to which our Holy Father, Leo XIII has been pleased to attach many indulgences, both plenary and partial.'

Shamus left me in the churchyard and I went back inside the church, going over to the altar rail and standing gazing at the incandescent bank of smoking hazy candles.

The steady and bright flame of a candle tells us much about that which is holy. It tells us about the unbroken flow of prayer which continues even after our private prayers have stopped. It tells of the light that Christ brings into our lives and into the lives of the people we meet. It symbolises the spiritual daring of Patrick's Paschal candle when he defied the evil demons of the Druids.

I took a candle and lit one for that boy in the Botanic Gardens in Belfast who had nothing to look forward to.

I took another candle and lit it for embattled Ulster in the prayer that a great ball of purifying fire would be rolled across the Province and that its frightened children be delivered up from the coils of this evil snake as, even now, it continues trying to squeeze the last vestiges of life from the community.

With the weeping rage of God in me I lit another that this Province might one day be delivered from the shadow of this man of lawlessness; that God might send all his holy angels to put an end to the weeping and dry all the tears.

I lit another in the prayer that the loving spirit of Columba, my dove, would return to this city and this church where it was first given majestic birth. I lit another with Elijah in mind who, after years of prayer and hope, saw the first clouds of rain on the horizon after a long, long drought.

God is racked with pain at this attack on His babies so we should all be lighting candles throughout Ulster that the hate now ebbs away and that this thing should come to an end.

Jesus said: 'I am the light of the world.'

FIVE
THE TOUGHEST PILGRIMAGE IN THE WORLD

LOUGH DERG·KNOCK·WESTPORT

There were about a hundred of us standing on the quay, all as quiet and thoughtful as communicants queuing up at the altar rail for the bread and wine. It was the greyest of mornings – a weeping morning – with the glittering still waters of the lake in front of us and the wooded low hills of Donegal behind. Far out on the lake a grey building with a green dome rose sheer out of one of the many islands and sat on the water like a magical illusion. It might have been a French chateau or even a Victorian prison but it was the Basilica of St Patrick's Purgatory of Lough Derg.

We were all quiet and thoughtful since each of us had just paid six pounds in the ticket office and were about to spend three days and two nights on the toughest and most penitential pilgrimage in the world.

As requested, none of us had eaten since the night before and already the hunger pains were clawing at my belly. I was with Felix, a small, bald man, as old as those hills and

with the lithe fitness of a flea. On the bus down here he had been teaching me how to say the Rosary and its prayers which, for the next three days, we would be reciting endlessly. *Hail Mary full of grace for the Lord is with ye. Blessed art thou amongst women and blessed is the fruit of thy womb Jesus Christ.*

Now you say it yourself, said Felix. Right. Now the creed: *I believe in God, the Father Almighty, the maker of heaven and earth . . .* Right. Now the Our Father. *Our Father which art in heaven hallowed be thy name . . .*

Felix had been to Lough Derg more times than he could remember. One year he had come with a bad back; it had healed up on the penances. 'You never take a cold home from Lough Derg,' he told me, but I knew that more than one penitent had died from the island's rigours. Then again, one man had made a grand total of fifty-six visits, the last when he was well into his eighties.

The sky was blackening and curdling with thunder as

the boat chugged across the water, sending out bobbing waves which whooshed along the banks of the tiny islands choked with shrubs and small ash trees. The water was slightly rusty – hence Lough Derg: the Red Lake. A peal of bells rang out and soon we were disembarking into one of the strangest encounters I have ever had with a place anywhere.

More than a thousand people were crammed together on this small island, some sitting on benches and others walking around the untidy brown stones which formed the penitential beds. All were barefoot and watched us silently as we came ashore and walked up past the dank lawns. It was their silence which was so difficult to come to terms with.

I followed Felix up to a dormitory where a nun, dressed in grey robes and with wide severe features that seemed not to have seen much laughter, told us to take off our shoes and socks and leave all our belongings on one of the beds. I pressed my fingers into one of the mattresses, finding no give in it at all. 'They are hard,' said the nun, watching me. 'But when you do come to sleep here you won't even notice it.'

So, barefoot and holding a rosary in my fingers, I came out into the warm, damp yard where a fresh-faced priest with spiky ginger hair explained what I had to do. 'First you have to make a station. You start here at St Patrick's Cross where you kneel and say one Our Father, one Hail Mary and one Creed then you go to St Bridget's Cross . . .'

One whole station, I discovered, called for an hour of kneeling before and kissing crosses, circling the Basilica again and again, walking repeatedly around the stone beds of St Brendan, St Catherine and St Columba, kneeling on the shore facing the lake and pushing out your arms three times at St Bridget's Cross to renounce the world, the flesh and the devil. All prayers were to be said standing, walking or kneeling – but never sitting.

In between each station – which took a little over an hour each – you could rest but you had to accomplish at least three stations before the beginning of the all-night vigil in the Basilica.

I began my first station sticking right behind Felix and soon fell into a strange, uplifting, wearying pattern of prayer and discomfort circling around and around with the others. Bells rang out occasionally; now and then my feet slipped or I stubbed my toes on the rocks of the penitential beds which were the remaining ruins of the bee-hive cells of the first Celtic anchorites who once lived here. Their dampness made them difficult to walk on and even worse to kneel on.

I doubted if I was going to survive three days of this; in fact, at the beginning, I wouldn't have put money on lasting three hours.

But I did settle down and after two stations I was relaxed enough to begin nosing around to see what was going on. My most vivid and immediate impression of the place was the horrific ugliness of human feet. There were swollen feet with bulging blue veins and hammered toes. There were puffed-up ankles and feet with bunions and feet with corns. All of them were stinking dirty from walking through the mud of the penitential beds though even the thickest layers of mud could not disguise those awful patterns – some flat and others fallen, some twisted and others skeletal, some knobbly and others bunched with arthritis. We spent a lot of time discussing feet on Lough Derg.

Yet in between stations we discussed lots of other things too since the Irish clearly can't give up yarning, not even on a penitential pilgrimage. By and large they were a jolly, devout bunch with a lot of hunched shoulders and grey hair. But there was also a fair smattering of teenagers too, all eager to do their stations properly and not above telling the odd dirty joke just to show how worldly they really were. 'So this priest asked me if I had ever slept with a woman and I said that, oh to be sure, I must have dozed off a couple of times.'

Isolated on its island, the punishing regime of Lough Derg is suited to only the most determined of penitents.

No one bends the rules on food or rest, as I discovered from one of the priests, who told me of two women who came here and produced their own bottle of milk for their tea. The priest pointed out that this was not allowed and the women insisted that they had been given a special dispensation for their milk by the Archbishop of Dublin. A brisk row followed when the Prior, Gerard McSorley, was called and the next thing the two women, together with their bottle of milk, were on the boat back to the mainland.

Other pilgrims have been sent home for turning up drunk or, in one case, for bringing a rug to snuggle down under at night. An unbelievable amount of thought had gone into making you as uncomfortable as possible. You are locked out of your dormitory. There is no pulling of leg-warmers down over feet; without shoes or socks, feet get cold and stay cold. Sweets, chocolate and chewing gum are banned. Apart from the tea, the only other thing you may drink is Lough Derg soup: warm water which may be sprinkled with salt or pepper or even *both*. Mineral water is allowed which, for the purposes of the fast, is defined as anything that does not fizz – i.e. water.

Evening Mass is in the Basilica at 6.30. The Reverend Michael Hand spoke of love:

'Too many people are confused by what we mean by love. There are confused ideas particularly among the young. So what do we mean by love? Is it a feeling or emotion? Jesus' whole life is a living description of what love is. He always went beyond loving as himself. The essence of Christianity is to love to the point of death. Paul's is a perfect portrait of love: "Love is always patient and kind . . . never rude or selfish. Delights in the truth." How do we measure up to this idea of love? We must love people as they are. It is easy to love those who love us. But our love may meet with hatred and rejection sometimes. We must not be afraid to stand up and be counted. Jesus won in the end. He loved unto death.'

They were dressed in a myriad variety of jogging suits, football jerseys and jeans. They smoked a lot between the stations too, which I thought a bit unfair on us non-smokers since the cigarettes took the edge off their hunger. By now, mine was positively burning in the pit of my belly.

Later that afternoon we went for our first and only meal of the day: dry toast and black tea perched on a long bench next to a trestle table. As a meal it banked down the worst excesses of our hunger and most took it in good humour. There were also some flinty oatmeal cakes, so dry and unappetising they were largely left untouched.

For that service there were sixteen hundred of us packed into the three galleries of the Basilica – the largest number of pilgrims ever to come to Lough Derg in one day and two hundred and thirty-three more than the number who came on the same day the previous year. Back in the 1950's thirty-three thousand came in one season but this declined in the 1960's and 1970's. Just twenty thousand came in 1982. But, this season, it rather looked as if they were going to have the largest number ever, since, as one priest fervently believed, times of poverty and hardship were again encouraging people to return to the Lord.

With no curtains or flowers the lantern-shaped Basilica reflected the austerity which is the pure spirit of this particular penance. The nave was set before a plain white marble altar; a giant chandelier hung down from the roof like clusters of bright electric berries. The plain walls soared in clear straight lines, though it was the stained glass windows which provided the one touch of colourful vivacity, depicting the Stations of the Cross in terrific daubs of flaring yellows, reds and purples.

Announcements followed the sermon: 'If you haven't taken your meal for the day you should do so as soon as possible. There will be confessions at 8.30 for those who have completed three stations.'

After the service our little gang met again on the bench near the water's edge where we shared yarns, jokes and the odd bit of helpful advice. 'When you go for confession, go for the Pilgrim Priest cubicle,' said Danny. 'He's a Franciscan and absolves you from everything you've ever done. You don't even have to say much. They're flying out of his cubicle like bullets. Franciscans only ever get upset by sins against charity.'

Asking about, I found a great variety of motives for coming on this toughest of pilgrimages. Some had come to pray for employment, to seek a favour in examinations or to try to make a decision on whether to get engaged, move jobs or even leave home. Some had come in the spirit of thanksgiving for some Divine favour. One man had promised, forty years ago, that he would do this pilgrimage if his sister recovered from a serious illness. She had indeed recovered and so, a little late in the day, he was keeping his side of the bargain.

Those who came out of curiosity never came back; curiosity was soon satisfied here. Those who came for the sake of friendship found it the greatest possible test.

Come 9.30 p.m. and it was time for the night prayer and benediction. Two bats were flying around inside the dome of the Basilica, and there was the slight burble of conversation as we packed into the pews. Then we sang a hymn as, outside, the night thickened over the placid yeasty waters of the lake and the midges danced around in the lights in the yard. A boat came in, sending its wake chuckling up against the quay. Some would soon be going to bed but we, who had arrived that day, were getting ready for the Rite of Penance which would take us through a night of tributes to St Patrick for rescuing us from the devastation of sin.

The priest prepared us for the Rite with an amiable, if stern, lecture:

'Your beds must have been locked up and you must remember that you must not lie down anywhere or stretch yourself out. You must not get down on your front or your back or prop yourself up on your elbow. If you do we will have to ask you to sit up. When I do they always say: "But father, I wasn't sleeping." Stay off the grass. Let the grass look after itself. You must always sit with your back against something. Some even fall asleep standing up. But remember the pilgrimage is not invalid if you do nod off. It only becomes invalid when you cease to make a decent effort. All these things you are doing are to bring you closer to God. Remember also that even before the world was created God knew you would be here tonight. This brings us to the mystery of human freedom and God's plan to bring us together.

Lough Derg offers few distractions and even fewer comforts, but still the pilgrims, in their thousands, come here year after year.

full of grace for the Lord is with ye, he intoned, the words quickening and merging in a sort of long electrified buzz. *Blessed art thou amongst women and blessed is the fruit of thy womb Jesus Christ. Holy Mary Mother of God pray for us sinners now and at the hour of our death.*

The whole congregation kept moving around and around inside and outside the Basilica as we went through the Hail Marys, Our Fathers and Creeds. *Our Father which art in heaven hallowed be thy name . . . On the third day he rose again. He ascended into heaven . . . I believe in the Holy Spirit . . .*

Throughout the penal night we were to chant aloud an incredible three hundred and ninety-six Our Fathers, one hundred and twenty-four Creeds and six hundred and forty-eight Hail Marys. There is a strange Jesuitical cunning in this endless repetition of prayers since, as you soon find, it is almost impossible to let your mind stray from the words and their meanings as they echo through your consciousness. Any fantasies that begin forming are swiftly cut down. Even pretended prayer is impossible. It is the method of the mantra in which meaning builds up in layers. The words might mean nothing, then they might mean everything. One minute they might be the empty cries of parrots and the next they are the profoundest insights of the greatest prophets. They might drift to you from a distance before erupting out of the very core of your being, be as soothing as a lullaby or as painful and direct as a knife in your side.

And so we chanted on throughout the long shuffling night.

It was around four o'clock when the words clearly began to lose their edge. Often they became gabbled, run together so they sounded like the gibberish of a lunatic. When kneeling, someone next to you might sway and knock into you. It was hard on the knees; one man took off his cap, put it down on the floor, went to kneel on it then stopped, as if unsure if he could get his knees directly on to it. So he went down on one knee, rearranged the position of his

'Lough Derg teaches us the value of prayer; the value of being tough on ourselves; making time for God; being prepared to be a Christian in public. Faith must be the foundation stone on which all else is built. So keep your mind on the Lord and don't just sit there gazing at the bunion on the foot of the person in front of you.'

And so, with the ritual closing of the Basilica doors to symbolise those fearful hours when St Patrick battled with demons in the cave on this very island, the Rite of Penance began. A man ascended the pulpit and began reciting the Hail Mary into a microphone. We all joined in. *Hail Mary* cap. Immediately it was time to get up and begin walking again. *Hail Mary full of grace the Lord is with ye* . . .

At the end of each station we got off this constantly revolving, kneeling world for some fifteen minutes' rest. Line after line of us in the pews were nodding off like drugged budgerigars; one man was even snoring until a sharp jab in the ribs woke him up again. Others went out for a smoke in the shelter outside; with all the fug and the packed, tired bodies, it was starting to look like the waiting room of Bombay railway station.

One woman passed around a canister to spray our feet; the midges had been attacking our bunions and corns. Some of the old stagers treated their feet with methylated spirits, always seeming to take things so easily, with their large smiles and a little joke for everything.

Five o'clock came and, walking around and around the outside of the Basilica, I wondered if it could possibly get worse. It promptly started to pour down with rain but still everyone went trudging on . . . *I believe in the Holy Catholic Church, the communion of saints and* . . .

With the rain came a dawn as dark as a hangman's stare. Clouds of tiny moths seemed to be hatched by the glooming morning which was spreading out over the mirrored lake and the tiny granite fists of islands in a great dripping symphony of twisting greys and mordant blacks. The whole universe seemed to be spreading up and outwards like a growing bubble and it was then, as we continued our pounding around the Basilica, that I believe I glimpsed something deep and rich in the Irish psyche.

This was not the bomb-throwing Irish so beloved of the media but a nation in its purest and most noble posture. This was the seed-bed of the Celtic Church; the great spiritual energy of a fundamentally decent people still pre-pared to stumble, red-eyed throughout the night; still pre-pared to punish their knees in prayer before a holy God; still prepared to suffer the pangs of an outrageous hunger; still prepared to walk barefoot over stones as they chanted

their tiny litanies of love . . . all so that they could earn the right to drag themselves face to face with their beloved Patrick; that they might look up to the monumental majesty of their saint who suffered all when he bargained with God to ensure the faith and future of the Irish; the man who fought with demons in a cave on this very island for them. For them!

This damp dawn we were all there in community with Patrick. His ineluctable personality was there with us, next to us, below us and above us. We were now suffering as he had once suffered for us. We had come to pay homage to him; this complete man who comforted us still.

And so, with the night behind us, the rain stopped and we stumbled on into the day, somehow not so tired now that the night hours were no longer calling us to our beds, just moving around our stations in slow amiable trances and gathering down on the quay in between stations for a wee crack.

A few of us were sitting there with our aching feet dangling in the water when the cruellest thing happened. Someone in the priory was cooking bacon and egg whose smell drifted over the water towards us, churning over our empty bellies and almost lifting us up on tip-toe with the mesmerising deliciousness of its aroma. We sighed, but nothing was said. There was nothing to say.

This particular island has been a centre of prayer and penance since Patrician days but it was later visitors who made it famous – men like Knight Owen who, when left alone in the cave – which has since disappeared – saw a vision of hell as he struggled with demons, later being consoled by angels before walking into Paradise. It became a popular site for supernatural visions and experiences. People claimed that they had walked across drifting plains with rivers of fire winding through a landscape of night-

The Basilica of St Patrick's Purgatory, Lough Derg: 'It might have been a French chateau, or even a Victorian prison.'

mare. Souls withered in flames with just a small fragile bridge to cross over. There were reports of huge pools of ice and immense reptiles. Dante's *Inferno* was said to be indebted to reports from Lough Derg.

It was widely believed that anyone who could spend twenty-four hours with the unknown and unspeakable in the cave would be purged of sin and automatically go to heaven. Kings, grandees and pilgrim poets came from all over Europe, all to stay in this fearful place and converse with the dead. But in 1497 it was dug up and closed.

Pilgrimages to the island continued, however. The pres-

ent Basilica was built in 1920 and consecrated in 1931; it is widely recognised as the most disciplined institution in the Irish church. It is open for ten weeks each year from the first of June to the fifteenth of August.

I did go up to the dormitory later that morning to clean my teeth. Taking one look at the bed, I climbed on to it and was fast asleep within seconds. The nun with mirthless features came and threw me out. I hurried out without complaint or comment; she was as terrifying as a London taxi driver.

I sinned again soon after that. I found a can of Coca-Cola in my bag so I sat in the lavatory, my shorts wrapped around the tin to keep down the noise of its fizzing, and drank it down with grateful relish.

That afternoon I had a chat with one of the priests, an affable young man in a trendy cap by the name of Father Laurence Flynn. 'We get all sorts here,' he said. 'Some are determined to do it properly and others are more than happy to leave when we ask them. We leave nothing to the frailty of human nature. It's the island location that makes total control possible. There have been some changes but, by and large, people resist them. This year there is the option of having coffee instead of tea and they complained about that. A few had fractured their ankles on the penitential beds so we put in a few flagstones to make it a bit easier and they complained about that too.'

I had noticed that nuns were going to the confessional. What sort of sins do nuns get up to? 'Och, they're human too. They mostly worry about the people they work with, how they are getting on with them and that kind of thing.'

He'd had, he added, some very interesting confessions while out here, sometimes from men involved in sectarian violence. He made such confessions sound the very highlight of his day. 'But we always give them absolution if they seem contrite. It's not for us to act for the law, though we do get very tough on them if they have involved an innocent person.'

Then we were back for the last few hours on those penitential beds. Sluggish minutes crawled past on torpid feet. Some of the beds were ankle deep in mud from the rain; I could not have felt worse. I consoled myself with the thought that, in olden days, the pilgrimage here lasted for nine days with just bread and water for food. Some pilgrims died of typhoid; everyone had to plunge themselves into the lake three times each day as a symbol of cleansing. Pilgrims were also armed with long pins which they stuck into anyone who dozed off in the night vigil.

And so it came to 10 p.m., time for the night prayer and benediction and then bed. We stumbled to our dormitories and, without a word and without even taking our clothes off, climbed into the rock-hard beds with the rock-hard pillows and it was Goodnight Vienna. No sooner had my eyes closed than it was time to get up again. It was the deepest, most dreamless, most complete and refreshing sleep that I had ever had.

After morning prayer it was a joy to get our shoes and socks on again. To the call of a bugle, we all filed down to the boats. Father McSorley sang us the traditional hymn of farewell as we moved off.

It had been a remarkable visit; a bit like moving on a time warp back into the fifth century. Even as I looked around at the brown and grey hills and the ruins of houses long since deserted I was still not sure what had hit me. I had not done battle with demons or seen fiery rivers or been attacked by reptiles or heard fearsome howlings in a dark cavern. But even a few weeks later I still felt a deep and mysterious sense of renewal.

It was an encouraging feeling. There and then, on that boat, I promised that I would do Lough Derg again but better the next time. There would be no slipping into bed, no mineral water that fizzes or any heretical stuff like that.

The *Galway Express* went racing down through the twisting country lanes of Sligo, past small dusty villages and the misty symmetrical tableau of the Ox Mountains. We were clearly moving through very poor country now, evinced by the terrible pocked roads and raggedy farms with patchwork hedgerows. Donkeys went about donkey business in poky backyards; men in boots sat yarn-

Knock. 'The very first thing you notice is the glittering torrent of plastic rubbish piled up over the counters, like some great beast hatched in the very maw of Woolworth's.'

even if it was covered with such a patina of seediness you wanted to run amok with a duster. The streets were full of Victorian ironwork and the chimes of doleful bells.

We left Sligo and I was dozing when I found a wasp on my lap and brushed it off. The wasp lay on its side in the gangway and I was lifting my rolled newspaper to bash its brains in when I looked up and noticed for the first time the nun sitting behind me. She must have got on at Sligo. I asked if it was a sin to kill a wasp, she shook her head so I gave the thing a hefty belt and missed. Still the wasp was hobbling around so, with a smile and a nod, the nun lifted her foot and crunched the poor insect flat with her black polished shoe. Murder on the *Galway Express*.

Today I was on my way to Knock and had to get off at Ballyhaunis for another bus. The wait was very long but I was in a sunny mood and told a woman one of my favourite little stories of the two men late for an appointment and needing a bus fast. They went down on their knees to pray for a bus which came immediately and went straight past them since, deep in prayer, they failed to signal it to stop. The woman went to stand on the other side of the pavement for fear, I imagine, that I might try and tell her another one.

Knock turned out to be a tiny and bewildering village built around a main street in a low spin of green Mayo hills which, on first blush, had all the convivial vulgarity of a long and amplified belch. A sign in the middle of the place managed to sum it all up: *Confessions*, one way. *Holy Water*, the other. *Post Office*, this way. *Tourist Office*, that way. *Holiday Home*, up there. *Jeweller*, down there. *Assembly Rooms*, over the road.

The place could well have been the ugly offspring of a mating between a circus big top and a holiday camp, all crushed up into a hamburger with lots of chips and a single votive candle flickering on top of the lot.

There were the great grey vistas of the car parks and the huge space-age church which not so much resembled a

ing on the top of low stone walls while their burly women-folk scattered feed before crowds of agitated chickens.

This bus could clearly be thumbed down anywhere. As we moved through village after village, men kept getting on with strange objects in cardboard boxes and women with baskets overflowing with vegetables got off. One man with a cat in a box came and sat next to me, the cat's thin piteous mewlings echoing around and around the bus.

Cottages smothered in climbing roses dotted the side of the road and we passed the sea where swans were swimming in the bays. The town of Sligo seemed lively enough, church as a rocket launching pad. Tiny rows of souvenir stalls stood next to the restaurants. There were admin offices for this and admin offices for that and fast-food restaurants with even faster prices catering, miserably, for the hungry pilgrims.

The truly fatal feature of Knock – fatal because it is the very first thing you notice on arrival – is the glittering torrent of plastic rubbish piled up over the counters like some great beast, hatched in the very maw of Woolworth's, growing and multiplying like that monster in *The Blob*, soon to devour the very church itself with the jaws of its kitsch crassness.

On one stall alone I found plastic crucifixes, magnetic car badges, polythene bottles of Holy Water (thirty-five and eighteen pence), a pile of pink shillelaghs of rock – *A Present from Knock* written through them (twenty pence each or six for a pound) – Knock baseball caps, holy bottle openers, pious key rings, autograph books and photograph albums, Knock pencils, Celtic crosses made from polystyrene, horse shoes, mirrors and six-feet-long wooden rosaries. I liked one plaque, though: an Irish toast – *May you be in heaven half an hour before the Devil knows you are dead.*

There was a small old church which was amok with a wedding that afternoon. The lovely bride was standing in the porch with the smile on her lips frozen with the purest fear. Every now and then she tried to broaden the smile, but it was as if the corners of her mouth had been put in deep freeze. The smile stretched a shade, collapsed and died. Crowds seemed to be drifting in and out of the nave with other pilgrims walking around and around the church fingering rosaries and chanting their Hail Marys. Before the wedding service began, a beautiful Irish tenor voice up in the gallery sang John Denver's 'Annie's Song'.

'We have come here to marry Thomas and Mary who have loved one another for a long time,' said the priest. 'We ask Our Lady to keep their love faithful and undying.

The Christian home makes Christ present in all things. Love is his constant calling – his fulfilment and help.'

After the wedding vows, people made their way up to the altar for communion. It occurred to me then how important a role the Church still plays in life events – of how it is always there and active in matters of births, marriages and deaths. Even at a time when many see the Church as stumbling and failing it is still the very cement of society, interpreting and declaring God's eternal purpose, overseeing life's cycles of feast and fast, Sunday and weekday, Christmas and Easter, the sowing and the harvest.

We need to go back just over a hundred years, to a rainy August 21, 1879, to understand the story of how the huge shrine of Knock came into being.

These were famine-haunted years, with the potato crop failing repeatedly and the farmers plagued by evictions by the army, rack rents and typhus fever. In just thirty years the country had lost one third of its population – a million dead by famine and two million in despairing flight. Now, in the summer of 1879, the crop was about to fail yet again.

At 7 p.m. on that fateful August day in this poor, peaceful and unknown village in County Mayo, just outside on the gable wall of this very church, all heaven broke loose.

The sky was slate grey with a strong northerly wind blowing when Margaret Beirne locked up the church for the night and set off home along the heavily pitted road. A fine drizzle began seeping out of the twilight when she noticed a large orb of light on the gable end of the church but, the evening being wet, she continued on her way. Later, at 7.30 p.m., she left her home and took another look and decided that some white statues had just been delivered there. 'Why didn't you tell me that the priest had got new statues?' she asked her friend.

The pair went back to the church to investigate and found

The marble statues at Knock commemorate the divine visitation of 1879. Barely ten days later, the first miracle cure took place here, and the marketing of Knock was under way.

white cloak fastened at the neck with a crown on her head. There was a beautiful mystical rose on her brow. Her hands were raised as if in prayer and her eyes turned upwards to the drizzling skies. Her face, said one witness, was a slightly yellower white than her cloak.

On her right was St Joseph with slightly greying whiskers and on her left St John the Evangelist dressed in the sacerdotal robes of a bishop, holding an open book in his left hand and, according to one child, wearing 'a little roundy hat'. Behind St John was an altar and, completing this fantastic arrangement of ice and flame, a cross and a lamb.

Who could even start to describe what must have poured through the veins of those fifteen visionaries as they gazed at this apparition? This was their beloved Mary, the Queen of Heaven and Mother of the World, clearly come with a mother's faithful love, to tell her hungry children that she had not forgotten them as they struggled through their dark night.

One of the villagers wept. Another said the rosary. They noticed that the ground where the figures were standing was completely dry. One ran off to get the local priest, Archdeacon Cavanagh. But being cold and wet after his rounds, he refused to go to the church, saying that the apparition was probably just a reflection in a stained glass window.

The apparition ended when Mrs Trench, a seventy-five-year-old woman, threw herself at Our Lady's feet to find that the figure had no substance. 'Nil lada ariseo,' she said in Irish. There is nothing here. Nothing, that was, except the soft cold rain sweeping up against the gable wall.

that the statues were moving. 'It's the Blessed Virgin,' said Margaret. Others were called and soon fifteen villagers in all were standing there in the pouring rain gazing at an apparition which, subsequently, was to seize the imagination of the Irish nation.

Three figures in all moved backwards and forwards slowly around an altar like glittering holograms. Each glowed with a light more startling and pure than the very sun; the edges of each apparition were evanescent with the flashing wings of hovering angels.

The central figure of Mary was dressed in a brilliant

People were flinging handfuls of confetti over the bride and groom. The bride was indeed very lovely, more relaxed now that it was all over, with a great broad grin lighting up her face. The groom could not stop beaming either, his nose curled up and chest puffed out like an extremely happy parrot.

On the gable end of the church there is now a glass oratory in which the three figures of the original apparition have been recreated in white Carrera marble. The glass doors of the oratory could be slid back and pilgrims were now queuing up to kneel before the statuary. PLEASE DO NOT TOUCH THE STATUES, read the inevitable notice.

I continued to feel uneasy. Looking around the oratory, I found a golden rose which had been presented to the shrine by Pope John Paul. The rose was somehow in the character of the place. I recalled a poetry contest in Spain where the third prize was a gold rose, the second prize was a silver rose and the first prize was a real rose.

Right in the middle of the complex was a huge stone cross erected in memory of the Papal visit on September 30, 1979, 'The greatest event in Irish history since the coming of Saint Patrick.'

Later, I went to have a look at the huge new Basilica which had been built a few hundred yards away. With the space and functionalism of an aeroplane hangar, its interior echoed with the cries of distant children. Though full of light, there was very little colour; whatever once there might have been seemed to have seeped away into the grey concrete support pillars. The chairs were small, cheap and wooden. There was no stained glass and no way of kneeling. Up above was a control room for radio and television while the altar sat in the middle of it all, cold and unadorned – a funeral pyre in the centre of a circus big top waiting patiently for a client.

I decided there and then that I wanted to see no more of Knock. However inquiries in the administrative block suggested that I might be able to meet the man behind it all, Monsignor James Horan, the next day. He is something of a legend in Ireland so I stayed on and signed into a gloomy hotel next to a farm where nothing quite fitted and the smell of something vaguely unpleasant hung in the carpets.

In the evening after dinner, I left the hotel for a constitutional. Night was now striding down over Knock with a light grey mackerel sky and one long bank of fluffy black cloud moving over the distant horizon. In the main street a man was speaking so loudly in an illuminated *Telefon* kiosk his voice carried clear across the road. A huge flock of starlings were roosting on a tall television mast – great bundles of black musical notes dotted over the lines of the wires.

I walked back down to the shrine, strangely peaceful and even faintly beautiful in the glimmer din with just a few children playing near the glass oratory. The statuary looked like white fish in an incandescent aquarium. Three women were sitting inside the glass walls gazing up at Mary. Now one of them stepped forward and kneeled at Mary's feet. A lorry went roaring past. There was the sound of car doors slamming.

I went down to look at the new Basilica again but, even in the encroaching darkness, it still failed to accrue much splendour to itself. It aspired to the proportions of a cathedral yet had no cathedral atmosphere. But for the odd motifs of crosses carved into the walls – so crude they might have been medieval arrow slits – it could just have been any old pre-stressed concrete office block. It gave the unfortunate impression of being done on the cheap; even the tall spire was the colour of rust. It aspired without accomplishing; it had none of the authority that comes with age; it had no authenticity or intelligence.

Three women walked past arm in arm and humming. Everyone seemed happy and contented enough here, which was all that mattered, I guess. Even vulgarity can make people happier than small babies. Vulgarity can be fun though, for myself, I believe that vulgarity and holiness are inimical. Holiness loves the old, regular and unadorned which is strewn across the beaten path of our ancestors. Holiness makes worship a wondrously attractive love affair with God and draws people to it. Holiness sets up an

argument so pure there is no escape from it. Knock seemed to have no such quality.

I walked back to the road. That wandering bank of cloud remained low and incredibly thick. Hardly anyone passed the oratory without stopping to look at the statuary and cross themselves. The man was still speaking loudly in the *Telefon* kiosk. A few midges bit into my neck like tiny stabs from sewing needles. A tractor came roaring down the road, headlamps blazing and trailer piled high with hay. There was that pungent aroma of burning peat and I knew that I was back in my beloved Republic of Ireland again; back in the country which had given me many hours of gurgling happines and peace.

The next morning I went over to have a chat with silver-haired Father Michael Casey, who runs the Knock medical bureau which verifies miracles.

He explained the long and tortuous process. First they had to get all the doctors' certificates stating that the disease had existed. Then there were the certificates stating that the patient had been cured. After that the patient will be examined again to ensure that the cure has been maintained. Then the doctors decide for themselves if a miracle has taken place and, if so, they send the dossier to the patient's Bishop who then sets up a committee of inquiry. It is then up to the Bishop to proclaim the miracle.

They recently had in a man from Clare with a cancerous lump on his hand. Soon to go into hospital for an operation, he came to Knock and the lump just fell off. 'A good cure but not much chance of being proclaimed a miracle,' said Father Casey, with the nostalgic sigh of an angler talking about the big one that got away.

His best bet for a cracking good miracle, it turned out, was a man with spinal injuries and in great pain when he came here. At about three o'clock he felt a strange sensation

in the base of his skull which stretched right down to the base of his spine. After that his recollection became hazy. The next moment he was clearly aware of himself; he had stood up and walked fifty yards from the wheelchair. His wife, unaware of the significance of what had happened, began shouting at him for being so rude in walking away from his friends.

There is a long and moving history of cures in Knock. Barely ten days after the apparition, a girl was cured of deafness and pain in her ear. Seven weeks later a Commission of Inquiry was set up, examining all the fifteen villagers and finding their testimony trustworthy and satisfactory. Thereafter the lame, the afflicted and the merely depressed, the diseased, the grief-stricken and those without hope, all the casualties of nineteenth-century Ireland took the hard road of penance as they struggled to Knock. In carriages, donkey carts, pony and traps they came, but many more arrived on foot, seeking favours from Mary, graciously coming to this Mayo backwater to start the first flowering of a pilgrim church.

Soon the meadow around the church became a swamp as the lame walked and the blind saw again. All the cement on the wall where the miracle occurred was picked out and taken away. Those who had been cured festooned the wall with crutches, surgical boots and leg irons. The first mass pilgrimage came from Limerick in 1880 and in that year alone three hundred cures were recorded. One man coughed up a growth from out of his throat, another reported that his ulcers had been cured and yet another found that his deformed hip had been put right. Even a leper was reported to have been cured here.

Then they started flooding in from abroad too; from America, Australia and New Zealand. There was the Childrens' Peace Pilgrimage, the National Pilgrimage for the

Peace and Protection of Ireland, the Society of African Missionaries, the Volunteers of Suffering, the Carmelite Regional Pilgrimage . . . Great shuffling armies – four million in the year the Pope visited Knock – now around two million a year, all sending up huge pyramids of prayer, all come to the market for miracle.

The Sacred Congregation of the Council in Rome issued guidelines for pilgrim behaviour:

> Pilgrimages must always have a truly religious character; they must be conducted as acts of Christian piety and must be clearly distinguished from journeys undertaken merely for recreation. It is most important to point out that all unnecessary and immoderate use of intoxicating drink is out of harmony with the spirit of devotion and reverence so necessary for pilgrims. Pilgrims are earnestly requested not to give scandal in this matter.

Later I met Tom Neary, the affable chief steward of Knock who told me about their marriage bureau and how it had been set up to try and correct the sexual imbalance in the West of Ireland following the tendency of many of the girls to emigrate. 'Fellas just couldn't get anyone to marry,' he explained, 'so we got them to fill in some forms and tried to introduce them to the right girl. We introduce, not arrange, marriages, but the people we deal with are as varied as the human race itself. Some men have up to twenty-five introductions but, if they need such a lot of introductions, they are not usually successful. It shows they are too fussy. They won't lower their sights.'

It seemed a bit odd for a holy shrine to be in the lonely hearts business yet I thought I understood quite a lot about the oddity of Knock after I met the big boss of the shrine, Monsignor James Horan. He is a large ruddy-faced man who does not smoke or drink but enjoys the odd game of golf. He says he will not see sixty again and is much given to riotous guffaws and immodest self-congratulation, whose little jokes and quips are obsequiously laughed at by his lieutenants – 'all kinds of characters' – who help him run the place.

Most tellingly of all he is a man in whom worldly pragmatism and prayerful spirituality have come together to create that most unusual animal – the politician priest with a penchant for the power plays of big business.

He clearly understands the needs of the reporter and talks in brief vivid bursts with much good humour. Mostly we spoke of his running battles with the owners of the souvenir shops and right old ding-dongs they have been on occasions. Once he managed to clear the unlicensed traders off the roads and he even brought the shopkeepers together a few times to try and fix their prices. 'But they couldn't agree. Some wanted to charge more than others. Some wanted to charge less. But let's remember those shops wouldn't be there at all if there wasn't a demand. I can't interfere or they would say that I'm a dictator who should stick to the gospels. I can't tell them what to charge for a piece of chicken.'

But then he added that he did his duty irrespective of what people said. He wanted put on his tombstone that he did according to his lights. 'No one can please the people all the time. I've fought for and against the shop-owners and they once gave me a small presentation recalling that I brought the Holy Father to Knock. I have never neglected my parishioners. I went to every place I was sent. Everything that has happened to us has been for the best.'

We talked finally of his favourite project; the much-publicised airport just then waiting for three million pounds to be completed. Built at a cost so far of ten million pounds the airport is a fantastic tribute to the sheer force of Father Horan's ebullience; to the way he has been wheeler-dealering with finance companies and politicians to get it moving. 'The airport, you might say, is in the hands of

Monsignor James Horan, the driving force behind the building of Knock's multi-million-pound airport: 'I've fought for and against the shop-owners, I brought the Holy Father to Knock, but I have never neglected my parishioners.'

that was important but the effort they made in getting there.

But Father Horan wasn't much impressed with what I said, and dismissed it with a soft snort.

The time had come to go but Tom Neary suggested that, as it was the last Thursday of the month, I should go to the invalids' healing service in the Basilica. I'm glad that I did. It was a sad, weeping service – jam-packed with hope and consolation – a high essay on how a concerned church can bring comfort to an afflicted flock.

'Lord, he whom thou lovest is sick! Lord, that I might walk! Lord, that I might see! Lord, that I might hear!'

All the chairs were packed with people – toddlers climbing over women's knees, men in rather shabby suits, tight starched collars chafing red on their burly necks. Most hands were clutching softly clicking rosaries with, here and there, the white drifts of nurses' caps or the black patches of groups of nuns.

Down next to the altar sat row after row of invalids in wheeled circles, blankets around their legs and shawls around their shoulders. One woman's leg stuck straight out. Some hobbled down to the front on sticks; others, bent double with arthritis and old age, were helped to their seats by stewards in blue suits and green sashes. *Hail Mary full of grace the Lord is with ye, blessed art thou amongst women and blessed is the fruit of thy womb Jesus Christ.*

A young priest lit the candles on the altar. *Our father which art in heaven . . .* A hand went up to stifle a yawn. 'The first three rows are for the anointing of the sick. Only those for anointing should sit in the first three rows. The anointing is only for those with a very serious illness.' *Forgive us our trespasses . . .*

God. It's going according to schedule but more money is needed. Pennies from heaven or millions from the Government. We need to get people here easily.'

I didn't agree with him on that score and told him so. Pilgrimage needs to involve an effort with the journey as important as the arrival. Certainly the pilgrims of old suffered much; some even travelled the roads bringing their own cows with them for milk and chickens to lay eggs. The journey was the pilgrimage and when those three kings travelled to that manger in Bethlehem with gold, frankincense and myrrh it was not the value of the gifts

Some were grotesquely misshapen with tiny shoulders and huge hips. There were club feet and tiny pathetic claws of hands. An eye bulged outwards hideously. *As we forgive them . . .*

A trolley carrying an effigy of Our Lady was pushed to the front of the altar followed by twenty-four priests in white robes. At the end of the altar was a sparkling cluster of silver communion chalices. 'My dear pilgrims I welcome you here today.' A reading from St Paul's *Letter to the Galatians* followed and that familiar smell of peat smoke drifted over the heads of the congregation. Cameras flashed amidst the odd squall of bad breath.

'Lord, he whom thou lovest is sick! Lord, that I may walk! Lord, that I may see! Lord, that I may hear!'

The priest widened his hands and smiled. 'You my dear sick people are the commanders in the army of the church. Maybe you did not know about this.'

The smell of peat mingled now with that of incense. The sun swooped down through the windows in triumph, exploding joyously over the altar.

'My dear invalids you are privileged in so many ways. Those who are suffering get a chance to reflect more than other people, to reflect on the love of God. You can come close to God in infirmity. You have something which requires a great courage and fortitude. Families which bring up invalids can be gentle and kind. You are commandos of the church. You look to God for strength. We have a Catholic father here who received a bullet in the brain in Belfast. Protestants got him an ambulance and rushed him to hospital just in time to save his life. My dear invalids, the Lord invites you to lay down your suffering for Him. Rejoice in your suffering.'

The huge white circle of priests moved around the altar preparing for the sacrament of the sick. There were now some thirty of them and they all held up their hands, bare palms facing the congregation.

A hymn followed and lips moved in unceasing prayer as

Only by travelling on foot can the pilgrim fully savour the character of Ireland. Most are whisked in and out by jet plane or air-conditioned motor-coach.

the priests administered to the sick, anointing their foreheads with a cross and then making a sign of the cross on both hands. *May the Lord who frees you from sin save you and raise you up. Through this holy anointing may the Lord in his great love and mercy help you.*

They lifted up their faces in abject entreaty as the damp thumbs made signs on their foreheads. Their mouths were tight with serious emotion. Their eyes suddenly flickered with life as they were animated by a terrifying hope. The priests waded through the shoulders of the sick who came to them with hands outstretched. A baby was crying. *May the Lord who frees you from sin . . .*

And so I felt the very bloodstream of the Irish flowing hot and deep again. I felt them gather at the feet of their beloved Patrick again, hands raised and using that old language of love. The body of the church was communing with the body of the people.

The priests handed out the communion wafers and you noticed that they all had different styles, some making a little circular flourish as they held the wafer up in the air, some with their little fingers stuck out as they put the wafer on the tongue or in the hands. *Body of Christ.* 'Amen.' *Body of Christ.* 'Amen.'

There were two long dindling chimes of bells and the golden glittering host was raised again. Father Horan said the final prayer: 'I hope that God will bring you many graces, many blessings. We will all pray that God will bring consolation to you.'

The service ended with a blessing of pious objects, held high by the congregation. *As it was in the beginning so it shall be in the end. Amen.* 'The Mass is ended.'

So the sick, who had been encouraged with words and the lame, who had been anointed with the laying on of hands and the deformed, who had been fed with the wafer and the old and frightened, who had been reassured by God's continuing love, were all now told to go in peace.

I walked out of Knock intending to hitch-hike to Wesport, but the local motorists appeared to have other ideas. They seemed oddly resentful of my outstretched thumb, some giving me a satiric wave, others accelerating away as soon as they spotted me.

After an hour I was still without a lift. It was clear that the only way I was going to stop a car was either to build a barricade across the road or fling myself under the wheels.

The greatest curse of the hitch-hiker in this, a good Catholic country, seemed to be the enormous number of children all crushed into each car, their tiny hands all over the windows and row upon row of black eyeballs regarding you. Somewhere deep in this hillock of kids would be a short fat lady with grey hair – the grandmother – handing out sweets.

But there was no haste – which is ridiculous in Ireland anyway – so I tramped along the roads happily enough. Cows' teeth ripped up the grass and others came over to inspect me with their big eyes deep with daftness. A cat and her kitten came and looked out from around the corner of an abandoned school. 'How are ye?' a farmer asked.

'Fine. And ye?'

'Fine. Aye.'

Sometimes I recited Hail Marys to the dancing gnats, keeping quiet and prayerful and, indeed, often so abstracted that I forgot to put out my thumb when I heard an approaching car.

Finally a lorry took me the last mile into Claremorris, followed by a London bus inspector on holiday who took me a few more miles to Castlebar and then it was a lad from Glasgow who took me along the road to Westport and my first sight of the highest mountain in Ireland, Croagh Patrick, The Reek, a huge black colossus shrouded in cloud.

It was this, the great holy mountain of Ireland, that I had

come to climb – along with some forty thousand other pilgrims – the following Sunday. Soon after undertaking the toughest pilgrimage in the world at Lough Derg I was now going to tackle the highest.

Westport turned out to be a convivial jumble of terraced houses, Wimpy bar and sawdust pubs scattered around a turbid stream, thick with weeds and empty lemonade cans where, now and then, you could just spot a darting trout. It had dowdy cafés, a church, shops bulging with postcards and souvenirs and a hotel with a tricolour and the stars and stripes fluttering above its porch, thus keeping most of its options open and a few closed.

Around these hilly streets – where the faint but definite whiff of the holiday camp came strutting around every corner – everyone went very intently about their business. Within half an hour I encountered a burly woman beggar with a baby in a shawl and a gnarled palm permanently outstretched; an actor, who enthused all with his bar-room tales of the famous, home from New York to see his mother; two drunks who seemed to be locked in an argument in the Octagon Square that was going to last a year and countless men, with thick boots and flat caps set at jaunty angles, sitting on walls and kicking their heels as they had a good crack.

The dark bars were alive with stumbling drunks with Guinness stains down the front of their shirts; black-eyed colleens who would show you the hem of their petticoats for sixpence and wild, mad characters with raggedy, oily clothes and billowing grey beards who played accordions in the, often forlorn, hope of a free drink. Come 9.30 p.m. and the bars filled up with folk bands – some good and some rotten – who soon had the very sawdust dancing with their screeching Irish music, screeching non-Irish music or, in one case, just plain screeching.

Hovering over all the good cracks in the bars and those pleasant meals in those dowdy cafés, The Reek just stood there as proud and implacable as a turbanned Sikh. Some-times mists rose from the jagged slopes as if they were on fire. If it was dark and damp The Reek seemed to move away from the town, distant and sullen. If it was fine the very mountain seemed to be about to stand on your foot.

Come to my slopes and I will teach you all about pain and outrage, The Reek seemed to be saying. Come to me all ye who are heavy laden and I will break your bones and your spirit and then, when you think you have nothing more of yourself to give, I will break your heart too.

So six o'clock came on the Saturday night before the great pilgrimage. I had climbed halfway up its slopes and was sitting in a bothy with just my sleeping bag, planning to spend the night out on her rocks. By now a heavy rain was streaming down off the mountain's summit, gusting over the grey slopes and down on to the patchwork of fern and heather below. The polythene cover on my bothy was flapping around; shards of broken glass and hundreds of bottle tops were embedded in the earth floor. Perhaps I could have slept the night here but, somehow, I did not fancy sleeping on all that glass, even if this was the only dry spot on the mountain.

As recently as five years ago this climb was made during the night. Of late, though, the order had been changed for it to be done at the break of dawn. But even in this darkening drizzle, some were already wending their way up the jagged path, a few in their bare feet.

Down below me a path twisted and turned until it reached the small village of Murrisk. Here, in a shop, a woman had loaned me the stick that would help me on the climb. Already the mineral water men and sellers of pious objects were setting up stalls at the bottom of the path, ready for the mob who would arrive early the next morning.

The view of the surrounding countryside was quite staggering: a rolling mist-shrouded vista of feudal Ireland, where peat bog sat next to mossy hummock and huge splintered meteors of rock lay scattered in the gorse. Even the sheep found it difficult to forage in this barren land. Now that they had been shorn, their ribs stuck out in the protruding emblems of famine. This was land which could not have changed a jot since St Patrick came up here and fasted for forty days and nights while bargaining with God over the future security of the Irish.

I had been out wandering in that countryside over the last few days and everywhere I found that things had gone to picturesque rack and ruin: the dry stone walls which zig-zagged one way and t'other before they collapsed into an incoherent rubble; the trees shorn of their foliage and bent double in humble obeisance to the savage westerly winds; the neat marching banks of grass which were once potato beds. I found an old ruined cottage with weeds and saplings growing on the rotten thatched roof. FOR SALE, it had daubed in yellow paint on one of the walls. PHONE WESTPORT 387.

Down near the falls I saw a salmon make a triumphant leap out of a still pool, tail bending almost double in an arc of flashy exuberance before it dropped back into the water leaving behind just the glimmering dartboards where its body had broken up the still surface. Between the grey sky and the dull greens of the sod there were the odd splashes of colour too – the fluffy white heads of the bog cotton nodding in agreement with the flamboyant phrases of the breezes; the tiny scatterings of the buttercups and, just along a lane, a whole wandering hedgerow of fuschia with masses of tiny red bells, each with purple trumpets inside them and long stamens poking down with black tips.

Once or twice I stumbled across the stones of a ruined oratory, a simple house of prayer where a monk of old may have sat listening to the music of the winds, watching the waves, smelling the flowers or tasting the warmth of the sun. Down in Murrisk itself there is a lovely Augustinian abbey, a charming rubble of dry stone walls from which the roof has long since fled.

Way out in front of me as I sat in my bothy was Clew Bay with its three hundred and sixty-five whorled and green islands: one for each day of the year. I could just spot the occasional upturned curragh on the grey shingle shore. A light wind blew bits of froth off the breeze-chopped sea, making them dance across the pebbles like stampeding bits of candyfloss. Mussels were gathered here too and sometimes you could watch the gulls picking them up in their beaks, soaring into the air and dropping them down on to the rocks to try and break open their shells. When the shells refused to yield the gulls picked them up in their beaks again, flying higher now and dropping them yet again.

I gazed around me at the rolling wet mists scouring the slopes of this sacred mountain as if engaged in an eternal struggle to make them clean. A stream was bursting in riotous laughter as it drained the rain out of the belly of the mountain. I could hear the sticks of the pilgrims striking stone as they made their way to the summit, the faces red and blustery with the mounting cruelty of the weather.

Finally I decided to stir my dreaming bones and make my own way up to the summit. I am not at all sure why I decided to leave the dry bothy; by now the rain was sheeting down something awful. Quite soon I found my hands and feet scrambling on piles of wet, mossy rocks which wanted to dance as soon as I stepped on them. Visibility was now but a few feet; the winds howled all around me. Occasionally the dark figure of a returning pilgrim emerged out of the dripping greyness and greeted me cheerily before disappearing in long sliding crunches of stone.

I passed a few rubbled outbuildings and by now was thoroughly cowed since I had not seen anyone for at least half an hour, the rain had seeped right through my clothes and I had gashed my knee in a stumble. I could not decide if it was easier to carry on or go back. The sheer immensity of those slopes was so frightening – everything so savagely durable beneath my frail, panting, non-too-hardy body. The Red Indians say, 'Only the rocks endure forever.'

When I did stagger out on to the summit it was a strange and singular sight, curiously Biblical, with shivering donkeys standing next to piles of stones and makeshift stalls with men and boys huddling beneath tarpaulins like Bedouins in the windy desert as the rain continued sheeting down. The black shapes of a few pilgrims were doing their stations around and around a small cairn, known here as St Patrick's bed. Just along a bit was a tiny whitewashed chapel in which I sought shelter.

Inside a man was hammering together what looked like a communion rail with some five people sitting like penned cattle in small wooden stalls. I stripped off most of my wet clothes and dried myself with the inside of my sleeping bag, chatting with the man with the hammer, telling him what I was up to and whatnot. A writer out on his business of writing always does well to ingratiate himself with whoever seems to be in charge. He was the chapel caretaker, he said, and he always came up here the night before the big annual pilgrimage to make sure that everything was ready.

More dripping, sodden figures came into the chapel and I spoke to two hotel girls from Castlebar who were busy eating an enormous pile of sandwiches. Why had they come on this climb? 'Oh that would be telling, wouldn't it,' one of them replied, giggling. There was a crusty old-timer from Westport who did not make too much sense and had been climbing up here every year since the 1940s. 'St Patrick brought the mountain here, so we've got to look at it,' he told me, straight-faced.

Gale-force winds kept bashing against the walls, demented, as we all settled down to spend the night in the chapel. I had never spent the night in any sort of church and certainly never expected that it would be as comfortless

as this. Giant draughts came romping in under every door and into the small main room. An altar cloth flapped around on a makeshift sort of stand that looked suspiciously like a biscuit tin. Water poured down into butts in various places in the chapel, spilling over on the floor with a positively malevolent glee. The whole place simply stank of animal dung.

But anything – just anything – was better than being out in that storm. I was settling down in a dry, if smelly, corner of the chapel for a long night vigil when the caretaker announced that the chapel was closing and everyone had to leave. Right in the middle of the night in the middle of the wildest storm! I could barely believe my ears. My mouth opened to squeak some sort of protest when he looked at me and said, 'You're all right. You can stay.'

His words were as welcome as a last minute reprieve from the gallows and I could never remember feeling so relieved. It really does pay to ingratiate yourself with whoever is in charge. But my relief was tinged with strong edges of guilt nonetheless as the others picked up their belongings and walked out into that terrible storm. The caretaker locked the door behind them and now, where some forty thousand were expected, there was, for the moment, just one – me.

Sleep was out of the question as I stretched out on the cold hard floor in my sleeping bag, tennis shoes as a pillow, gazing up at the leaking chapel roof. My legs were stiff with the cramps and my knee was sore too as I tossed and turned. Every half an hour or so some pilgrim knocked on the door and cursed piteously when he found that it was locked.

Later it went quiet again. My consciousness was flickering between waking and sleeping when what sounded like a huge group turned up and began moving around the chapel chanting Hail Marys into the teeth of the storm. Around and around they went . . . *Hail Mary full of grace . . . blessed art thou amongst women . . . blessed is the fruit of*

your womb . . . and even as I was stretched out on the chapel floor like a Plantagenet king in the guttering darkness I saw, for the first time, what the bodies of those saints of old must have felt as they lay in state and pilgrims came from far and near to chant devotional prayers around their tomb.

My eyes kept opening and closing when I just had to smile at the expanding absurdity of the notion. What would those sodden pilgrims have said, I wondered, if they had realised that, far from muttering prayers to the glory of their great Irish saint, they were in fact circling a damp Welsh bloke with a gashed knee lying in a sleeping bag with a pair of tennis shoes as a pillow?

The prayers died away and the rains gradually ceased too. But the winds kept pounding against the walls in the steady rhythm of breaking waves. Mighty winds are very evocative of the whirling mysteries of God, I think; so too are the summits of mountains where the imagination can liberate us from our puny forms and set us in a greater picture – way above the earth itself and resting in the hollow of the Lord's palm.

There was the bright brittle music of breaking glass from somewhere outside. Singing rose up and died away in eddies. Finally I dozed off and dreamed a strange dislocated dream of churches and chapels. I was wandering from altar to altar when I broke into a run ending up sliding across freezing ice. The ice cracked and I fell only to be held by the hand of Etheldreda herself. 'There's no milk for the tea,' she said softly before bearing me up and dropping me over a cliff from which I fell for a brief eternity.

With a sudden shuttling of bolts the caretaker opened the door to let in as glorious a dawn as I have ever beheld: the rain and mist had been vanquished by a cool ebullient sunshine with ravishing views of the Twelve Pins of Connemara, the scattered islands of Clew Bay and, beyond, the pine plantations approaching Donegal. Dotted over the brown patterned fields were cut turfs of peat stacked with

The slopes of Croagh Patrick on the West Coast of Ireland. St Patrick beckons to pilgrims toiling up the slopes from the village below.

such precision they might have been mysterious Druidical pyramids.

We were, I now could see, at the apex of a grey-green cone of rock. Sunshine swarmed down behind the clouds and anointed the heads of the thousands upon thousands of pilgrims who were making their way up the slopes. Many were barefoot, mud squeezing up between their toes, others were in climbing boots and yet more in sandals. But all were smiling as they scrambled up the last sheer yards to pay homage to their patron saint.

They might have been a medieval army on the march – a meandering crocodile stretching the three miles to Murrisk. All sorts of people came stumbling along with their hazel walking sticks: young girls in shorts, old women in long black coats, men carrying children on their shoulders, brawny men with delicate rosaries in their hands, press photographers with cameras, mountain rescue men in white safety helmets and carrying stretchers to deal with broken ankles and crushed toes. Priests were among them, their working clothes tied up in a bundle as they toiled up the slopes to relieve the pressure on the others now taking confession in the chapel, dogs bounding around in the excitement of it all, mules hauling up yet more mineral water to sell at a pound a time. All this ragged army was surging up for the first Mass of the morning.

One huge house of a man, barefoot and with his trousers rolled up above his knees, came stomping over the jagged stones and, taking out a rosary, kneeled in prayer at the entrance to the chapel. His feet and legs were badly gashed, not that he seemed to give a hoot as his fingers worked their way through the rosary beads.

I walked over to the other side of the chapel and bought a cup of tea off one of the Bedouins for a pound, not begrudging the price either, knowing what they had gone through during the night. He told me to go and warm myself next to the peat fire where another man came and stood next to me. He had a face which looked as if it had

been the victim of a thousand lost fights; his suit was torn and ripped. He said that he had spent the night in the men's lavatory and kept shivering as he held his steaming mug of tea with both hands. I suspected that he had got into a drunken brawl – something of a remarkable feat on a holy pilgrimage – but, try as I might, I could get no straight answers from him.

Thin wisps of mist were chasing one another over the mountain. Already a thousand, maybe two thousand people were surging around and around the chapel in the wiffling peat smoke. *Hail Mary full of grace . . .* And there it was again – the massed, marching, haunting music of the Irish at prayer.

I crowded back into the small chapel where I had slept. It was so packed it might have been the bob bank for a rugby international in Cardiff, elbows digging rudely into sides, feet crunching on other feet. The service was in Irish but despite not understanding a word – and even in such a crush – I was uplifted again by the sheer effort which the pilgrims here have invested in paying tribute to their Patrick.

As the service continued I closed my eyes and thought of the doughty old saint, up here alone, bargaining with God and his angels. He was tormented by fire, ice and swarms of blackbirds but still he would not be gone from The Reek until his demands were met. 'I am here to kindle the undying fire of faith in the land of the Gael,' he kept saying.

'But what is it exactly you want?' asked an angel.

'I want seven persons out of hell on Doomsday for every hair on my chasuble.'

'Your wish is granted, now get thee gone from The Reek.'

'It is also my saintly duty that I be allowed to sit on the Day of Judgement and personally judge the people of Ireland.'

'Your demands of God are excessive and obstinate. Such a sanction cannot be obtained.'

'God alone could grant such a blessing and unless He gives it I shall not be gone from The Reek.'

'God so grants it then.'

'Blessed be the bountiful King who has so bestowed. The faith of the land of the Gael is secure. Now shall I move down from The Reek.'

And so too, now, it was time for me to move down from The Reek and I walked down the slope feeling a great sense of gladness. I chatted with a photographer from the *Irish Press* as we descended into the gaudy circus of souvenir stalls and mineral water men in Murrisk. Abba was blaring out on a loudspeaker to attract people to a car raffle. Already the pub was doing a roaring trade. I was exhausted. I went off to my hotel bed calculating that, by now, I had done enough penitential pilgrimages to sin, with impunity, until I dropped.

SIX

THE FAIR FLOWER OF WALES

HOLYWELL·ST ASAPH·LLANGEFNI·BARDSEY·ABERDARON
ABERYSTWYTH·ST DAVID'S

The shrine effortlessly imprisoned you with the purity of its passion as soon as you stepped into it. It was something to do with the sweet cool shadows of the early morning and the carvings on the ageing stone pillars. It was something to do with the centuries of prayer cobwebbed in the air. But most of all it was to do with the magic of the gorgeous morning sunlight sparkling on that spring of water; the way light and water bubbled and swam together; the pure energy of that current bursting up out of the smooth brown and green rocks. Yes, it was that water that best spoke of the pure passion of the shrine.

I had come early – just after eight in the morning – and changed into a bathing costume inside a canvas cubicle. I was still the only customer. My skin was goosepimpling riotously, more at the thought of what was to come than the warm reality of a midsummer morning. The water, the man at the ticket office had told me, was as cold at this time of year as it was in the middle of winter, which is another way of saying that it was very cold indeed all the year round.

Built directly over the wall was a huge stone gazebo. Just next to it, right at my feet, was a long tank of cold water, large enough to hold four coffins piled up on top of one another, with an iron rail on either side. The gazebo, in its turn, was surrounded by an old stone chapel with fan vaulting and small, witty sculptures of little animals and flaking cheerful faces. Many of the faces had been disfigured by the weather though one, facing me, was the perfectly distinguishable carving of one pilgrim carrying another through the pool on his back.

Just outside the building, in the dandelioned sunlight, there was a small swimming pool with a few brown leaves skulling around on its surface in the manner of empty abandoned coracles. A huge stone sat on the floor of one side of the pool. St Beuno's stone.

I stared down at my reflection again, face featureless, legs white and arms holding my chest comfortingly. I placed my foot slowly into the water and took it out very quickly indeed. The water was so cold it was as if my foot had gone completely numb and I had to dance around the shrine, as if engaged in inventing a new one-legged waltz, before the blood got working through the ankle again. Somehow – and standing there at that moment I could not quite see how – I was going to have to get the whole of my body under the water and through that Arctic pit *three times*. I wished then that I too had an obliging pilgrim to carry me through the water – someone tall enough that it meant that only my knee-caps would be grazed by the perishing water.

This was Saint Winefride's Well in Holywell, the Bethesda of North Wales and possibly the most famous healing well in Wales. I was standing, my knees knocking, on a spot which is at the very heart of this great nation; a hallowed spot where the deaf came and first heard the bubbling of those holy waters; where the dumb found words of worshipful love flowing from their mouths; where the crippled abandoned their crutches and were able to dash across the fields outside; where the blind were first able to see and marvel at the lowering majesty of the nearby Snowdonia range.

Even in the violence-fouled days of the Reformation – when the shrine was locked up and broken down – pilgrims continued to come here, often at night and at considerable risk to their safety. Priests conducted the services in disguise and even when threatened with the dungeon, sword and the stake pilgrims continued to come, making this well the only place of unbroken pilgrimage since the seventh century. As you enter the shrine's door you read:

THIS IS HOLY GROUND
MADE HOLY BY
THE MARTYRDOM OF ST WINEFRIDE

THE PRAYERS AND THE STEPS OF PILGRIMS FOR OVER 1,300 YEARS.

I tentatively dipped my big toe into the water, and discovered that it was every bit as cold as I had at first thought – just behind me was a stone statue of St Winefride herself. She was 'The fair flower of Wales, hope of distressed pilgrims and patron saint of Holywell.' She had a crook in one hand and the palm of martyrdom in the other. A stone gown flowed around her shoulders with a crown on her head. Yet it was the thin white line around her neck which told her story; a tale as mysterious and inherently improbable as the fare structure of British Rail.

We must go back to one morning in November 660 when Caradoc, a Welsh prince from Hawarden, returned, hot and lusty, after being out hunting. The beautiful, if cool, Winefride sparked his sexual fancy and he made overtures, only to be firmly rebuffed. In a paroxysm of rage he pursued her, sword in hand, and, as she ran seeking the sanctuary of the church, his sword swung through the air and hacked her head clean off her body.

At this moment Winefride's uncle, St Beuno, emerged from the church and, in a holy fury, laid the curse of God on the murderer, whereupon the earth opened and swallowed up Caradoc. This very well sprang up at the spot where Winefride's head rolled. The miracles of the afternoon did not end there. The old saint prayed to God that the girl's life should be restored and, lo, he placed her head back on her body and life returned to her. A line remained around her neck for the rest of her life which she spent as a nun in a community at Gwytherin where she became an Abbess. Beuno moved on to a monastery at Clynnog Fawr.

It is another of those stories with very little sex but plenty of violence which have come down to us from medieval times. Perhaps it is best seen as an illustration of the great dignity of women in medieval Wales; a parable of the inviolable role she played in the position of the family and the dispensation of hospitality to strangers. She could never be struck or insulted although, according to tradition, a husband could strike her lightly with a thin twig just below her shoulders if she gave away his harp, cloak or cauldron.

So when Caradoc sought to ravish her, he was striking right at the heart of that open hospitality which was the peculiar glory of early Welsh life. When he attacked her he was attacking the inviolable status of womanhood. His actions were motivated by lust, the hallmark of the barbarian who would deny the Welsh their right to enter the kingdom of God – or so the Celtic theorists of old would have seen it.

This present-day theorist, though, had more temporal matters in mind. When I finally dropped my body into the water I must have frozen a good year's growth out of it. My very bones seemed to be breaking up into dust; I squealed out loud. The cold pounded against my shoulders and thumped down on my head; my chest tightened alarmingly. When I scrambled out on the other side my body had lost all feeling. I danced around and around the gazebo leaving a trail of wet footprints on the stone floor slabs until the blood began flowing again. There were blue patches on my skin, millions of goosepimples. And I had to do it all twice more.

Three is the crucial number in this particular pilgrimage since the pilgrim must come to Holywell for a period of three years and make three immersions each morning for three days. This rite probably came from the old Celtic practice of baptism by triple immersion though the number three is, in itself, the most holy number of them all. Christ prepared for thirty years for a ministry that lasted three and died at the age of thirty-three. One of three men on three crosses, he died after a three-fold betrayal by Peter at three o'clock in the afternoon – the traditional time for prayer – when three hours of darkness descended on Jerusalem.

And then, on the third day, he rose again and is now a part of the Holy Trinity.

I expected that the second immersion would be easier than the first. I was wrong. Whole sections of my body slumped into a frozen coma; thin shrieks of agony wriggled out from between my teeth. On the third dip I did not think I was going to make it through the trough at all. A rage of purple agony skewered the very core of my being; I could have told a torturer anything he wanted to know; the universe consisted of the purest pain.

Some, however, could survive the cold for ages. John Gerard wrote of his own pilgrimage here in 1593:

'Once I was there on November 3, St Winefride's Feast . . . there was a hard frost at the time and though the ice in the stream had been broken by people crossing it the previous night, I still found it very difficult to cross the next morning. But frost or no frost I went down into the well like a good pilgrim. For a quarter of an hour I lay down in the water and prayed. When I came out my shirt was dripping but I kept it on and pulled all my clothes over it and was none the worse for my bathe.'

A quarter of an hour! I might have been in that freezing water for a quarter of a micro-second as I hurried through my third dip. I certainly did not pause to pray. Then another pilgrim came out of the cubicle, went straight down into the water, bobbed up his head, held up his hands together in prayer, kissed the stone on the side of the trough and walked up the stone steps on the other side.

'Lovely that was,' he said to me. 'It was really cold yesterday.'

My eyebrows went shooting up into my hairline in amazement. 'What do *you* call cold, then?' I asked.

'This is warm. Smashing this is. You could sleep in this.'

He went down into the well for a second time and again said an interminable prayer. After his third dip in the well – I confidently expected bits of him to begin falling off – he got out intact and went over into the swimming pool

Holywell, the Bethesda of North Wales. Christians come here to pay shivering homage at St Winefride's icy well.

on the other side. Here he knelt on the large stone, saying another prayer with just his head sticking up out of the water. It is said that St Beuno sat on this stone when he was instructing Winefride.

His name, I discovered, was Kosta Nedic, a cheerful Yugoslavian Catholic with thermal skin and fur-lined bones who made his living out of laying tarmacadam. His mother-in-law had been cured in this well – 'she left her wheelchair behind' – and so now he comes whenever he can. 'See here,' he said pointing at the steps going down into the well. 'Every year on the anniversary of Winefride's death the steps here drip with blood. I've not seen it myself but that's what they say. See just under the water there.'

He rubbed his bushy hair and eyebrows with a towel. 'I've been coming here most of my life. There used to be crutches and surgical boots everywhere that the cured would leave behind them. But there's nothing like that around now, is there? It's the young isn't it? The young have lost their faith, haven't they?'

A lad in torn jeans with a large gold ring in his left ear came into the shrine and filled up a petrol can with water from the well. He had driven all the way from Worcestershire to get this water. 'Mum likes to have it around in the house. If any of the kids get sick she showers them with it.'

A few more people came in. Then an Irish lad borrowed ten pence off me to light a votive candle and two very dubious characters, with dirty oil-stained jackets and in need of a shave, proceeded to fill up empty whisky and cider bottles. Was there something alcoholic about the water that I didn't know about? The elder of the two men screwed up his whisky bottle and explained that the water had once cured him of soft legs when he was but four years old. The Irish lad, who had borrowed ten pence off me, then wanted to borrow my bathing costume so that he could do his three-fold dip.

'They're all bums,' Kosta Nedic whispered into my ear

with some vehemence. 'Wherever you go you can't get away from bums. Even in a holy place like this. Bums.'

A van pulled up outside and what seemed like hundreds of kids came dashing into the shrine, stripped off their clothes and began splashing about in St Beuno's pool like a school of demented porpoises. The man with them had the swarthy good looks of a Romany. 'I'm a traveller sir,' he told me, 'move about a bit, you know.'

The laughter and splashes of the children somehow went well with the spirit of prayer in the place; the shrieks of the young rising up to mingle with the prayers for the dead – an odd little conjunction for sure, as mysterious and joyful as a rock 'n' roll party in a church crypt.

The curator of the shrine did not find it all very joyful, though. He quickly shooed the children out. 'This is not a swimming pool,' he said to the Romany. 'This is a holy shrine.'

I thought it a shame that the children were kicked out of the water which they were clearly enjoying so much. Places of prayer should be places of fun, too, and I rather fancy old Beuno would have enjoyed seeing the children play. He wasn't one of those terribly crusty old saints who never changed his boots from one Easter to the next. He was a funny bold man, a master of monks, challenger of tyrants and a friend of the helpless. Anyone who set about trying to convert the difficult and obdurate peoples of North Wales must have had a great sense of humour.

The day before I had spoken to Father McGrail, the priest in charge of the shrine, and had met an amiable bearded fellow who had grown up in the shadow of The Reek that I had toiled up a few weeks earlier. This was his first pilgrimage job and he believed that pilgrimage was basic to Christian belief. Some twenty to thirty thousand pilgrims came to Holywell each year, he said, particularly from Liverpool and Manchester. They came in a spirit of penance and prayer. They came from all walks of life and many of them found what they had come for, oh yes. 'People would

not come in such numbers if they had not received some extraordinary answers to prayer.'

He recalled the case of a parishioner with a bladder complaint, who had waited long and patiently for a major operation. This man also had a bad rash on his hand. 'I told him to put his hand into the water of the well,' said Father McGrail. 'The rash was healed immediately. He also drank a glass of well water every day and, when he was called to the hospital, it was found that not only did he no longer need the operation but also he had none of the old symptoms.'

One Belfast priest put a paralysed hand into the water and, within minutes, it had straightened out and has been perfect ever since. I liked the story of Betty Lloyd-Hughes who had a raging headache, dipped her forefinger into the water and made a sign of the cross on her forehead. The headache disappeared immediately.

Towards eleven o'clock the sun streamed down on to the lawns and flowers of the well's garden and Bud Grant came to prepare for the service which is held here every morning throughout the summer. Bud is from Iowa and training to be a priest in a seminary in Rome. This is a vacation job for him, though they don't come any more unpriestly than Bud. He had a laughing manner, blond hair and the boyish good looks of a teenage pop star. Here clearly was a man who was going to be dogged all his priesthood by thousands of young impressionable girls falling madly in love with him.

He once had to hold the Pope's mitre in a mass in Iowa. 'My greatest regret was that I did not put it on. I was very tempted to give it a try but all those thousands of faces and television cameras put me off.'

He added that he was very nervous of all this business of saints, pilgrimage and relics when he first got here. 'But now I've come to understand it as a type of spirituality. I take the relic of St Winefride's fingerbone and explain to people why it is important and why people gave their lives trying to protect it. I explained to them that we can become holy by thinking about holiness.'

He had, he said, many regulars at the morning service. There was one ninety-seven-year-old man who travelled here for up to eight hours to fill up a jug of water. There was also another old lady with leukaemia who came and sat by the well where she cried so much she could not pray. 'I always take her hand and bless her.'

That morning a dozen people, as well as the gypsy's innumerable children, gathered around the well for the service. Bud spoke of the strength of prayer in the shrine and how it was unique in the history of pilgrimage. 'Also consider what it means to pray to the saints, those who came close to the ideal Christ set in us. We can pray for these gifts just as we can pray for ourselves.'

After saying the litany of St Winefride we queued around the well. One by one we kissed her holy relic which Bud held up to each of our lips.

Afterwards I spoke to one of the worshippers, Derrick Dykins, a singular man looking a little like an old Indian sufi with long silver hair and brown broken teeth, dressed completely in black with a large silver crucifix around his neck. 'I'm just an ordinary Christian,' he said when I asked him why he had come. He added that he had been doing so almost every day for five years. Had he ever taken the waters? No. He suffered from arthritis and was afraid that the coldness of the water would make it worse. But surely the water could help to make him better? He regarded me for a moment with old suspicious eyes as if I had just told him I had come to cut off the gas. Well yes, he was a Christian but, to be perfectly honest, he had never thought of the waters in that way.

It was an odd reaction from a sick man who had been worshipping here every day for five years. Illness has nothing to do with the kingdom of God and perhaps its real insidiousness is that, deep in our hearts, we do not want to be healed.

Later that day I made tracks along the coast road to Bangor. As I walked I felt yet again a spasm of the joyful madness that had smitten me again and again on my journey that year. I fondly imagined that it was a form of holy dementia which had something to do with the motive power of the pilgrims of old; a peculiar joviality of the spirit which makes you want to sing out and waggle your hands around joyfully as you shuffle down the road; a springing sense of release from the imprisoning morbidities of the electronic age. The very spring of Christianity is something mobile, something on the move along the road. Faith and life come together in the spirit of the journey; the journey in which we tell our tales and think our thoughts; the journey in which we stumble and change as we abandon the known, the old and the familiar; the journey where we search in the darkness, safe in the assurance of Christ's victory over death, hoping to reach out and touch the features of holiness.

Another and more accessible way of thinking about the Christian journey – of which I am rather more fond – is when it is likened to a boat full of yo-yos which, on its voyage from Hong Kong to London, sinks twenty-eight times. Every time you go down to the depths you come bobbing back up again gasping for air and swearing that you are not going down again. Then you spring another leak and sink like a stone beneath another mass of bubbles laughing derisively at the poverty of your tenacity and you know that you have embarked on the hardest pilgrimage that there is – that the way of the Cross is hard and bitter with, more often than not, the rancid taste of defeat in your mouth.

Had I been rich in medieval times I could have avoided any such feelings of failure on my journey by hiring a freelance pilgrim to undertake my journey for me. I might have made a promise to undertake a journey when ill and, on recovery, decided that the penance was rather excessive. I could have hired someone to do the necessary, making sure that he took the long route, preferably on foot, on which he suffered a lot and then got a signed certificate from the priest in charge of the shrine confirming that all due prayers and penances had been properly performed. They were always happy to oblige with such certificates since the gifts from the lazy and absentee rich were also an important part of the shrine's income.

I think that some of my happiness that day had sprung from Bud's belief that we can only become holy by contemplating holy things. That line and variations on it kept jabbing about my mind like the hook of a pop song. I had always suspected that there was happiness in holiness; that happiness was one of the chief characteristics of holiness. You see this in the smiling serenity of men of the cloth. The perfection of holiness, it seems, precluded misery.

On the road to Bangor I called off at St Asaph Cathedral, a squat, womb-like church with a stout symphony of pillars, golden bosses on the wooden roof and stained glass windows which blazed with brilliant reds and astonishing blues. The cathedral was founded back in 560 by our old friend St Mungo when he was exiled here from Scotland by local chiefs jealous of his popularity. There is a Mungo window in the north aisle together with his logos of the salmon and the ring.

Is there an art form anywhere more lovely than stained glass? What could be more poetic than these coloured translucent poems set in pieces of glass held together by lead strips? They were the medieval counterpart of our cinemas and videos: the earliest of all the media used to tell ordinary people about parables and miracles, the angels and the Lord.

Everywhere I had gone that year these brilliant configurations of colour and light had been blazing vivaciously with heavenly visions and exploding with the goodness of creation. Those windows represented the media at its purest and most basic. Those windows represented the media without the distortions of corruption, violence and cruelty. Those windows were the 'Poor Man's Bible' showing people what they should think on that they may know God. There was an old catechism which said that as soon as you entered a church you should take the holy water, adore the sacrament then walk around the church and consider the windows.

I sat in the Translator's Chapel which commemorates Bishop William Morgan's translation of the Bible into Welsh which, in its way, was crucial to the survival of the Welsh language. It was while sitting there that I found a most beautiful prayer for pilgrims handwritten on a postcard. It was full of the questing spirit of love and concern for others which is the sign of true prayer:

O God our Father, we pray Thee so to fill this ancient house with thy spirit: here may the strong renew their strength and seek for their working lives a noble consecration: here may the poor find succour and the friendless friendship: here may the tempted find power, the sorrowing find comfort and the bereaved the truth that dark death hath over their beloved ones no more dominion; here, let the fearful find a new courage and the doubting have their faith and hope confirmed: here, let the careless be awakened and all that are oppressed be freed.

May all who come be drawn by the Lord and go home with doubts resolved and faith renewed: their fears at rest, their courage high, their purpose firm, their hearts aflame: through Jesus Christ our Lord.

I took a bus to Anglesey and holed up in the Victoria Hotel in Menai Bridge, taking time out of my holy pilgrimage for a pilgrimage of a somewhat different kind: one to the National Eisteddfod in nearby Llangefni. The great and sacred range of Snowdonia provided a majestic backdrop to this strange rite at which the whole of Wales and her dog turns up to celebrate the poetic heart of this ancient race and its love of great thrashing poems and singing visions.

As a child I always knew it was time for the Eisteddfod since it would bucket down with rain and everyone – but everyone – would roll up for a tribal gathering in the mud. This time, however, the sky was miraculously clear. Glittering shafts of sunlight rolled through the trees as we, in our turn, rolled around the field.

The main pavilion, which resembles an aeroplane hangar, is surrounded by a series of stalls where you can buy such items as a harp to take with you to heaven, a Japanese electronic organ, or a car sticker saying 'Keep Wales Tidy. Dump Your Rubbish in England'. But it is not primarily for such delights as these that the same gang rolls up year after year. Nor is it entirely for poetry or brass bands. This gang of shaggy-haired poets and teachers, of stern vicars and stooped grandmothers, of language activists and young girls flaunting the disposal of their bras have all come for a dip in this cultural Ganges largely to catch up on the gossip. The Welsh do not just send Christmas cards to old friends and forget it, they hang around the field to gossip at Eisteddfods and forget it. They embark on an endless circular tour of the field when, knee-deep in confidences, they can hatch plots, select the Welsh rugby team, bury old quarrels or start new ones, learn who has got who in the family way lately, assassinate a character, build up that storehouse of anecdotes which no Welshman can be without.

She used to be a right snob she did before she got divorced. That brought her down a peg or two I can tell you.

I just saw Wynford. He's still as fit as a fiddle.

Now tell me what happened to that girl you were in hall with . . .

And what happened to . . . She had a baby did she? Never . . .

And look, there's Geraint Evans over there. He's been putting on weight since he's been talking about retirement. That's that folk singer, whatshisname, Dafydd Iwan. He's getting fat for definite. Isn't that one on television a lot? Aye. Forget his name offhand.

Now tell me whatever happened to . . .

The Eisteddfod was begun at a time when every major family had its own poet. It was originally staged to clear up the proliferation of 'rhymers, bards and minstrels' who were fouling up the valleys. Today, the field might be the only place in the world where you could come across a group of men spinning out verses to one another.

Mindful of this august heritage the more serious-minded crowded into the pavilion where poets were chaired, choirs honoured and the Druids of the ancient Gorsedd came in their long nightshirts. Horns were held aloft and swords flashed. Music and brave declarations rang out. All eyes swam with patriotic tears on the occasion of the crownings when a name was read out and the new king shouted 'Yma'. The late Gwyn Thomas wrote: 'Each and every one of us, from the time he got the shawl out of his mouth and could shout "Yma" (Here) when the Eisteddfod conductor called out the name under which he had entered, was an Eisteddfodwr, a real gone guy under the banner of the festival.'

And so it was that all us real gone guys met in a huge sloping field where the jubilant syllables of Welsh sang out of the speakers and yellow masses of buttercups nodded in the breeze. Out in the hedgerow I found a wasps' nest and watched them zooming out fast and high but coming back low and slow, as if after some exhausting and distant battle. The breezes kept turning over the leaves of the trees, showing their hissing silvery undersides. Way out over Snowdon a bank of black cloud was coming together, dark and humourless, like the outriders of a war party from the Welsh Language Society. The summer was unwinding rapidly; I figured it was time to leave.

The glow of early morning sunshine on slate tombstones.

On yet more buses I made my way down the harebell lanes of the Lleyn Peninsula, past grey snoozing villages and ruined crofts (those rubbled relics of a lost past) in search of Bardsey, the sacred island of Wales.

Then it was Sunday morning and we were all huddled together in a small fishing boat as it chugged out over the softly swelling waves from the village of Aberdaron on the Lleyn. The village itself was a raggle-taggle of white-washed houses flung down in front of a sandy beach and around a gull-sentinelled chapel. Indeed the only feature of the village that seemed to have any symmetry was the graveyard with its lines of grey slate tombstones, as formal as parade-ground soldiers, marching line by line up the grassy incline.

Otherwise Aberdaron was a collection of shop, pub and inn around a stone bridge with, just at the centre, a small white tea-house known as The Big Kitchen where pilgrims of old, about to make the trip over to Bardsey and waiting for suitable weather, could claim a free meal. Not free any longer, of course: fifty pence for tea and up to three or four pounds for such as steak or scampi and chips.

A man was tugging on a rope ringing the chapel bell to invite people to the morning communion service but we were heading for our own service, out in the ruins of a monastery on Bardsey. Our boat bucked as the sea swelled and the row-boat we were towing behind us yawed wildly. We were now passing cormorant cliffs leading up to un-compromising headlands, barren of trees and dotted with mounds of spiky gorse the shape and size of giant pumpkins. On the other side of the bay behind us a whole gabbling gale of herring gulls were swooping in and out of the sea.

There might have been five hundred of those infernal gulls who had been creating the most hellish racket in the bay for the past four days as they fluttered above and dived on a shoal of whitebait who, in their turn, had been trying to escape from a shoal of mackerel. It was clearly no fun at all being a whitebait harassed from above and behind, and neither was it much fun listening to the cries and screams of those gulls.

The night before I had been lying in a bed in an hotel room right on the beach and the gulls had come right up to the window. The sounds were the very stuff of the most frightening nightmares and lying in that betwixt state – neither asleep nor awake – I had just lain there like someone being heavily menaced in a horror film. The noise was what you might have expected to have heard in the corridors of Bedlam. One second their calls were slow asthmatic gasps which built up in intensity and frequency until they changed abruptly into the crazed shrieking laughter of witches happily despatching their enemies with pins in dolls.

'That's St Mary's Well there,' said one of our group pointing at the wave-lapped headland. 'It's a fresh water spring which is covered by the tide but always manages to stay fresh. The pilgrims always used to use it. One of the Lord's miracles to help pilgrims on their way, they say.'

There were twelve of us travelling across the Sound that morning: Menna Hughes, a woman who had once farmed on the island and was today going back for the first time for years; a Scottish couple on holiday in nearby Pwllheli; a couple from Kingston-on-Thames; a man on holiday from his work in a creamery and an elderly lady who had once taught on the island for five years. We also had three children with us, all led by our skipper Huw Williams, a man with Shredded Wheat muscles and sprayed-on shorts. He sported a denim cap made in the People's Republic of China. I dubbed him Captain Birds Eye.

'Terrible storms there were when we were on the island,' Menna recalled. 'We could get caught out there for five or six weeks without a boat of any kind. Terrible it was. We'd run low on flour we would – all kinds of things went short. We'd go over the cliffs to get gulls' eggs to eat. What were they like? I'll tell you. They had a dark yolk and weren't very nice.'

We turned around the headland and I caught my first sight of Bardsey. As impressive as a good punch on the nose it was too, a huge volcanic fist of jagged rocks, some sooty black and the others as red as rust. One side of the island rose up mountainously with a thick tablecloth of mist lying around its summit while, on the other end, sat the white tower of a Trinity lighthouse. A cormorant flew past us, its neck as straight as a spear.

'See that rock there?' said Menna. 'They used to send messages from there to the mainland if they wanted anything. They had to light a flash, they did.'

I had found yet again that sense of a place set apart from the madding throng; that special isolation of the spirit which I had found in Iona and Lindisfarne; that quality of inviolate purity which was the prerequisite of a holy spot.

It was Cadfan, the patron saint of warriors, who first set up a religious house on this island when he came here from Brittany about 480. In the Middle Ages Ynys Enlli (Bardsey) became a great spiritual centre; something of what Iona was to Scotland. People wanted to come to die and be buried here to such an extent that the island became known as the Island of Twenty Thousand Saints. Pilgrims came here from all over Europe and Pope Calixtus II – 'in view of the perilous nature of the trip to Rome' – declared that three pilgrimages to Bardsey would, in future, be counted as equal to one pilgrimage to Rome.

But this same Pope, who also declared that two pilgrimages to St David's in West Wales were worth one to Rome, was not the thoughtful, avuncular type that we have today. He was an irritable old bore who kept dreaming up these formulae, not because he was worried about the perils to those on the roads, but rather because he wanted to try and thin out the intolerable throng of pilgrims who kept jamming up the streets and hostels of Rome.

The pilgrimage to Bardsey ended in the Reformation when the monastery was pillaged. From that time, its role as a spiritual power point faded. It was taken over by farmers and, at one period, became a hang-out for pirates. The island even had its own kings and when the last one, King Love Pritchard, turned up at the Eisteddfod he was welcomed by David Lloyd George as one of those Welsh 'from overseas'. These days there was just a hermit, a Franciscan monk, a tiny community based on a farm, and a bird sanctuary.

Captain Birds Eye rowed us alongside a small concrete jetty where a few launches lay on their sides and lobster

'Captain Birds Eye':
Huw Williams, Bardsey
ferryman.

pots were piled up high next to a shed. I struck out straight for the old Augustinian Abbey since I wanted to catch the service there that morning. Hurrying along the dirt path with alarmed rabbits dashing away from me and straight down their holes, my heart was soon gliding on great emotional breezes of happiness again. I stopped still a few times, smiling at the sun and warmed right through in the way that you get when you suddenly know that someone, somewhere in the world, is praying for you. There really was healing magic in the air on that island and I could have all but shouted out with joy, renewed in the feeling of the closeness of the resurrection in the morning; in the sense of the new being born out of the ashes of the old.

I was carrying with me a bucket of Lindisfarne holiness again; that very stuff of angels' dreams which hangs over a place completely surrounded by water, the pleasing tidiness of those fields shorn of all spare grass by foraging sheep and rabbits but, most tantalising of all – as I passed a clump of grey stone cottages – in the snatched sounds of hymnody being borne aloft and shaken around by a sun-drenched wind. Lovely things to the Welsh ear are such sounds which, like the smell of roast beef and the theme tune of 'Family Favourites', tell of all those plump Sundays of our childhoods when we lay around eating too much, listening to the radio as Mam washed up the dishes and worrying that, one day, she would stop loving us.

I only caught the final notes of the last hymn of the service though what could be a more beautiful setting for any service than this ancient rubble with the call of the birds in the rafters of a great blue sky; surrounded by, on one side, Anglesey, just here the mighty sweep of Cardigan Bay and, way over the sea, the Wicklow mountains in Ireland? The small congregation filed out through a grave-yard where, on a huge Celtic cross, there was the telling inscription: 'Is it nothing to you, all ye who pass by?'

When all of them had left I introduced myself to Brother

Nathanael, a Franciscan friar who said that, as soon as he had changed out of his vestments, he would take me down to his house for a cup of coffee. He was here for the summer to look after pilgrims and seemed positively abrim with the love and gaiety of his spiritual leader, St Francis.

As we were walking back along the path to his house a woman came walking across a field towards us. She moved as slowly as a publisher's decision, with tiny stooped shoulders, fingers bent with arthritis and a black cowl over her head. She smiled, showing a few gold teeth below a simply enormous beak of a nose and the large, sad brown eyes of a boxer dog. 'Your visitor might like this,' she said in a voice so soft you could barely hear it as she handed Nathanael a leaflet entitled *Tramping Down Death By Death*. 'You are both well, I hope.'

With this, and before we could say anything, she left us as softly and as slowly as she had come. She was Sister Helen Mary, the hermit on the island. She spoke but rarely, and survived on a small vegetable patch and a lot of prayer, Nathanael explained. She was one of the Sisters of the Love of God and had been living in the loft of some old stables for ten years now. If Nathanael ever complained to her about anything her reply was always the same: 'Pray, brother, just pray. Nothing else matters.'

As he made the coffee, Nathanael admitted that he did not know much about modern things. 'When I first came here no one had a fridge. There was no electricity, just calor gas lamps, candles or torches.' He also had the tattiest gown that I had ever seen – all patches and stitches with so many rips it would have been rejected by an Oxfam shop on a bad day. 'It's my second best,' he said when I asked if his vow of poverty meant just one gown until you died. 'I was going under some barbed wire the other day and tore the sleeve here. I fear it's on its last legs now.'

We talked of the island and he smiled as he said that it really was possible that twenty thousand had been buried here. Wherever you dug there were masses of bones. 'Any historical journal will tell you that, all along the coast right down to Aberystwyth, people always asked to be buried here. They would even have makeshift mortuaries where they stored the bodies if the weather was too bad to get over to the island. Indeed, I'm sure there are *at least* that number buried here.'

Just lately the island had been taken over by the nation after its owner had the absurd idea of turning the place into a sort of Club Mediterranee, even booting Sister Helen Mary on to the mainland for a while lest she upset the campers.

Nathanael was an Anglican Franciscan who tried to welcome every pilgrim to the island in the summer. At the moment he was friary-less since his last friary had been closed down and, at the end of the summer, he was going to be based in Llandudno as a part-time priest. Much of his time on the island was spent in prayer: the morning compline, midday office and evening prayer. Prayer, you sensed, supplied him with the pattern of fidelity crucial to his love of the Lord. In a way, his life was one long secret prayer.

Being a good Franciscan he loved the profusion of birds and rabbits. He was saddened when myxomatosis struck the island and many of the rabbits had died. Only that morning he had seen one such rabbit with its face swollen up and blind, bumping wretchedly against a stone wall. Even as he spoke, his gentle radiance told me much about the practice and presence of God. He was one of those rare and valuable men who mediate God to us; a simple good man in whom you can find the very icon of the risen Christ. We spoke for a while about another good man that I know, Canon David Watson, the great evangelist who had recently been stricken low by cancer. Then all of us sat around the table and prayed for David's full recovery; that God would send His angels to kiss the disease out of David's body; that he would be restored to us and his Church.

It was one of those prayers in which we all entered into a dialogue with the power of healing Love. When we had finished, there was nothing more to say.

We chugged back along the island's cliff shore where guillemots and shags stood guard on the rocky ledges. A puffin waddled from one rock to the next; the huge baleful eyes of a resting seal watched us as we went by. 'I wouldn't want to go back there again,' Menna said, looking back out over the waves to the island. 'It was such a hard life. Don't know how we managed to stick it really.'

There was a fine moment that evening, after dinner, when we were out walking on the promenade in Aberdaron. The sun was dipping out of the sky and sending up cascading bars of orange and gold with lovely breezes sweeping in and out of the village. Most of the day-trippers had gone but on the small quay next to an arcade jammed with fruit machines and space invaders a small group had gathered around a tiny foot-pedalled organ.

A man was handing out hymn sheets and we all stood there for an hour singing those great old Welsh hymns with the very music and poetry of the tribe surging up through them. Shrieking gulls wheeled over the church spire as the organ wheezed and puffed along behind us. We moved into 'Abide With Me' and there was a real power and passion in the singing when time dislocated itself again and my hands were steadying the coffin as the rain bucketed down on us and the winds tore at our faces like whips.

Abide with me; fast falls the eventide;
The darkness deepens; Lord with me abide
When other helpers fail and comforts flee
Help of the helpless, O abide with me.

Huge waves were piling on top of one another, rolling in with great engines of thunder inside them and collapsing into the shingle with a hissing sigh. We were all shouting at one another, some wanting to go that night and others wanting to wait until the morning when the winds might turn.

'Sing brothers,' I shouted as loud as I could, remembering what Sister Helen Mary had told Nathanael. 'Just sing. Nothing else matters.'

And so we sang those sweet songs of love, all rejoicing in the psalms of our native hills as, safe now, we pushed the boat out into the angry waves and that old organ wheezed and puffed along behind us.

The journey down south began at Portmadoc, waiting for the train to take us down to Aberystwyth and on to St David's. It was another of those spectacular days which had graced our lives so frequently that summer, the sun blowtorching into a clear blue sky as two butterflies danced around the brambles behind the platform on which about a dozen people, including a man wearing clogs, waited for the train.

It came on time with an ebullient blast on the horn and soon we were all rattling down the coast of Wales, past green marshes buttoned with white blobs of sheep and the tide, as full as an egg, gently swelling and falling up against the brown sea walls. Ugly pylons went trooping over the landscape and all heads jerked forward as the train's brakes screamed long and loud when we pulled into each station.

The guard was as genial as the day itself with a funny big nose and the impressively billowing grey whiskers of a character escaped from the pages of Beatrix Potter. He was very busy with those continually getting on and off: 'You've no time for yourself on a day like this,' he told me in a rare free moment. 'I'm not complaining though. Who wants to hear complaints?'

'Seagulls followed me everywhere I went that year.'

himself; black suede brothel creepers with inch-thick soles, bright silver lurex socks, narrow drainpipe trousers which stopped three inches above his shoes, a long green Edwardian jacket with a black velvet collar, a lace shirt and, joy of joys, a bootlace tie. His hair was piled up high to camouflage a huge bald patch with a DA cut neatly in the back. He sat staring ahead of him, impervious to our admiration. Astonishingly, this vision of male pride was accompanied by a truly scruffy harpy of a girlfriend with pneumatic legs that bulged hard against her jeans, a pile of barbed-wire hair and a recently blackened eye. She had a cold and kept wiping her nose with the inside of her palm and when she did speak to him – for he was too regal to speak himself – I understood not a word. The imagination boggled. Were they going to a fancy dress ball or what?

Two gypsies got on when the teddy boy and his girlfriend got off. Had it not been so early in the day I would have been sure that they were both paralysed drunk. Our attention then turned to a woman carrying a large child who was screaming his tonsils out since, it seemed, he had never been on a train before. The mother, clearly as nutty as the child, kept smacking his leg with one hand as she used the other to cover his eyes. 'Don't look out of the window then,' she shouted, smacking his reddening legs again and again. 'You just wait till I tell your father about all this.' Smack. Wail. Smack.

Aberystwyth is a Victorian university town, as amiable as a bookmaker on a winning streak, with its streets packed with shops, cars and the sounds of the sea. All day the smell of chips is chased around the pavements by the gusting ozone. In winter it is taken over by students but, come the summer, the holidaymakers move in, largely sitting around the promenade next to a rocky beach with a sea so swarming with seaweed it is all but impossible to swim in.

I had to break my journey for the night here. In the

We passed the lowering purple-patched range of Snowdonia and the mighty castle of Harlech set out next to a golf course. We clicked along steadily past some sand dunes and holidaymakers, rattled over a wooden viaduct above many launches anchored on the whiffling waves. On the platform at Barmouth there were lots of children shouting at one another and running around, their red buckets filled with sand.

A teddy boy and his girlfriend got on at the next station and everyone fell silent and slack-jawed as they studied this splendid vision from the fifties. He was getting on for fifty tourist office I found a Bed and Breakfast (or *Gwely a Brecwast* as the Welsh say). For cheapness and efficiency, such establishments have become the accepted watering hole of the modern pilgrim, high on spirituality if low on cash. Some B & Bs can be horrible, others pleasant. This one – ten pounds a night down by the harbour – had a tone all of its own. The following list of regulations, written in a spidery hand, was pinned on the lavatory door:

WELCOME
Breakfast 8.20 a.m. Door-key available for any late function.
No baths to be taken without permission and showers not to be taken after 10 p.m. and before 7 a.m.
Shower 20p Bath 30p per person.
Evening tea, if requested, served until 10 p.m. @ 15p a cup (and if not out ourselves).
Rooms to be vacated as soon as possible after breakfast on the day of departure. Never later than 10 a.m.
Thank you.

The residents' lounge was also the owner's private domain, festooned with piles of chinaware that would never be used, polished brass candlesticks and souvenirs from trips everywhere. Notes were dotted on shelves saying not to touch this and on no account to touch that. The boss herself was a frail woman, the shape and hue of a bottle of milk. She was eternally dressed in a pinafore; she had tight grey curls, hands that kept wringing one another and two very rampant bees in her bonnet which buzzed about like fighter jets in close formation – her health and money:

'Oh you know they are going to take me back into hospital soon, so they are. I've got this narrowing of the

St David's Cathedral: 'a weird cocktail of this and that, built out of the rich gifts of fourteen hundred years of continuous pilgrimage.'

aorta, you see. They didn't know what it was at first. Do you want a cup of tea do you? Just fifteen pence. No? A glass of pop then? It's cheaper to have pop here than in the shop. I get bulk deliveries, you know. Well, first of all, when I got into hospital they thought it was trouble with my gullet . . .'

I tried to edge nearer the door. As the torrent of words poured out she barely stopped for breath, head bobbing from side to side like that of a demented budgerigar as she chattered on, as relentless and unstoppable as a Welsh mountain stream.

'I was that ill I could barely speak. I was choking here in this lounge. Choking. All I could say was my doctor's number. My husband called him. He was so good to me, my husband. He called the doctor and stayed with me as I was taken out on a stretcher. I told him that we'd had a great life together. I thanked him for everything he'd done . . .'

Now she was crying with real fat tears, dabbing one eye with a handkerchief and then the other, but still talking ceaselessly. 'He said I would be well soon but I said no, my heart's gone now, my darling. Thank you for all you've done for me. I'm very emotional, you know. I took his hands and told him that my aorta had gone . . .'

Later I discovered that everyone else in the place came back on tiptoe in the dead of night with hands over their ears. To avoid her, some even gave breakfast a miss altogether.

The sky had blackened and was gurgling with threats of rain when I got off the bus at St David's, the smallest cathedral city in the kingdom and the most westerly point of Wales. This is a holy place for the Celts and one with an important place in the history of pilgrimage since it was here that St David, the patron saint of Wales,

founded a religious community which became one of the greatest shrines in Christendom.

But there was little sense of a holy place set apart when I first wandered those cold damp streets. The day-trippers – disappointed at not being able to sit on the nearby beach – were trooping dispiritedly up and down the narrow main street dragging bored, crying children in their wake. At the foot of the stone monument in the square two callow youths were taking it in turns to swig from a flagon of cider. A row of hotels, guest houses, shops and restaurants straggled along one side of the square. Down in a steeply sloping dip on the other side sat the great cathedral herself, surrounded by a meadow and the ruins of the Bishop's Palace.

One of the first people I located in St David's was a Miss Timmis, a blue-eyed English lady of some elegance who had been living here for eleven years and conducted pilgrimages around the place beginning every Tuesday morning at 11 a.m. sharp: *Bring own lunch, walkers at their own risk.*

What Miss Timmis did not know about St David's, I had been told, wasn't worth knowing. Apart from the cathedral itself, she took her groups around the four chapels and an old Roman Catholic church. We learned where John Wesley spoke from the steps of The Black Lion; of the yews out at nearby Nevern which bleed just like crucified flesh; of the Penitents' Bridge which medieval pilgrims were supposed to cross on their hands and knees; of the Sparling Bridge which shrieks when corpses pass over it; of St Non's Chapel, the oldest religious building in Wales where St David was said to have been born and of the nearby well famous for its healing properties and specialising in eye complaints. A good Welsh characteristic that: if you want to get ahead, get a speciality.

I asked Miss Timmis if any of her pilgrims had ever had any miraculous cures. 'Just people never wanting to work again.' Witty too.

She kept a diary recording all her pilgrims and some of the groups had been very heady mixtures indeed. Only the other week she'd had two nuns from the Sisters of the Poor Child Jesus; two Jewish people ('I kept off crosses that day'); a Halifax clergyman keen on the charismatic movement; three nonconformists; an old Dutch Catholic and someone who had worked with lepers.

She flicked through the pages of her diary again. 'That was a very good week, that was,' she added, but there were three weeks when no one at all had turned up in the car park. 'Pilgrimages, I'm afraid, are not what they were.'

Neither were the times, she clearly believed. Just by her front door was an enormous knobkerry big enough to crack open the heads of several dozen Irishmen.

That night a local drama group staged a *Son et Lumière* in the Bishop's Palace and very moving the production was too, even if the cold of the evening made my knees hurt. Amidst a whirlwind of flashing lights and bursting puffs of smoke the narrators told the marvellous story of St David, made all the more compelling by being acted out against the backdrop of a great ruin big enough to once house all the bishops of Europe as well as the numerous pilgrims who made their way here throughout the Middle Ages.

We learned of those evil and troubled times before the Age of the Saints; of societies torn apart by tribal conflict and competing Druids. We were told of strange and dark gods fashioned out of fear and of how rainbows would form over the Welsh coast to tell the people of the coming of a great holy man who was going to free them from the slavery of fear. 'The new man was to be a thought from God: a holy riddle.'

Everywhere at this time prophets were abroad. Gildas, a holy man, told the people that 'One Non will shortly be delivered of a son endowed with a greater portion of the divine spirit than has ever yet fallen to the share of any preacher in this country. To him must I resign my situation as better able to fill it and this an angel of the Lord has declared to me.'

David was born in a storm, the son of Non and Sant, a Cardigan chieftain. A single shaft of sunlight lanced down on to Non's heaving hips, the very angels applauding as this new and beautiful prophet of God fell, face forward, out of his mother's womb. She supported herself on a stone which retained her fingerprints.

David grew up in the fields around here. He was instructed by the dove which was to become his emblem. His flower was the daffodil. Later he became a priest and left his home, travelling the country teaching the Gospel. He went to study on the Isle of Wight, made a pilgrimage to Jerusalem where he was consecrated as a bishop. When he came back he set up monasteries in Glastonbury, Bath, Croyland, Repton, Leominster, Raglan and Llangyfelach.

He was thirty when, with his disciples, he returned to this kingdom of Menevia. He set up a community on the bend of a river valley, next to a spring of fresh water and about a mile from the sea. The order of the day was exacting rigour with each man eating one meal a day and drinking only water. No oxen were allowed in the fields; David declared that every man should be his own ox. He also introduced Opus Dei, a daily round of ordered worship and would, himself, pray through the night.

A giant of a man, nearly seven feet tall, David – also known as The Waterman – became a great charismatic leader renowned for his healing miracles. His thundering eloquence was such that mounds were said to spring up beneath his feet whenever he spoke to crowds. He could bring forward springs at a command; white doves came and sat on his shoulders to advise him.

'The day is close at hand,' he said when death came near. 'I am glad to go the way of my fathers.' When news of his dying went out, crowds came from all over Wales to be near him. He told them: 'Brothers and sisters, be joyful and keep your faith and do the little things you have seen and heard with me.'

Clearly a life of abstinence and hard work must have something going for it since he was reckoned to be a hundred and forty-seven years old when he died on March 1, 589.

Later that night, with the shadow of yet another great man crushing down on me, I walked up through the graveyard next to the cathedral. A strong wind was blowing black sea mists over the spires and shaking the leaves of a sycamore. Blackbirds were flapping about the squat central tower or perching in rows along the parapets, every now and then erupting into the greatest imaginable row. The noise of the birds was whipped along by a dog who barked with even greater violence helped along by, of all things, the honking of a donkey tethered in a garden near the Deanery.

Turning around and around on this tomb-dotted darkling plain, I still could not lift the insistent grip of David's 'little things' from my shoulder. I turned again, taking a big sniff on the breeze. Gusting black mists were swirling around the belfry. I turned back and caught hold of something evil rolling out of the night; something dark and mad and big; something crawling out of the dark forests of the Mabinogion and now at loose in the streets of the land again.

The next morning I joined a tour around the cathedral conducted by Roddy Williams, a splendid fellow who sings bass in the choir and is a retired classics master from Durham University. He kept the fees for the tour in an empty golden syrup pot, clutching it to himself lest some brigand try and make off with it. He showed us around a church that was a weird cocktail of this and that, built out of the rich gifts of continuous pilgrimage for over

Above: St David's has much to delight the visitor: a gorgeous nave ceiling, elaborately carved choir stalls, a fine tiled altar.

Right: St David's commonplace exterior gives little hint of the treasures within.

eral times, the church was totally rebuilt by the Normans who deliberately made the tower short and squat to make it less visible to pirates. There is a clock face on three sides of the tower but not the north since the people in the north of the village gave nothing to pay for the clock to be put up. Just over the south porch he pointed out a head rather resembling a disconsolate Harold Wilson having just lost his pipe. It was, he told us, meant to be Queen Victoria.

If rather ordinary on the outside, St David's is quite stupendous inside. There is a gorgeous nave ceiling of richly carved Irish oak, one of the most perfect celebrations of the woodcarver's craft. In the salt air it has hardly darkened over the years. The stone columns of the nave splay outwards, giving a surprising effect of space and distance for such a small church. Abundant shafts of daylight ricocheted everywhere while my eyes kept swivelling around at the sheer richness of the detail – the twelfth century arcading, the fourteenth century choir screen, the sixteenth century ceiling and the twentieth century organ case.

The wooden choir stalls, with elaborate carvings of chortling pilgrims, were limericks in wood. The bishop's throne, with its three intricate canopies and cascading wooden waterfalls, is finer than anything of gold and rubies. There are seats for the chaplain and a special seat for the sovereign. Cromwell's men desecrated this place too, taking the lead, bells and brasses for weapons and breaking the original medieval windows, but the altar still has one of the finest sets of medieval tiles in Britain. The portable altar stone might have been used by David.

The old saint's shrine was also looted and scarred in the Reformation but it is there still: a simple bare stone structure with holes for the pilgrims to kneel and touch the oak box containing David's bones and others for them to put in their offerings. The bones have now found a new resting place in the beautiful and chaste chantry chapel, but are now only displayed for television. For television!

fourteen hundred years, bashed down and built up by thousands of workmen under the guidance of dozens of tampering bishops until today when we have one of the richest, oldest and most unusual churches in the land.

It is always better to have a real living guide to show you round, rather than rely on a dry handbook. Certainly Roddy Williams is one of the best guides I have come across. He has an enthusiastic delivery and a lively sense of scandal. It was Bishop Barlow who pinched the lead off the roof in the sixteenth century, he told us, to help provide dowries for his five illegitimate daughters. Destroyed sev-

That afternoon I went to see the Dean in his handsome Victorian manse and found a man with a BA in despondency; a man weighed down with the problems of running a cathedral in a secular age, trying to cope with two hundred and fifty thousand visitors a year, more than any other church in Wales, with four Welsh and English services every morning.

The whole job had fagged him out, I thought, even made him a little bitter with the unequal struggle of paying heavy bills and the continual round of restoration, refit and upkeep that inevitably comes with maintaining such an old building. 'I'm now corresponding with the architects over the repair of four clerestory windows at fourteen thousand eight hundred pounds. Then there is this iniquitous VAT on ancient monuments like ours. That's fourteen thousand eight hundred plus VAT – we've got to pay the government for the right to spend money here. The renewal of the drainpipes is going to cost three thousand six hundred. I asked the architects if they were proposing to put in gold pipes.

'We've never had much money but people will it to us and we have a good society of friends. Sometimes I have to act on faith as when we needed thirty-six thousand pounds to restore the organ and we only had eight hundred in the bank. We appealed to everyone we could think of and, within a year, had the money. One didn't worry about money when we started here but I do now all the time. Do you know even the local oil company as rich as Esso just gives us fifteen pounds every Christmas? People's hackles rise if you ask them for just a pound. They don't mind giving in kind but not in cash. They also don't mind paying to see the ruin of the Bishops' Palace but won't pay to see the church.'

Clearly all this business with money was getting him down. He should play some sport or something, I suggested. Well he had once played rugby for Llanelli and used to play golf every Monday. But in the last twelve years he had only had nine games of golf. 'Those days are over. If I take a day off one of my parishioners might die. You can't bargain for people dying.'

I left feeling rather sorry for this beleaguered man who, presumably, was once called to preach the Gospel and was now struggling with damp in the crypt, kids rifling the collection boxes and people like me coming and telling him he should play some sport or something. There was clearly more fun in having all your teeth pulled out than running an old cathedral. There are indeed fates worse than death.

The next day sunshine glazed the puddles as I walked down towards the sea, stopping briefly to watch a weasel chasing a rabbit across a field. The rabbit was squealing with fear, yet the odd thing is that they can outrun weasels any day. They just become paralysed with fright, and get caught.

Down in another field I came across the holy well of St Non, enclosed by a stone arch. Some coins were lying on the stone bed beneath the clear moving water; freshly cut hydrangeas were moving around on the surface. Further on again was the restored chapel, a light stone structure on the site where David was born. It was a most beautiful spot this, powerful with wild Wales. On one side is the low crouch of the Pembrokeshire hills and, on the other, the steady grumbling of the sea to the rocks.

I was walking out towards the sea and my spirits quickened when I saw a rainbow, breathtaking in its perfect arc, sweet in its promise that the Lord will not drown the earth again. Might it be the same rainbow that once appeared to the people all those years ago telling of the coming of a new prophet of God? They say there is only one yawn in the world which travels everywhere at the same time entering the backs of necks and stretching mouths. Might it be that there was also only one rainbow, eternally re-inventing itself through the ages, drifting through a constant state of reincarnation, so beautiful and difficult a creation it just could not be made for one appearance and then thrown aside?

Gazing up at that rainbow I saw that the story of the saints like David had come to bestride my modern pilgrimage just as surely as that coloured arc of refracted light. Everywhere I had ventured that year they had been around. What a gang they must have been. Facts are often lost in the alleyways of legend but we know that Patrick came here regularly to see his chum David; that Mungo once exchanged croziers with David and Columba; that Aidan journeyed from Columba's Iona. We know that they all had great powers of healing and were on first-name terms with a dozen angels; that they came into a world in chaos to rekindle the fire of faith.

I could see them coming down that Pembrokeshire coastal path now, framed by that colossal rainbow, all chattering to one another as they went past the caravan park. Fourteen of them, many wearing bracelets with combs of bone in their long hair, shaven on the forefront from ear to ear, their long habits the natural colour of wool, great hooded cloaks swirling around their feet, satchels full of books flung over their shoulders and single bells tied on to the cords around their waists. They turned right at the ice-cream stall and vanished from view.

SEVEN

A UNIVERSITY FOR THE SAINTS

LLANTWIT MAJOR·CARDIFF·CHEPSTOW·TINTERN
GLASTONBURY·ISLE OF WIGHT

Over the hills and out to sea they drifted. Yellow-bellied from the rising sun they went one by one and two by two, hurrying along with the winds, being shunted to wherever clouds are shunted before they fade away and are no more. Above them the long vapour trails of climbing jets sliced up the grey-blue dawn into giant white squares, bissected here and there by the endless caravan of those clouds . . . four, five, six . . . eleven, twelve, thirteen . . . marvellous fluffy frontrunners in a floating marathon across the heavens.

Autumn was foreclosing on the summer with the dark nights drawing in when I came to Llantwit Major, a small town in the Vale of Glamorgan, to resume my search for holiness. It was a time of earwigs and the sudden rifle shots of cooking apples falling in the orchards. Gardeners were out lighting bonfires and scraping up the first of the dead leaves into dank piles. The tomato plants were withering in the greenhouses and, everywhere, there were lots of daddy longlegs, all spindly limbs and tiny black bodies, looking menacing as they lurked around in porches like plain-clothes men trying, but failing, to look unobtrusive.

This morning, standing counting the clouds out in the village streets, the very rooftops were singing with the kiss of an Indian summer which had come bragging to the yellowing leaves on the trees, making the morning dew sparkle as she glided her majesterial way from lane to lane, as gorgeous as a queen on her way to her coronation.

Only the postman and the milkman were up and about their business: the rest of the village snoozed on behind drawn curtains. The pubs scattered around the stone monument in the square were as closed and still as hangovers. Just a few tiny snails with delicate white and red shells were out strolling over the pavements. Johnny Jones's cockerel greeted the day with a few thin calls but there was none of a cockerel's normal jubilant exuberance in the thing since, as Johnny Jones says, the bird is now nearly fourteen years old and full of sleep.

I was walking out towards the ruined church at Tresilian when, down in a green-grassed gully, I stopped on a stone bridge to watch the brook chattering over brown and grey pebbles, its sides swollen full up against the mud banks after a week of rain.

And what rain it had been, driving down hard when I had arrived the day before, trudging around from winding street to winding street, with cold drips dribbling down my back as I looked for a bed for the night. At one point I stopped still and lowered my head, cowering in a sudden spasm of fear when something louder and faster than lightning went shooting through the dense rain mist above.

It was, I realised after it had gone, merely a jet from the nearby airfield at St Athan. But for a split second, as I held up my arm over my head, it could have been something straight out of the Inferno or, perhaps, that bald witch with one tooth called Mollen who, the locals say, regularly roams the night on a broomstick above the Town Hall, on the look-out for naughty boys to frighten out of their wits.

I ambled along the lane out to St Donat's, turning off and crossing a cow-patted field where dopey-looking cows with huge black eyelashes stared at me balefully. The ruins of the church at Tresilian were being used as compounds for farm animals and, where once there was a nave, there were now piles of mud stamped with the hoops of cows' feet. As I stood on the high ramparts of the limestone cliffs, looking out at the sun cranking herself up over the muddy waves of the Bristol Channel, swarms of seagulls fluttered over the rock pools looking for something by way of food. Almost everywhere I had gone that year there had been seagulls.

I took the cliff path back to Col-hugh valley which, in its turn, leads back up to Llantwit itself. Just at the mouth of the valley is another of those squalid caravan parks, now abandoned for the coming winter. The real emblem of Wales is no longer St David's daffodil or the leek; it is the caravan. As I sauntered past I saw that a wren had somehow got itself trapped in one of them, fluttering up the window and falling back down again, trying to find a way of escape. The door was locked, as were all the windows, so I picked up a brick and bashed in one of the windows to let the bird go.

Feeling a good deal better, I continued on up the brambled path which brought me back into the town. In another caravan site on the other side of town I called on Myles Jones, The Author, who had been struggling the long night through writing The Novel. An agent in London had expressed an interest in it, he told me. Now sixty-two, he has a soft Welsh voice and lots of ragged holes in his jumper. His caravan was piled high with newspapers, records and assorted dusty books with a sheet pinned on the wall above his table containing such injunctions as: SUSPENSE. GET WORKING. NO WET TALK.

Since retiring from teaching Myles has been living here for some three years, listening to Brahms and Schubert, brewing his own beer, working on The Novel in longhand and then getting a secretary to type up his scrawls. 'I've had six and they've all had nervous breakdowns.' He was very secretive about what the magnum opus was all about – not even revealing the title – but, as the whole town knows, he is still very bitter about the break-up of his marriage and the book might just be read as an act of revenge.

Myles is but one, if eccentric, example of a literary tradition in Llantwit that stretches back through fifteen centuries from his dusty caravan to another sort of scholar altogether. This was St Illtyd, who founded the first university in Britain here. As saints go St Illtyd was pretty much second division but his achievements were still considerable. Not only did he perform miracles (when thieves stole his pigs he turned them into stone which is no mean miracle

In a church probably very much like this Sir Arthur Bryant wrote: 'All English history – its strength, its sleeping fires, its patient consistency – is here, contained in its speaking silence.'

by any standards) but he also clearly had a brain the size of a small planet: 'Now this Illtyd was the most learned of all Britons in his knowledge of the Scriptures, both the Old and New Testaments and in every branch of philosophy, poetry and rhetoric, grammar and arithmetic; and he was most wise and gifted with the power of foretelling future events.'

He also had the typical medieval saint's rapport with animals. Once, upset by the constant cries of crows, he gathered them together in his church and imposed a vow of silence on them. He also gave shelter to a stag fleeing from King Meridian and, thereafter, the stag stayed with him.

But his greatest glory was his university. Three thousand students were here, accommodated in seven halls. Eight hundred small wooden cells were built on this spot, *pulcherrimus locorum* – this most beautiful of places – as St Illtyd's biographer called it, surrounded by the ditch and mound which comprised the Llan or sacred enclosure. They built a tiny wooden church for prayer and meditation and instituted the old monastic rules of *Laus Perennis* – praise without end. The students were divided into twenty-four groups with each group responsible for one hour of worship and adoration, ensuring that ceaseless praise ascended to God around the clock.

All types of people came here to learn the great truths: scholars and poets, ecclesiastics and missionaries, beggars and royalty. There were even three saints from Brittany studying here – Samson of Dol, Gildas and Paul Aurelian – who, in their turn, spread news of Illtyd's work throughout their own country to the extent that we still find Illtyd's name attached to many Breton churches.

St David also studied here and the story goes that one of his teachers, Paulinus, had lost his sight and though many students had looked at his old eyes none could understand the reason for his affliction. Only David would not look since, he said, he had never raised his eyes to his master's face. Paulinus praised this humility but asked David just to touch his eyes and when David finally agreed the old teacher could see again.

Some say that St Patrick – or Maenwyn as he was called in Welsh – was studying in one of these classrooms when the place was invaded by a gang of Picts and he was taken off as a slave to Slemish. But apart from all these stories there is now hardly any evidence of St Illtyd's old university of the saints. It survived up to the Norman conquest but little remains apart from the memorial stones and crosses in the church itself, all carved with the characteristic Celtic interlacing designs. There were, I was told by the church's assistant curate, the Reverend Peter Reid, no special plans to celebrate the anniversary of Illtyd's death on November 6 – and so we have another saint lost in the marsh mists of the centuries; one whose ghost comes back to brood, perhaps, on this holy site where once he educated scholars to do battle with the evil of an age.

The next day I went back to investigate the church which John Wesley once described as the most beautiful as well as the most spacious parish church in Wales. It is indeed a very attractive jumble. Two churches in fact built around a central tower, all set in a gully next to a stream with a neat, jammed graveyard dotted with palm trees.

Even though it is periodically vandalised and the parish council has asked for the church to be locked it has been decided to leave it open to keep faith with its original purpose as a place of prayer and retreat. 'It continues to get done over and they even let off a fire extinguisher in the vestry,' said Peter Reid. 'But we would hate to have to lock it.'

Indeed on the back of the collection box I found a note clearly written to dampen the ardour of any would-be thieves: 'This box is emptied daily so do not expect to find more than a few pennies in it.'

I was sitting in one of the pews when I heard squirrel-like noises coming from behind the organ and found that it was an amiable old man, Ernest Brook, setting up his gear to photograph a tombstone built into the wall. He had an extremely small head with gaunt skeletal features but, as he spoke, you realised that there was little that was small about his brain.

He was, he said, a retired headmaster who spent much of his time in his remaining years studying old churches. 'I collect old tombstones the way some collect old violins.' I asked him what was so interesting about this place and he launched into one of the most amazing, energetic and vivid lectures I have ever heard as he took me around pulling up

carpets and pushing aside cupboards, his mouth a veritable machine gun of knowledge and insight which even hours later had left my brain quite dizzy.

'You can see that this gravestone in the chancel must be about 1624. We know that because the cross went out in about that year. And look here. Two brothers dying on the same day, a Christmas Day, in 1756. That must be unusual. See this. The mason couldn't fit in all his lettering so he jammed it all in there. Why didn't he chalk it out first? You tell me. This man would have been put in there in the year that Walter Raleigh was executed. I've been studying this other stone for some time. The problem is that the Latin is wrong. They had to strain the grammar to get it to fit. This tombstone says he was one hundred and twenty-nine when he died. It is clearly a lie. He might have been twenty-nine and some eighteenth century vandal added the one. It's nice to think they had their own vandals too. I love this one. See the crudity of the lettering . . .'

And so this amiable and engaging crank went on, rather making me realise just how superficial my examination of many of the churches had been on my pilgrimage; how they had evolved over the centuries in a way which meant that every corner had its own story which it yielded up only too happily to a little study and thought. He was one of the real gems of my stained glass hours was Ernest Brook.

I t is difficult to talk about something you know well and I know Llandaff Cathedral in Cardiff very well since I grew up in the shadow of that pencil-sharpened spire poking up out of a vista of conker trees. The bells that were even now ringing out, in a great thrilling romp over the damp fields, were the bells of my childhood.

Even as I stood there that morning, beneath the great chestnut tree whose fanned leaves were falling slowly and

Llandaff Cathedral: 'I grew up in the shadow of that pencil-sharpened spire. In the cathedral graveyard our first cigarettes stung our throats and made our eyes water.'

hurriedly around me, I could hear the sounds of all those dog days of school and first love. I could just see myself, a snot-nosed kid with scuffed shoes, scouring the gutters looking for money or marbles, picking up cigarette packets to see if there were any left inside, kicking around those brittle dead leaves looking for the green spiky cases of those shiny brown conkers which I took home and tried everything from baking them to soaking them in vinegar so that they would become rock hard and enable me to smash my foe's conkers into smithereens. I was also an ABC minor with a badge to prove it.

Yet, as I walked towards the cathedral, I can't say that I felt any particular warmth towards the place. Lovely though the building undoubtedly is, the congregation was always unbearably snobby, the services always manned by ushers with starched smiles and frowns crouching in their eyebrows. You could easily come here every Sunday of your life and none of them would talk to you. The men were the kind of men who would go to services three times on a Sunday and then complain bitterly if you parked your car directly outside their house. The women were the kind who, if they found you dying of some terrible wound, they would take you in but first take your shoes off so you wouldn't dirty up the carpet. That's the way they were in Llandaff.

The bells were still ringing out to herald something or other and there were lots of parked cars around the green when a double-decker bus, on charter from the corporation, pulled up and disgorged a large posse of dignitaries in Moss Bros suits and billowing hats who filed down the slope to the cathedral. There was clearly some special service going on in the place this morning, now fully restored after one of Mr Hitler's boys dropped a bomb on it during the war. Another of the same lot dropped a bomb on my home in nearby Cathedral Road which did not go off and went straight down the chimney, lodging itself behind the fire-grate in my bedroom, only to be discovered thirty years later when the bomb squad was called in. I spent most of my youth sleeping within a few feet of an unexploded bomb.

Around in the cathedral graveyard we cut up lengths of creepers and lit them, thus making our first cigarettes which stung the throat and made our eyes water copiously. We would drop ants on to spiders' webs watching, with our blood running cold, as the tips of the spider's long black legs appeared and stalled, watchful and suspicious, moving out very slowly as the ant heaved and struggled when, with a lurching dash, the spider would pounce on the ant and wrap him up in a bundle before hauling it back down into its hole to have for tea.

I asked a passer-by if he knew what was going on that morning and he showed me an invitation card for the Centenary Service for the University College, Cardiff. Having gained a third in philosophy and being unique, in my year, in then managing to fail my Dip. Ed. I was slightly pained that I had not been invited myself. But I let it pass and decided that, when they had all settled in, I would sneak in unseen. There might be an open door around the back and there wasn't much I didn't know about sneaking into cinemas and football grounds in Cardiff though this was the first time I had ever tried to sneak into a cathedral.

I went down past the south wall where there are the stone carvings of all the sovereigns' heads beginning with Richard III and ending with the uncrowned head of Edward VIII. The heads continue on the north side with George VI and down to Elizabeth II. It is said that when the north side is full there will be no more kings and queens of England.

I passed beneath the toothy smile of a gargoyle – a hideous thing warning that all vices must be renounced – and tried a few doors around the back, but they were all good and locked. There was no alternative; I would just have to gatecrash the party. I opened the front door as the congregation was singing the first hymn and somehow bluffed my way past an usher who seemed less concerned with my credentials than with my lack of a collar and tie. He duly put me in the back row where, presumably, no one could see this scruffy bounder come to foul up the cathedral without a collar and tie, by Jove.

There, squeezed in between extremely fat people, amidst the smell of boot polish and expensive suits, I sat again in the church where I had been confirmed, looking up at this lovely airy place. It is dominated by a concrete arch which contains the gilded organ case, held up by Sir Jacob Epstein's *Majestas*, a simply massive unpolished aluminium sculpture of the risen Christ, his body long and holy with huge hands and feet and great sad eyes looking up at the wooden roof. I have always wanted to wrap the thing up and take it home. Its unreal length is a poem to holiness; a striking testament to how Christ was a great deal different from all of us in his majesty.

'We have come together in this Cathedral Church,' said the Dean, 'to give thanks to God for the blessings he has bestowed upon our University College of Cardiff since its foundation and to pray that he may continue to pour his blessing upon us and all who contribute to its well-being.'

This cathedral was founded by St Teilo, another Welsh saint who was supposed to have accompanied St David on his journey to Jerusalem, and who then came here in 560 to build a tiny church. The Normans built the cathedral in 1120 and Urban, the first Norman bishop, arranged for the bones of yet another Welsh saint, St Dyfrig, to be brought from Bardsey Island to Llandaff, thus making him the first bishop of Llandaff and providing a shrine to attract a pilgrim cult and the money they brought with them.

St Dyfrig had a marvellous status in medieval legend, being the Archbishop of Caerleon as well as crowning King Arthur. He is the 'Dubic, the high saint, chief of the church in Britain' in Tennyson's *Coming of Arthur*. His chapel is just up on the left of the altar, an enchanting glade of stained glass and old stone, thick with old shadows and now reserved for private prayer.

But the building has had very bad luck over the years. It has been torn up by storms and bombs, and once was even turned into a beer house by Cromwell's troops. The chapter library books were burned and the font used as a pig trough. In 1656, troops shot at some parishioners taking communion in the Lady Chapel. In 1703 a famous storm brought the tower tumbling down through the roof. The walls of the nave collapsed too and, soon, ivy was growing over the sad rubble prompting one observer to describe it as 'this poor desolate church of Llandaff'. It was restored late in the eighteenth century but then on January 2, 1941, a German pilot hit the cathedral fair and square, making it, next to Coventry, the most damaged cathedral in the war. It was not fully restored until 1958.

But now, this damp morning, it was as splendid as any cathedral in the world. Magical swords of sunlight slashed down through the stained glass windows and played on a whole swelling sea of gold mitres, spangled vestments, chains of office and wave after wave of stuffed shirts. Such coloured shafts of sunlight well suited the heaving sense of triumphalism in the air as the speakers spoke of such as John Viriamau Jones, the first principal of the college. Ringing rhetoric was the order of the day: 'The search of the intellect for the truth and the cry of the heart for salvation,' or that old favourite, 'The strength of a country is in its learning.'

The Archbishop of Wales was speaking when a member of the congregation, sitting just on the other side of the aisle from me, flaked out. People milled around him in alarmed circles, some dashing off to get help and others shifting their weight from foot to foot anxiously. Yet, among all the fuss, the man managed to look serene and almost beautiful, his head slumped forward on his chest, a tiny deaf aid in one ear, his eyes closed, his gold half-moon spectacles perched on the end of his nose, his podgy hands resting delicately on either knee.

But when two ambulance men came to look at him he suddenly revived. Though the colour had drained out of his face, he looked very worried by all the eyes turned towards him, upset that he had caused such a fuss. He let the ambulance men take his arms to help him out. He seemed a good man, a retired academic perhaps, now giving over the remainder of his days to studying the Gospels, port, and the odd cigar.

Afterwards I bumped into Reverend Bruce Davies, my old college chaplain, a man with a healthy cherubic grin and a lovely line in humour. 'That service went on a bit, didn't it?' he complained. 'Services should never last for more than half an hour. God puts down the phone after half a hour. He gets earache.'

I told him about the man who had flaked out. 'I had a chap die in one of my services once. And I didn't get the funeral either, dammit. That went to the chapel down the road.'

The old market town of Chepstow is built on a great cliff rising out of the west bank of the River Wye, as you can see immediately you get off the bus. All the streets slope so steeply it is a wonder the place is not a forcing-ground for mountaineers. One is even called Steep Street. I looked around at this strange wonky jumble with its shops, gabled houses and old buildings. It has a leisure centre and a bingo hall. There is also a huge stone gate over the main road which has been bashed and dented by a century of traffic. The ancient tribe of the Silures built the earthworks of the town, the Romans fortified it, the Saxons traded in it, the Normans built a castle on it and now Chepstow has the slightly pained air of distressed country gentlefolk, broken down by the twin perils of traffic and the twentieth century but, somehow, managing to hang on to a few vestiges of dignity and self-respect.

In Hawkers Hill Street there was an ancient inn with the strange sign 'The Five Alls' – which would, doubtless, have delighted that fellow-traveller around Durham who collected pub signs. The name derived from the five portraits on the sign: the king – 'I govern all'; the parson – 'I pray for all'; the lawyer – 'I plead for all'; the soldier – 'I fight for all' and the devil – 'I take all'.

There wasn't a bus to Tintern for another two hours so I asked a man how I could walk there and he told me that I would be far better off if I stayed in Chepstow. 'There have been some good murders here you know,' he said. 'In a bungalow just over the way there a woman had a shotgun and blew a lad clear across the living room, she did.'

I disregarded his advice and followed the road out past the race course, keeping a watchful eye on a spaniel who, in his turn, was keeping a watchful eye on me. But there was no fight, and I trudged along the grass verge down into the wooded valley quite happily, whistling to myself and the falling leaves.

They were as grand as I had hoped they would be, those falling leaves, drifting across the road in clouds of brown confetti and crunching under my feet. Leaves drifted past me in ones, twos and great rattling storms. Leaves went tumbling over the road like acrobats; I could hear them scratching the surface as they went, soft but distinct like the faint rasp of fingernails on a blackboard, many suddenly dancing demented jigs in the draughts of passing cars as yet another breeze shook loose another crackling shower of leaves across my path.

A helicopter chattered overhead and hundreds of black-headed gulls stood around in a field, all facing the wind, as motionless and formal as a wartime cemetery. On one bend in the road I stood on the edge of a pond watching a duck when, in a furious flutter of wings, another duck broke cover from the reeds near my feet and they both flew off

Tintern Abbey, 'this incredible ruin, squatting at the bottom of the valley, guarded by the river and framed by a huge orb of pale shimmering sunshine and autumnal woods.'

to wherever ducks fly for some peace and quiet. Everywhere there was that rich, yeasty smell of autumn; that lovely fat scent which so perfectly describes a season putting up the shutters and closing down for the winter.

The woods thickened and moved away in misty banks – here a despondent and dead elm; out there a green line of Christmas trees wading down through a sea of brown. A magpie went foraging through the bare branches and, far away, I could hear the aggrieved clinking of a blackbird. When the breezes stopped twirling the remaining leaves on the branches the woods were as fresh and still as a mountain tarn, the giant creepers curling everywhere.

Woods have the same effect as electric trains and model sailing boats. There is something about them that makes you young again; something about them which shrinks away the years and holds you in their protective and mysterious magic. In one clearing there was a whole lake of brown curling beech leaves, just begging you to come and roll about in them, flinging whole handfuls of them up into the air.

I was walking on down the road picking some leaves out of my collar when I glimpsed the River Wye curling along the valley floor. I continued moving along the road, sipping on a can of lemonade. Another clearing, and there was Tintern Abbey. It was the strangest sensation: the first flash of a lovely dream and my heart was smitten with delight. I just stopped walking and said, 'Oh boy' softly to myself, standing there on the side of the road while looking down at this incredible ruin, squatting on a flat tableau at the bottom of the valley, guarded by the river and framed by a huge orb of pale shimmering sunshine and autumnal woods.

Although it had no roof the abbey was almost a complete building, sitting there, disdainful in its own majesty, serene in the mellow certainty that comes to the very old. I understood immediately the power of its charm; the way it had attracted painters and poets to those 'bare ruin'd

choirs where late the sweet birds sang' with those rows of gaping glassless windows and the great seven-light window on the west wall, standing up erect against the blue sky like a huge pair of closed pincers.

It might have been on this very spot that William Wordsworth wrote his 'Lines Composed a Few Miles Above Tintern Abbey on Revisiting the Banks of the Wye During a Tour', later to be published in *Lyrical Ballads*. J. M. W. Turner came here in 1790 to paint an ivy-clad ruin shot through with shafts of light, fallen bosses and promises of eternal praise. By 1800 it was a busy tourist attraction, surrounded by beggars and bringing boatloads of visitors down the river from Chepstow, all escorted by innkeepers from Ross and Monmouth 'so that the ear is not pained by the coarseness of language so frequently heard from the navigators of public rivers'.

But, these days, the ruin was attracting some hundred thousand visitors a year and I was but one more plodding down the hill, past a cloud of whirling gnats, in search of somewhere to spend the night.

A shopkeeper directed me up a back lane to a Bed and Breakfast and very pleasant it was too, run by Barbara, a handsome Welsh lady with big eyes and a soft heart, who not only talked too much but knew that she talked too much. 'When you've had enough just walk away. I won't mind.'

She said that my best bet for dinner was the Anchor Hotel, just next to the abbey itself and I must say that I have never found an inn quite like it; a wondrous melange of the old and the new, somehow exactly summing up what a modern pilgrim might expect to find when, in the year 1983, he came to pay homage to those beautiful, mad Cistercian monks who first built the abbey in 1130.

In the bar there was an old cider press with a huge stone wheel sitting next to one of those one-armed bandits with PRESS and HOLD and so many lights and buttons you needed an electronics degree to figure out how to work it. Taped

Thirsty visitors to Tintern can refresh themselves with a Cromwell's Conquest, a Wolsey's Wallop or a Raleigh's Ruin. A nice cup of tea might be more in order.

muzak percolated through speakers somewhere in the black wooden rafters. But nothing would prepare the modern pilgrim for the menu. It was unique in my travels. Starters were described as Matins. You could choose between *Holy Order*, a 'bowl of homemade soup fit for a serf'; *Abbot Wyche*, a prawn cocktail, or *Nicolaus of Llandaff*, which was fried scampi.

Then there was The Feast itself: *Catherine of Aragon*, grilled fillet steak; *Jane Seymour*, grilled T-bone steak; *Anne Boleyn*, scampi provencale; *The Reformation Charter*, grilled lemon sole; *Thomas Cromwell*, succulent sirloin steak and *William Wordsworth*, salmon from the Wye poached in white wine.

For Compline you could have *Cistercian Rites*, once commonly known as profiteroles, or *Tynterne Order*, which turned out to be homemade apple pie. The special liqueur coffees came as *Cromwell's Conquest*, with cognac; *Wolsey's Wallop*, with whisky; *Raleigh's Ruin*, with Tia Maria or *Cardinal's Nightcap*, simply coffee.

I ordered a *Holy Order* with a medium-rare *Catherine of Aragon* followed by *Cistercian Rites* and a large *Cardinal's Nightcap*. Despite the curious nomenclature it was delicious and beautifully presented. I later discovered I had caused something of a panic in the kitchen since the barmaid spotted me making notes on the menu and everyone assumed that I was an Egon Ronay inspector. 'We've only just applied and we thought you were the man,' said the landlady. 'A right old fuss you caused.'

Later I went out to look at the abbey again. Its spiky towers stretched up against the darkening blue of the evening, spectral, black and holy. It is said that, by night, you can hear the Gregorian chants of long-dead monks in those ruins but, standing there with my hands on the railings, all I could hear were the faint sounds of birds roosting and burbling in the rafters. Through each window I could see the star-smattered sky while the air was wet with river mists with just the faintest taste of woodsmoke.

I was peering through the encroaching darkness at the twin doorway and some of the elaborate wall panels when a car came along the main road, its headlamps slicing through the trees and rolling over the giant pincers of the west wall, making them shiver and dance like something erupting out of a giant firework, then all went dark and quiet again. I put my hands in my pockets. Far away there was a shrieking commotion of farmyard animals, while down by the Anchor Hotel the red and yellow flushes of neon on a dark river flowing silently on its way.

The next morning I went out walking over the bridge and up through the forest to the Devil's Pulpit. A long climb it was as well, following the path through silvery patches of mist and gusting showers of brown leaves. The leaves on all the trees were, incredibly enough, several different colours ranging from the orange and yellow blazes of the beech trees to the deep crimson of the rowan and the pale brown of the ash, all catching the sunlight and turning it into magical sparkles as they fell. A few of the oaks were still holding on to their leaves, standing above the others like great golden cathedrals. Whole pools of yellow poplar leaves swirled around my ankles with the odd patch of purple hawthorn. As I walked I felt that this morning, the womblike forest belonged to me alone.

The Devil's Pulpit is an unusual heap of grey granite from which you can see over to the Forest of Dean, the distant Severn and the Black Mountains. Smoke curled upwards from an embowered chimney. But always the eye is drawn back to the abbey, always you turn to gaze again at the abbey's lovely face as it sits down there in its wonderous setting of meadow, river and wood.

The abbey owed its beginnings to murder; one Walter de Clare slew his wife, Eva, in Chepstow Castle. Her ghost kept coming back to torment him so, on the advice of a priest, Walter became a pilgrim crusader. On his return, he poured all his money into building the abbey. He invited a Cistercian order of monks to join him and the first service was held in 1131. Later the building was expanded by the fifth Earl of Norfolk, Roger Bigod, who employed the finest craftsmen in the land to create this exquisite poem whose very form and intelligence manages to marry a sense of lightness with enduring strength.

The Cistercians carried on their daily pattern of worship here for four centuries, praying around the clock, copying manuscripts, teaching the novices, sleeping in the great dormitory, eating in the dining hall and caring for the sick who, alone, were allowed to eat meat. But those old monks eventually turned their backs on God and, when they did that, God gave them up. They became notorious for their avarice and decadence. Many of them drifted away and when the abbey was dissolved and surrendered to Henry VIII's commissionaires only a handful were left. The abbot was given a small pension and sent packing; the lead and bells were stripped from the roof. Masonry was taken for use in other buildings and the valuables were catalogued, weighed and sent to the Royal treasury. And that was the end of Tintern Abbey.

I walked back down from the Devil's Pulpit and went in search of the abbey's chief custodian, Roger Plaister. He is an affable man with the large black eyes of a thoughtful sheep and a fondness for ghost stories. It seems that he has written quite a lot of such stories including one, *A Ghost Story for Christmas*, about a ferryman in neighbouring Brockweir 'with the face of a corpse in a sickening grin', which was published in *Welsh Country Life*.

Imagine his surprise when, a year later, the *Sun* newspaper ran a series on people who had seen ghosts and there was this Tintern man talking about the ghost of Brockweir 'with the face of a corpse in a sickening grin'. It turned out that the man had merely retold Roger Plaister's short story

Glastonbury Tor, epicentre of a thousand legends, a totem pole suffering from an identity crisis.

to the gullible reporter, who then presented it as fact to his equally gullible readers.

But, said Mr Plaister, he had once seen two real ghosts brawling in a nearby field. He knew of one woman living near the abbey who had seen the ghost of an old Cistercian monk in her living room so many times she had been forced to go and see a psychiatrist.

Mr Plaister did not blame Henry VIII for having the abbey pulled down, however. 'He was led by his passions that one,' he explained. 'You should read his letters to Anne Boleyn. She really had him where she wanted him. It was Thomas Cromwell who was behind it all. Still, the money from the Dissolution did secure the reign of Elizabeth and the future of the monarchy so it can't have been all that bad. The church had become corrupt anyway. Arguably, the ruins are better than the real thing.'

Certainly you can feel the centuries of belief as you walk around inside this Gothic ruin. You can sense deeper truths when you look out through windows in which there is no stained glass but something larger and lovelier in the ravishing views of river and wood. Sunlight smashes down on the broken pillars. Lumpy carved stone bosses lie around on the neatly cut lawns with the only tomb being under the north arch. *Hic: Iacet: Nicholaus: Landaverists* – Here lies Nicholas of Llandaff. All along the side of the nave are bird droppings and fluffy pancakes of white moulted feathers.

I asked one of the men working on a wall what sort of birds hung out here. 'All sorts,' he said. 'There's about fifty of them but most are racing pigeons who've dropped out on their way home. They're a nuisance, if you ask me, but you can't do anything. One of the boys tried to scare them off once with a gun and shot one through the neck by mistake. There was blue murder over that. One man came in here shouting that God's creatures could not be killed in God's house, and all that kind of thing.'

I loved the notion of the drop-out pigeon, a sort of cosmic cowboy of the skies, falling in with a bunch of

like-minded ne'er-do-wells, in the eaves of a majestic ruin owned by a benevolent God who would brook no harassment or evictions of the squatters on his property. Still drunk with those golden hours in the falling leaves, I was on the road again. To Glastonbury.

I took the road to the ancient and sacred kingdom of Glastonbury sitting up high on the passenger seat of a builder's lorry. The cab reeked of oil and a broken spring pressed into my back. Scaffolding shackles and dusty crumpled newspapers were scattered around my feet. The driver was a burly man from Bristol with strong arms and a bold bullfinch nose. He didn't talk much, and left me to look around the countryside quietly.

We went lurching through the hummocky Somerset hills, past a group of people standing at a bus stop, the warmth of their breath vaporising into long plumes in the coldness of the air. A police car overtook us in an effortless burst of speed and, standing on the corner of a lane, a man was eating chips out of a newspaper.

It was then that I caught my first sight of Glastonbury Tor, standing guard over the town, a high conical hill with a building atop it, strangely at odds with the low rolling fields all around. The Tor bobs up in all kinds of roles in all kinds of books. Some say it is the seat of Gwyn ap Nudd, the Lord of the Underworld. Others say it represents the final great monument to the mysteries of the Druids. I say it looked like a totem pole with an identity crisis, when the lorry driver changed down and rounded a corner making the Tor disappear behind the light brown roofs of a council house estate.

The driver dropped me off in the square, leaving me to wander around the main street with its clothes shops, Indian curry house and fifteenth-century church. There was a shoe shop called Camelot and bookshops called Helios and The

Glastonbury Experience. Small herds of aggressively scruffy teenagers wearing studded leather motorbike jackets, with safety pins in their ears, wandered around the pavement and, I was to learn, went slowly ricocheting around the streets all night too.

But there were other more exotic inhabitants as well: the space cadets with their embroidered kaftans, slumped shoulders and every-which-way hair styles. Now and then you saw them sandalling about clutching their fat books and looking extremely ill, lost in clouds of being and nothingness. Some of the unusual advertisements in the shops told you they were thick on the ground too: ads for things to do with cosmic menstrual cycles and mystic origami; others to do with the wonders of Sufi and the way of Zen.

For never forget, man, this place is one of the world's power points; the home of sacred geometry and the ley line, all overhung by the astrologer's zodiac and other assorted holes in the head. This is where, in 1920, one Alfred Watkins had a paranormal vision and became aware of a whole network of lines, standing out like glowing copper wires all over the country, intersecting at important sites like churches, castles, ancient stones and burial mounds. These were the ley lines or prehistoric direction indicators.

I followed a ley line along the pavement to the George and Pilgrims, a hotel at least five hundred years old, said to be the oldest in Britain and, to be fair, looking every minute of it. You can see its age in the ecclesiastical stone front and the mullioned windows; in the flag-stoned hallway and polished brass handles on the windows. Pilgrims have been staying here since 1475, it says in the hotel brochure, and I envied their being spared the one-armed bandit in the bar and the artificial flames of a gas fire which lapped, hungrily and hopelessly, around a pile of fake logs.

The welcome was pretty modern too: whey-faced wenches staring at you blankly and a po-faced demand to take an impression of your credit card as soon as you arrived. I was left to carry my own bag and find my own room. I sat at the end of the bed wondering why I hadn't followed another ley line to a different hostelry since, even after paying a stiff twenty pounds a night, I still only qualified for a sachet of powdered milk to put into my tea.

Times had clearly changed since 63 A.D. when that 'good and just' uncle of Jesus, Joseph of Arimathea, came here together with a hundred and fifty disciples. It is reported that he brought with him the chalice cup used at the Last Supper – a present from Pontius Pilate. He was also thought to be carrying two cruets containing the sweat and blood of Jesus. When he came to nearby Weary All Hill Joseph put his staff down into the ground where it turned into a bush and burst into blossom. Henceforth it became known as the Holy Thorn which still blossoms at Christmas, when a spray is sent to the Queen.

Joseph decided that the flowering thorn was a blessing from the Lord and settled in Glastonbury where, after a visit from the archangel Gabriel, he built the first above-ground Christian church out of wattle and daub. Another version of the story is that Joseph, a rich merchant trading in Cornish tin, brought the Virgin Mary and the Christ himself here. As a young carpenter, the Lord might well have worked on the church.

Almost alone in Britain – even if only in such legends – Glastonbury is associated with that pale Galilean, full of grace and truth, who came to serve the world and show us an unequalled glimpse of surpassing tenderness and beauty.

Joseph is also said to have buried the cup in Chalice Hill. As if his story were not enough for one place, it then attracted a further body of legend around King Arthur, who was searching for that same cup, known as the Holy Grail. Camelot Castle was reputedly built near Glastonbury and even nearer was the Isle of Apples – Avalon – where King Arthur was brought to die after his last great battle.

Glastonbury's 'special atmosphere' draws countless visitors each year. 'The Americans just can't get enough,' says a local organiser of magical mystical tours.

In 1191 Glastonbury monks claimed that they had found the tomb of King Arthur and his Queen, Guinevere.

I talked about the special atmosphere of Glastonbury to Jamie George, a large young Scot with a soft musical voice who ran Gothic Image, a shop near my hotel, and who also specialised in Mystical Tours.

'There *is* something about the place,' he agreed. 'I was working in television in London when I came here one day and I was taken by its stillness. I packed it up in London and came here, first signing on the dole before getting my shop together. Yes, that stillness hits you like a club.'

Soon after setting up his shop, which sells almost everything the fringe has ever dreamed up, he began taking pilgrims on tours around Weary All Hill, the Chalice Well, up the Tor and, finally, around the abbey ruins. He gets a lot of Americans, Europeans and Japanese. 'The Americans just can't get enough.' Accordingly he is now setting up tours right around the ancient sites of Britain and, when we spoke, he was about to go to Los Angeles to set up new business contacts. The pilgrim business was clearly going international.

Later in the afternoon I went to see the abbey ruins where I hired a tape recorder at the gate and got a very posh colonel voice telling me what was what, and what to do next. 'Right, now go and stand at the wooden cross and then switch off,' he boomed with military precision, though it often sounded as if he was slurping on a large gin and tonic and eating a chicken sandwich as he spoke. 'Right, now take three paces down the path and stand next to the yellow marker . . .'

I saw the Holy Thorn – 'in fact this is a Levantine thorn', the ringing voice proclaimed – and the small museum with a scale model of the reconstructed abbey before going off to look at the ruin of St Mary's, better known as St Joseph's Chapel – a gem of ecclesiastical art with lofty windows, the remnants of rich panellings and elaborate carvings on each door. This was the site of the first church referred to as Lignea Basilica, the spot on which some say the Gospel was first proclaimed in Britain. True or not, we do know for certain that this spot was once associated with yet another great holy man, perhaps the most famous Anglo-Saxon saint of them all. This was St Dunstan, born here in 924. He became abbot in 940, and later Archbishop of Canterbury.

A man of immense culture, Dunstan revived organplaying in the church and also set up the monastic custom of ringing bells to celebrate services. He asked for louder peals on special occasions. He was educated by scholars and seems to have suffered from sleepwalking long before anyone knew anything about such things. After taking holy orders he came to live in a cell in Glastonbury, building up the abbey in a series of reconstructions. His relationships with two kings were very volatile but he always continued with his learning as well as making bells and playing music. He became the patron saint of goldsmiths, jewellers and locksmiths. The devil once appeared before him, it was said, so Dunstan took a pair of blacksmith's tweezers and seized the devil's nose, so putting it out of joint.

I was ordered in no uncertain terms to move up to the abbey itself and stand at the red pole of the nave near the grave of King Arthur. Here, on the site of the churches St Peter and Paul, there were the broken-jawed remains of what must have been a great church: part of a lofty arch, rubbled walls and little piles of earth left by the worms in the lawns. The ruins were not so complete as Tintern – your imagination had to work harder to get at how it might have been originally, how the lines of the pillars joined up and how the roof sat on those broken arches – but something of that same sense of loneliness was there nevertheless.

The abbey was gutted by a great fire in 1184. A contemporary writer movingly described the reactions of the monks:

'What groans, what tears, what pains arose as they saw what had happened and pondered over the loss they had suffered. The confusion into which their relics were thrown, the loss of treasure, not only in gold and silver, but in stuffs and silks, in books and the rest of the ornaments of the church, must even provoke to tears, and justly so, those who far away do but hear of these things.'

Two years after the fire the monks were reported to have discovered the bodies of Arthur and Guinevere lying in the hollowed trunk of an oak deep within the abbey grounds. They also found a cross saying: 'Here lies interred the body of King Arthur with Guinevere, his wife, in the Isle of

Avalon.' Her golden hair was said to have crumbled when a monk's hand touched it.

It is all a pack of lies, of course, as insubstantial as that golden hair. The monks probably made it all up to get tourist loot to finance the abbey's reconstruction. Any fool knows that King Arthur never died anyway. He is alive and well and merely asleep in a cave near Avalon from whence he will come again to save our lost and fallen tribe.

When I was walking on Iona earlier in the year a Canadian had given me the address of the Ramala Centre in Glastonbury's Dod Lane. It is described, in one book, as 'part of a seminal spirit path, the bed of an invisible stream along which the souls of the dead are conveyed on their passage to Avalon, the Western Isle'.

Dod Lane looked pretty ordinary to me, when I found it: new bungalows, cars on drives, a man delivering milk. I even spotted a colony of plastic garden gnomes. At the top of the lane, I found a large red-brick house with two huge oak trees and a wooden geodesic dome in the garden. This, not surprisingly, was the Ramala Centre.

David and Ann Jevons live there, together with their children and a very fat greedy cat called Merlin. Over tea they told me of the pilgrims who came here, often just turning up, some saying that they had been divinely directed. There were Anglicans, Roman Catholics, Essenes, British Israelites, Companions of the Well and the Arcane School. Yes, they got a fair few nutters too. 'We've often had visitors claiming that they were King Arthur or Jesus Christ,' laughed Anne. 'We don't mind that. It's when they claim that they are both that we know we're in trouble.'

David believed that places such as Glastonbury have a sort of cosmic aerial. People make contact with the energy and find themselves drawn subconsciously here to its source through an ethnic line of power. 'Glastonbury has been

'The broken-jawed ruin of what must have been a great church.'

becoming alive over the last fifty years,' he explained. 'More and more people come each year, all drawn to the centre of the power. It's much the same power as draws Mohammedans to Mecca.'

The Jevons' faith and the books they write are centred on Christ – something they call the Christ Expression – but not the church as such. Twice a day, at noon and in the evening, they, together with anyone who wants to join them, sit in their wooden dome for a period of meditation. The dome is very pleasant inside, with deep-pile blue fitted carpets and various objects such as quartz stones scattered around on shelves. It had the thoughtful, fussed-about atmosphere of a much-loved home.

Ann added that she had a relationship with the two oak trees – Axil and Omega. Axil told her to build a bench around its base to bring visitors closer to it. The oak, the Druids believed, symbolised God. The Druids also believed so firmly in reincarnation they accepted that any money borrowed in this life was repayable in the next. So, if you are ever lucky enough to meet a Druid, tap him for a fiver immediately.

The next morning I visited the Chalice Well at the bottom of the Tor; a walled garden containing a laid-out spring of such dainty ornamentalism it seemed to draw its inspiration more from the gaudy world of Walt Disney than the ascetic world of the medieval pilgrim. The well, which bursts with an inexhaustible torrent of water, is said to be connected with the burial of the Holy Grail. It has long been regarded as a curative shrine, and reports suggest that ten thousand people came here in 1751. It is also known as the Blood Spring: the waters often run red with rust.

Later I flogged up the serpentine path of the Tor itself, following a path over a stile and across a gently rising meadow, stepping over the dark pebbles of sheep dung and the tiny hillocks of earth thrown up by many moles, past a few people coming back down, ever higher as the surrounding countryside stooped lower beneath my feet. The morning was again shot through with a magical vein – the same sense of the closeness of watchful angels that I had felt down in those Glastonbury streets.

Up high on the Tor you can see the spire of the cathedral town of Wells, the Mendips, the Polden Hills and even the distant Cheddar Gorge but, this morning, banks of mist hung over the fields and trees like burly ghosts stretched out on a siesta. I could pick out the gentle curve of the breast of Chalice Hill and the wooded slopes of Weary All Hill. The rest of the country crept away and hid beneath the swirling, secretive mists.

I stopped and turned around and there was absolutely no sound except the dull throb of my heart. Directly ahead of me was the strange oblong of a church tower that seemed to have mislaid its church. Down below was Glastonbury, this Avalon of the Heart, looking mystic in the mists. It was lovely just to stand and look when the morning began playing with my spirits, swirling them around the Tor on the quiet breezes drifting up and down. I understood why so many had seen visions on the Tor; why people up here have felt that they were inside the very lungs of God, sensing his breathings, giant but soundless, sustaining and feeding life, with incredible power, into the very bloodstream of the creation.

It was early evening and raining on the castellated, redbrick spires of Quarr Monastery on the Isle of Wight. The rain was tadpoling down the leaded windows with the wind bashing against the doors and walls. Suddenly, two soft chimes of bells hung in the weeping night. Yet, inside the monastery walls, there was a silence which swept all around. It moved through the darkened crypt, hung around the pointed arches of the cloisters and was all but deafening in the high wide church lit by just one guttering candle. Another few bells.

Doors opened around the cloisters and men in black billowing robes slippered silently down to the refectory. It was time for the 7.30 supper and, after bowing to the figure of Christ pinioned on the wall, some twenty-three of them stood behind wooden chairs as one led the Grace and the others responded.

They took their knives and forks out of huge, white linen napkins which they stuffed into their collars and ate a plain meal of beetroot, scrambled egg and bread. In the glimmering half-light they made no sound – apart from the scrape of cutlery on plates – and sat some three feet away from one another.

Many were old, grey and balding; some had ruddy faces and others were pasty with more than a few being young men, short of hair and with bright, animated movements. A man in a small, brick pulpit – according to the Benedictine rule – read a book as they ate. The reading was slow and incantatory. Tonight it was the life story of Orione, a man who had just been beatified.

You noted that they all ate very fast since, it appeared, no one wanted to keep anyone else waiting. First and last this was a community of men in which sensitivity to one another was finely honed. Yet the brevity and simplicity of the meals were very much a part of the lifestyle of Quarr – perhaps the most simple and unadorned life to be found anywhere in Britain.

After a short period of recreation more bells heralded the start of Compline or evening prayer. Within these walls bells were the music of the nights and days. They struck off the hours, announced the beginning and end of prayers. There were tiny, tinkling bells, fat, echoing bells and huge romping gongs which pounded right down into the very foundations of the crypt.

I had come by train to Portsmouth, crossing on the ferry to Ryde where I took a taxi to this strange, beautiful place. I had been graciously received by these pained, unworldly men who were afraid of cameras, unwilling to look you directly in the eye and who only spoke when spoken to and then with a great deal of effort.

Compline was a sight of religious beauty, stirring both to the spirit and the eye. The robed monks took their places in the choir stalls, and almost immediately, the lights were turned out and there was but one burning candle. As they chanted and knelt before God, their black, rounded shapes revolved around and dissolved into one another in the flickering light. Their voices, amplified by the empty nave, were astonishingly strong as the Gregorian chants carolled out, sometimes in unison and sometimes duelling as the sacred mysteries were celebrated. At the end the abbot sprinkled holy water over all as a purification. Catch a drop on your cheek and it seemed to burn.

At nine came The Great Night Silence when all that could be heard was the wind hurtling around the monastery walls and shaking the branches of the pine trees in the gardens. *May the Lord grant us a quiet night and a perfect end.*

Even in the long silence of the night there were still tiny bells, ringing soft and sweet, redolent with the jubilation of Christmas carols. And there was the sighing wind and the gentle swish of the pines until, at 5 a.m., the cloister bells pealed out again, fat and assertive, stirring the monks out of their slumbers in readiness for Matins.

Matins is the only service of the day in which the monks don their hoods. This is the coldest time of the day; Benedictine tradition holds that a donned hood reinforces the desired feeling of isolation and oneness with God alone. It is a service of psalms, hymns and scripture reading.

In the half an hour between Matins and Lauds, Dom Matthew Taylor had a period of silent prayer in his room. The monastic life, he told me, was just one long process of coming close to God. 'Yet the closer you come, the further away he seems to be. He is nothing like his created reality. The more you understand the more you realise that you don't understand at all. He is only like himself.'

These are mystical, lonely thoughts, though in the constant cycle of prayers, silences and chants in the monastery you sensed something of the mystical, lonely search for God. In the steady, almost punishing rhythm of their days you sensed the barren loneliness of the wilderness into which Christ was driven alone to overcome the blandishments of Lucifer and grow in isolation in his love of the true God.

Here too the doors were constantly being locked to protect the monks from outside interference; bolted to allow them the tranquillity in which their faith could grow. There was no television or radio to poison their ideas.

Father Joseph Warrilow, whose long fingers wove and shaped the air as he spoke, has been a monk for fifty-four years, thirty-three of them here. He confessed to a difficulty in learning to love God, even though he knew that God loved him. 'The Psalms give such a mixed picture of God. Perhaps I haven't given it enough time.' He did once have a mystical experience when he was shaving, he said, when he *knew* that he was one of God's creatures. 'Many believe that life here is too ceremonialised, but I don't think that we should change it. Life becomes more and more an act of faith. Most of us have come through some kind of crisis. You learn to feel truth. If you can feel it you know it to be true. Our days are much the same as they were in medieval times. We must keep witness to faith when so many others are losing theirs.'

Quarr was now around half full since there was a shortage of the right men with sufficient sympathy for Benedictine ideals. One such right man was Brother Denis Bradley who had been here for seven years. 'Yes. I feel quite well absorbed now,' he told me. 'I don't believe that I will ever leave.'

The base of the monastery is academic, rather than physical, and Brother Denis tried to spend at least three hours a day studying theology with a view to finally becoming a priest. He enjoyed the full balance of the monastic day and actually laughed a lot which came as something of a surprise since most of the others were solemn, devoted men. They own nothing at all – even their clothes are given to them. 'But we've really got quite a lot.' That laugh again.

Outside in the monastery grounds a brown, brackish sea lapped against a beach littered with debris and driftwood. A car tyre waltzed around in the waves and a tree had fallen over. Some monks were out working in the gardens, a few were chopping wood. They try to grow as much of their own food as they can. Those bells floated out on the damp breeze again.

The centrepiece of the day was the full Mass and Communion in the middle of the morning. The monks wore bright red robes and walked into the church chanting together. Just before communion they all hugged and kissed one another to underline their brotherhood.

Here, surely, I had found the real meaning of holiness: men prepared to endure any hardship or sacrifice to break down any barriers to their relationship with the King; men righteous, just and fearful of the holy wrath of God which is the beginning of all wisdom; men loving one another and weaving a great web of prayer for the world with Christ at its heart.

Here on the dark days approaching the end of the twentieth century were holy men fulfilling a contract with God. They were giving him the prayer that he loves to hear and, in so doing, trying to save the world from drifting into a new Dark Age. They could see a time when God, in his rejected and disappointed wrath, would send in floods and tempests that might last for years, when people on those darkling deserts would be forever lost and crying out with pain since they could no longer even touch those they loved.

These men – like Columba, Aidan, David, Patrick and Dunstan before them – were giving up their lives so that others could keep theirs. They were keeping the flames of love alight at a time when an ocean of evil was flooding every corner of the world. Theirs was real faith. Theirs was real sacrifice. Theirs, surely, was the path of holiness.

EIGHT
LOST ON THE OLD WAY

WINCHESTER·GUILDFORD·AYLESFORD·BOXLEYABBEY·CANTERBURY

It was a cold day, deep in winter, when I got off the train in Winchester to resume my journey. Squalls of acid rain came sweeping in over the station car park and a man suffering from gargoylism walked past me. Bodies were bent low, struggling against the squalls and, up near the shopping centre, a bearded tramp was sheltering in a doorway. He was muttering evilly to himself, his possessions tied up with string and newspapers, scattered around his feet.

A green bus roared past, smashing up the carefully composed rain puddles and making them leap around in demented grey sprays.

It was the coldness of the wind that was the worst, slicing through your trousers and making you grit your teeth and whistle thinly to yourself at the pain of it all. The wind made great polythene sheets flap around noisily on a building site in front of the cathedral. Occasionally a bird broke free to fly wild or a crouching figure dashed across the cathedral lawns and disappeared through a stone arch. Yet, even in the cold rain, it had to be said that the cathedral looked mountainous, spine-chilling, infused with the careful craftsmanship of centuries.

All those cold and bare branches of the trees lashing the air forlornly seemed to suit Winchester. This was the most ancient and austere of cities. You saw its tremendous age in the buildings leaning at crazy angles and the exposed half-timbering on the house fronts. Everywhere the winding streets and old stone walls spoke of antiquity. It might even have been built old, sprawling around, as it was, with its empty spaces full of rain and the mocking calls of rooks.

Facts and figures about the place were carved in stone on the front of the Guildhall: its latitude, longitude, height above sea level, distance from London, Portsmouth, Southampton and Salisbury, and so on. It might have added, but didn't, that we were a hundred and twenty miles from Canterbury and that these two ancient cities were connected by The Old Road: a meandering, disappearing track hallowed by centuries of travel and the footsteps of millions of pilgrims who had started their journey here after sailing into Southampton. They took this road to pay homage to Thomas à Beckett after he was murdered in Canterbury Cathedral in 1170.

Winchester and Canterbury were both great centres of English life. The former was once the capital of the Saxon kings who founded the kingdom of Wessex. William the Conqueror had his court here. This was where the Doomsday Book had been kept. Canterbury has always been the spiritual centre of England so I had come, armed with maps and guide books, to follow the Pilgrim's Way between these two centres, walking the whole distance just as the pilgrims of old would have done, sleeping wherever I happened to find myself. What is more, I was going to do it very slowly at what was once known as the 'Canterbury gallop', which later passed into our vocabulary as the word 'canter'.

However, it seemed as though the cathedral authorities were anxious to speed me on my way. The dean refused to see me, saying he was about to go on holiday. The verger had retired and gone away the week before. I asked a woman a question and she said 'I don't know' and walked away.

The welcome in the cathedral itself was hardly joyful either. As soon as I walked in, a forest of placards suggested I cough up some money. A black-coated attendant stood next to the collection box, wearing a mugging smile. I didn't talk to him either. The lady in the cathedral shop was a treasure of frostiness. She knew absolutely hundreds of super people who knew all kinds of things about pilgrimage, but none who'd welcome me knocking on their door. Oh, no. Absolutely not. This was Winchester. People had to make proper appointments in Winchester.

In the end I knocked it all on the head and went to see a James Bond film. All year I have been entertaining this little fantasy that, on one of my pilgrimages, I would meet this old monk who would take me down to a small jetty on the shore of a lake and row me across to a secret island. We would walk through immense woods, watched by white stags, until we came to a cave where, deep down inside, he would show me all the jewels that his fellow monks had hidden from Cromwell's grasping clutches in the Dissolution. There would be rubies and chalices and gold orbs studded with diamonds. There would be silver crosses and, just inside a distant grotto, the Holy Grail itself. As it was I was sitting in this damp and cold flea-pit, with a man snoring behind me, watching Sean Connery flinging an assortment of villains through plate-glass windows. Perhaps that was what a pilgrimage added up to these days. In his way, James Bond is maybe the true icon of the modern world.

When I went back to the cathedral the next morning the rain had held off. This time, I would let the building itself do the talking – I wasn't up to another bout of offhandedness. It was indeed lovely and ravishing. The sheer height and splendour of the nave – with twelve bays, the largest Gothic nave in the world, they say – engulfed you like a great symphony as soon as you walked inside.

But it was walking down the side of the nave and coming across stone steps, worn down by the footsteps of an endless progression of pilgrims, and moving through ancient shadows that I felt something of the real spirit of the place. I turned and turned and felt the era after era of prayer that must have flowed up through this warren of archways and alleys and cloisters. I noted the cleanliness and smelled the polish and saw the sheen on the wood and understood the pure love that had been poured into every inch and corner of the place. I could faintly hear the canticles of the monks of old. I just knew that I was approaching the foothills of the Lord.

I suppose it was in that cathedral – perhaps more than in any other – that I had a sense of how much buildings

Winchester Cathedral: 'Era after era of prayer flowed up through this warren of archways and alleys and cloisters.'

mortuary chests containing the bones of Anglo-Saxon kings even, some say, those of King Canute. On the north aisle of the nave I found the tombstone of the novelist and princess of irony, Jane Austen.

I have never been sure why being near to such tombs always makes me feel so peaceful or why I always get such a deep and inexpressible feeling of human continuity staring at the face of unknowable death. But I *was* drenched in peace as I moved past those chantries. I was on knowing terms with the unknowable and might even have been dead myself. Perhaps this consoling sense of peace sprang straight out of all this architecture of death since it represented, for those so interred, the ultimate freedom from anxiety and pain; it symbolised a chortled shout of triumph that they were finally shot of us and our absurd and exhausting demands. You can't mess us around now, this architecture said. Sort your own problems out. Take your daft demands elsewhere.

The stained glass works were beautiful, particularly the tribute to the Anglican angler, Sir Isaac Walton. But my favourite part of the whole cathedral was the marvellous grey stone altar screen, so detailed and elaborate it might have been modelled on a great waterfall or even Niagara herself. If you gaze at it for a long time and then begin blinking it really does seem to start running.

This cathedral was built on the cult of St Swithun and here, again, we come across a rather different sort of saint. He performed no great miracles, nor did he scourge the land with fiery prophecies; in fact, he was an unparalleled celebration of simple human ordinariness. He was born in Winchester in 800 and, even when he became bishop, he only ever ate plain food and travelled around the place on foot. He built chapels and houses for the people and asked that, on his death, he should be buried outside the cathedral, without pomp or ceremony, where the rain fell and the feet trod. He died in 862 and was buried in the churchyard.

He lay out there for around a hundred years until the

grow like multiplying amoeba over the years. Wherever I looked I could see how a bit of this had been added to a bit of that, all somehow cohering into a graceful, even holy whole.

The cathedral's most unusual feature was the striking number and variety of the chantries, chapels and tombs. There were painted effigies of bishops lying in perfect Plantagenet repose. Knights were stretched out with their legs crossed. I found a shrieking skeletal figure on one tomb who looked so charred and upset he might just have been pulled off the electric chair in Sing Sing. There were also

Bishop of Winchester, clearly keen on cashing in on the pilgrim cult, ordered that his remains should be brought inside. On the day that the body was to be removed, July 15, 971, it rained so hard – and continued to rain so hard – that the body could not be moved for forty days. In that rain, it was believed, were the tears of the old saint anguishing at his disturbance. Even today it is believed by some that, if it rains on St Swithun's Day, it will then rain ferociously and without stopping for forty days.

In the cathedral library I met Mrs Barbara Carpenter Turner, a former mayoress of Winchester, whose husband was once the cathedral architect. 'Trying to follow the Pilgrims' Way are you?' she asked. 'You've read that book by Belloc, I suppose?'

I had indeed.

'It's all bosh, you know,' she told me. 'Pilgrims just wouldn't have taken the route that Belloc described. Pilgrims were always afraid of robbers so they would have stuck to the main roads, not all those lanes that Belloc talks about.'

Although she was an historian and working on the cataloguing of the library she said she knew almost nothing about St Swithun or, indeed, much about the pilgrims who came here. 'We only know of one small miracle that he performed. A poor lady was running down the street with a basket of eggs and dropped the lot. Swithin fixed them all up and restored to the lady even more eggs than she had broken.'

I thought that was a pretty smart miracle. Not very theatrical, perhaps, but smart nonetheless. 'Have you got much that's valuable in this library?' I asked.

'I'll show you if you like. But you're not a thug are you? They're all wired up to burglar alarms, you know.'

She showed me some illuminated pages of various Bibles, including the famous Winchester Bible of the twelfth century. The initial letters were particularly astonishing, both in the vivacity of their colours and their breathtaking detail.

The one B, the first letter of the first word of Psalm 1, Beatus (Blessed), depicted David, the writer of the psalm, rescuing a sheep from a bear and a sheep from a lion. Another initial showed Christ driving an evil spirit out and saving souls from hell. The Harrowing of Hell was a favourite medieval theme.

'Aren't they lovely?' Mrs Carpenter Turner asked me. 'You know it would take the skins of two hundred and forty sheep just to make one vellum Bible.'

Afterwards I went down to the shrine of St Swithun, at the rear of the nave. Cromwell cleared it out and complained later that all the jewels were fakes. It is not absolutely certain where the old saint's feretory was placed though there is now some sort of horrible contraption on the supposed spot, just sitting there sadly like some spaceship built on the cheap and out of petrol.

Much of the area is now cold and unadorned, rather different to the way it must have been once when the pilgrim would have approached a whole riot of mural colours and masses of gaudy ornaments. Yet the remains of some of the original wall paintings can still be seen in the Chapel of the Holy Sepulchre and the Guardian Angels' Chapel. Here, from the ceiling, dozens of big-eyed angels peer down on you still.

The carvings on the stall-ends of one of the chapels show you what the pilgrims were like: fat, thin and disagreeable; on foot and horseback; carrying staffs, Bibles and scallop shells; rich and poor; aristocratic and working class. All are as different and individual as life itself.

Stop and listen. Hush and you can hear their footsteps even now as the pilgrims come, with a gambler's hope in their hearts, that they will be cured of all ills and their souls saved by the sacred bones of St Swithun. See how they stretch their hands through a Holy Hole to touch them before getting on the road again and making their long, arduous and perilous journey to Canterbury.

Before setting out for Canterbury, any modern pilgrim

must first visit the Hospital of St Cross and Almshouse of Noble Poverty, just down the road in St Cross. Apart from being one of the oldest institutions in the land, it was probably the first staging post for the journey to Canterbury where, even today, pilgrims can still claim the Wayfarers' Dole: a meal of bread and beer.

It is a curious complex of buildings, erected in 1136 by Bishop Henry Blois as a soup kitchen after the failure of the harvest. It has a huge chapel and an old quadrant of flats topped by high, almost industrial, chimneys where twenty-five brothers – eight red coats of the Noble Poverty Foundation and seventeen black coats of the Hospital Foundation – are now living together in reasonably amicable retirement.

This was the place that inspired Hiram's Hospital in Anthony Trollope's great work on the twin perils of Christianity and senility, *The Warders*. It features in his other Barchester novels as well. On looking around trying to find someone, I half expected Obadiah Slope to come sliming around the corner at any second. Instead, I found a caretaker who gloried in the wonderful name of Mr Heavens.

'We still give out the bread and beer to pilgrims, oh yes,' he said to my enquiry.

I stood waiting and arranged a sort of hungry gleam on my face.

'Go on, you've just got to ask.'

'Ask for what?' I asked pathetically. 'What do I say?'

'You just ask for the dole. All you've got to do is ask.'

'Can I have the dole?'

'Oh most certainly you can. It would be my pleasure. Yes.'

Mr Heavens tottered off into his office and came back holding a round wooden salver with a small cube of bread on it and a tiny glass containing such a small drop of beer it wouldn't get a fairy drunk.

'It's just symbolic now,' he said when I expressed misgivings about the size of the meal. 'Just a token, you know.'

Mr Heavens introduced me to one of the brothers, William Dalgetty, and we had a most agreeable chat together in his cosy flat with its exposed beams, theological books and various photographs and mementoes of what had clearly been a life which streamed with love. He was a spritely, retired civil servant and had been living here for six years paying six pounds fifty a week towards the heat and light.

He liked the life well enough, he said, pottering around the garden and, now and then, jumping on buses with his pensioner's pass and exploring the countryside. He had been to Dorchester and Portsmouth a lot and liked to investigate churches too. Just lately he had discovered a Greek Orthodox church in Southampton that he enjoyed. 'I like the Greek services. There's just no telling what's going on.'

We talked a bit about theology. 'As you get older you understand that there is some reason behind it all,' he said with a nod and a faint smile. 'You just know that it can't be all for nothing. But what the reason is I couldn't be sure. It *is* very puzzling.'

After tea he showed me around the chapel which had some lovely modern stained glass work as well as an early sixteenth-century lectern with a parrot's head, eagle's body and webbed feet. 'The parrot's head is to remind us that we must read the Bible prayerfully and not just like a parrot.'

And so, fortified by my cube of bread and tot of flat beer, I left Brother Dalgetty and set out to follow the Pilgrims' Way, taking the North Gate out of Winchester. I followed the Jewry Road, so-called because it was formerly the centre of the Jewish community in the city, once in the very thick of the city's commercial life and past whose money-lenders all traffic would have proceeded. Or so it said in the book which I was using to follow the Way, *The Old Road* by Hilaire Belloc. I went past a statue of King Alfred hoisting his sword aloft, ambled past a closed pub, made a deft swerve around some dog mess and I was on my way at last.

Winter had caught the land in a relentless clamp and the lanes were as quiet and dull as council planners. Now and then chilly winds erupted through the bare hedgerows, hissing angrily and shooting out tons of dead brown leaves which shot around me like so many fusillades of bullets. Everywhere the earth was thick with chalk, slippery and difficult to walk on, even in my studded walking boots. The branches of the trees hung over me like cats o'nine tails. I wondered if, in winter, the trees have the same shape above ground as below.

I passed a wood with a sign saying BEWARE OF ADDERS, though I would have thought any self-respecting adder would have been curled up and fast asleep in its warm hole at this time of year. Practically nothing was growing anywhere – just the pendulous catkins shaking in the breeze and the odd snowy waterfall of old man's beard on some of the trees. In a churchyard, however, I did discover a shy stammering of snowdrops.

It was the sheer chilly emptiness of the chalk–dotted landscape that was so forbidding. No one was out in the fields and slivers of ice sat in pools in ditches. Soft winds moaned quietly into the dead brown bracken. A crowd of black rooks sat around in one tree, now and then exploding into knowing parliamentarian guffaws. The bang of a shot-gun rang across the fields, its echo moving emptily along the side of a wood, making the rooks rise up in a black circling cloud before they all settled back down again.

The joints in my none-too-fit legs were squeaking a bit when I finally signed into the Swan Hotel in New Alresford, the same town where Belloc had spent his first night on the same journey. I was worried by the aches in my legs since I had hoped that I would be able to do the whole journey on foot. I had conceived it rather as a private journey of toil, a tribute to the suffering of the pilgrims of old, something for God.

New Alresford, I later discovered, was a very English sort of place. Foot scrapers stood outside the doorways and the curtains were so thick you could not see inside. One of the pubs had lots of ferocious animal traps dangling off the wall together with a group of farmers hogging the fire, slapping their thighs with big red hands and chortling a lot at loud blue jokes.

Down in Old Alresford I found a lovely old church, St Mary the Virgin, where, I discovered on a memorial plaque, one Mary Summer had, in 1876, formed the Mothers' Union. It was the first of many pleasant discoveries in what was to turn into a massive church-crawl. I came to love those moments when, after getting the keys from the rectory if the place was locked, I could wander around those old damp churches alone. Usually I was tense with the expectancy of being disturbed, but I always read the Bible left open on the lectern to see what had hit the congregation the Sunday before. Sometimes I found notes on the last sermon, or sweet papers secreted behind a pew.

Those old English churches were jam-packed with sur-prises: a scratch dial near the door, for instance, by which the sun would show the times of the various ancient ser-vices. I found a church on that journey which had once been run by the vicar who had invented the multiplication sign and another where there was a plaque in the porch commemorating the theft of a statue 'by persons unknown'. Always, but always, you found near the altar a beautiful spray of freshly cut flowers.

Sir Arthur Bryant, in another English country church, once wrote: 'All English history – its strength, its sleeping fires, its patient consistency – is here, contained in its speak-ing silence.'

The next morning was warm and welcoming with the dull coin of the sun making a valiant attempt to shine through the thin clouds. I made my way out past watercress fields, geometric terraces with damp green clumps of cress and flowing rivulets of water laughing from one level to the next. At one time they produced so much of the stuff here that the local railway, which took it to London, was known as the Watercress Line.

I wandered on towards Alton. A dog came bursting out of a garden yapping its head off. I withdrew back down the lane, which was clearly a mistake, since the beast, emboldened by my cowardice, came after me. I changed tack and began barking and growling, running straight at him and waving my bag around. The dog took off faster than a four-bob rocket.

The sunshine was bejewelling the dew which was still thick on the fields and, to be honest, I was not now at all certain that I was on the Old Road. Every time I thought I was heading in the right direction the track disappeared into a ploughed field or ran straight into a brick wall or a deep snouzling river. Sometimes you could follow it through a wood and then it came to a dual carriageway with traffic zipping back and forth. All I knew for certain was that I was stumbling eastwards to Canterbury, a half-eaten bar of chocolate in my hand and my head stuffed with daydreams.

The track of the Old Road was clearly arbitrary anyway. 'You must pass by that well,' Belloc had been told. 'It is sacred' . . . 'You must of ritual climb that isolated hill which you see against the sky. The spirits haunted it and were banished by the faith, and they say that martyrs died there' . . . 'It is at the peril of the pilgrimage that you neglect this stone, whose virtue saved our fathers in the great battle' . . . 'The church you will next see upon your way is entered from the southern porch sunward by all truly devout men; such has been the custom here since custom began.'

Later that afternoon I signed into Alton Abbey for the night, finding that my feet had begun to bleed not to mention several rioting patches of blisters.

It immediately became clear that, although Benedictine also, this place was not another Quarr since the monks spoke to you and smiled a lot. Indeed Brother Francis, a cherubic man with a cherubic smile, just could not shut up. He was a man on whom the vow of silence would hang as easily as the death sentence, you fancied. He told me about the place and how they had a television and were even now hoping to get a video. A what? 'Oh yes, the whole lot of us watch "Dallas" every week.'

They also, I learned with mounting horror, were much taken by the idea of having a microwave oven. What kind of monastery do you call this then?

They didn't bother to try and grow their own vegetables any more – 'It's just too expensive' – and neither had they any animals. They had all been given their marching orders. 'We used to have three peacocks here,' Brother Francis explained. 'They used to make a shocking noise too until one night they were unwise enough to get on the window of the Abbot's bedroom and wake him up. They went soon after that.' They also had beehives but they were empty too.

There were four other guests in the Guest House – all college friends and ministers who met for a week each year to revive and encourage one another. It turned out that one of them kept bees also and he'd only been stung a couple of times. 'They only sting if you get in their flight path.' He'd had a queen bee die on him recently so he arranged for a new one to be sent to him for five pounds. It came through the post buzzing inside a match box. The problem then was to get the bees to accept their new queen. Sometimes they did and sometimes they just flung it out through the door. That's what they did to the one that came in the match box. They just killed her and threw her out.

Royalists would doubtless be pleased to learn that complete social anarchy followed this dastardly act with the whole structure of the hive going to pot, workers doing no work, soldiers messing about when they should have been on guard duty and nothing much by way of honey being produced.

However, I soon discovered that they ran an old people's home as well as providing further income from making communion wafers and incense. This operation was run by Brothers Benedict and Bede – a sort of holy double act. Brother Benedict explained that, together, the two of them turned out some hundred thousand wafers a month, making up the paste, baking them into sheets and then punching holes in them with their shining new machine. 'We just had that old puncher before. Murder to work that was.'

When the Pope came over they worked their little sandals off, making half a million wafers for the Coventry Mass alone.

It turned out that the Carmelites made most of the wafers with Alton filling in a few gaps. 'No, we could't assemble colour televisions or anything like that. Our work has to be compatible with the religious life.'

Did he think that watching 'Dallas' was compatible with the religious life?

'Oh, it gives us something to talk about.'

Brother Benedict also took me to his little cobwebbed room, a sort of scented Prospero's cell where he made up his special incense mixtures such as Rosa Mystica, Madonna, Festival and Special, all at six pounds ninety per pound plus VAT. He let me sniff some of his ingredients such as essence of geranium, hyacinth, sandalwood, jasmine and lavender. I took a good sniff on his patchouli and said it rather reminded me of a Bombay brothel. Realising that I was speaking to a holy man I flushed, but he merely took the vial off me, sniffed it and said, 'Yes, I suppose it does.'

So what did a Benedictine monk in Alton Abbey know about a Bombay brothel?

Oh, I would be surprised at what he knew, he said, since he had once sailed in the Merchant Navy with Shaw Saville and Union Castle lines. I too had once worked with both those lines as a seaman, as it happened, and our eyes briefly caught each other's; an odd moment to be sure – two men discussing incense in a monastery and in a sudden spasm of common insight, realising that we both knew of a world that was as far removed from holiness and incense as it was possible to get.

After the evening service, I chatted with the Abbot, Mark Gibson, a large man seemingly built out of circles with bullfrog jowls and a surprising light music in his voice. It was while talking to him that I understood why the abbey was so happy and relaxed: the boss was as happy as the day is long with a permanent smile on his lips and it seemed to rub off on everyone.

The first thing I asked him was why he was allowing all his charges to watch 'Dallas'. I just could not get over the notion of all those men in their sandals and Benedictine gowns sitting there, in front of the box, watching the activities of J.R., Sue Ellen and Miss Ellie.

'I find television a good way to relax,' he said, his smile broadening. 'I recently had an accident and spent all day watching television. It was lovely. Now they're all saying that they want a video so I suppose I'll let them have it.'

I thought such things were terrible in a monastery, and were sure to turn them into an Athenian rabble.

'Well, you're quite wrong on that, since Benedictine monasteries have always been in the vanguard of the modern world. One monastery in Belgium even uses computers. Benedict always saw us adapting to the world we live in. It was not part of God's plan that we live in sixth century Italy.'

They'd be reading newspapers next, I sneered.

'Oh, yes, we do that too. Brother Francis likes to read newspapers. They give him subjects for intercessory prayers.'

The trouble with these monks is that they've all been given Jesuitical training. They've got an answer for everything.

The morning sun was breaking through cloud and whispering enthralling promises of a coming spring when I left the abbey. At the bottom of the hill I passed a white Siamese cat with huge blue eyes sitting in a patch of sunlight by a privet hedge. Later I came to the town of Alton itself, a charming mish-mash of old and new, sitting at the head of the Wey Valley with a fine chapel and a church door, battle-scarred after having been under fire from the Roundheads. I passed the grammar school and was soon back in my wintery landscape of chalk again.

Today, at least, I was on the Pilgrims' Way for sure. It followed the main road from Alton all the way to Farnham, right next to the same river that provided water for the pilgrims of old to drink and wash in.

In *The Old Way*, Hilaire Belloc suggested that the one hundred and twenty mile path passes near thirteen existing or ruined churches – King's Worthy, Itchen, Stoke, Bishop Sutton, Seale, Puttenham, St Martha's, Shere, Merstham, Tilsey, Snodland, Burham, Boughton, Aluph and Chilham. In the case of eight of these the path went right up to the south porch.

Belloc also claimed that there were three main factors in the survival of the Old Way: the pilgrims themselves, the eighteenth-century turnpike system – which meant that travellers would want to avoid toll charges on the main roads – and, most importantly, the chalk. This viscous and spongy stuff, he said, would have been shaped and sculptured by the endless procession of walking feet. The chalk would always hold the shape and path of the Old Road; indeed, you could often spot the trail scything through the hillside ahead of you.

Belloc writes a marvellous hymn to all that chalk which lay scattered, white on brown like hundreds of broken and old teeth, over the fields around me:

'The chalk is our landscape and our proper habitation . . . The chalk filtered our drink for us and built up our strong bones; it was the height from the slopes of which our villages, standing in a clear air, could watch the sea or the plain; we carved it – when it was hard enough; it holds our first ornaments; our clear streams run over it; the shapes and curves it takes and the kind of close rough grass it bears (an especial grass for sheep), are the cloak of our counties; its lonely breadths delight us when the white clouds and the flocks move over them together; where the waves break it into cliffs, they are the characteristic of our shores, and through its thin coat of whitish mould go the thirsty roots of our three trees – the beech, the holly and the yew.'

The last few miles into Farnham were murder. The weakness in my left knee, which had first bothered me that Easter on the Fens, had come back again. I could barely walk at all and hobbled into the darkened market town where I signed into the first hotel I came across, the Bishop's Table. It was hideously expensive but when I complained, the manager knocked five pounds off the nightly rate. Grateful for small mercies, I promptly put myself to bed for a couple of days to give my knee a chance to heal.

It was a grey, sobbing morning when I picked up the Old Way again in the village of Seale, nestling in a vale in the shadow of the high, long escarpment of the Hog's Back. It is a place of some charm populated, I guessed, by retired brigadiers and those who had finally hung up their bowler hats.

I went into the church, built in the early enthusiasm of the pilgrimages, finding a six-hundred-year-old porch and, in one corner, a copy of the will of one John Fylpot who, in January 1487, bequeathed his soul to God, tuppence to the cathedral in Winchester, a further tuppence to the high altar, one sheep to the light of the cross, one sheep to the light of St Nicholas and one sheep to the light of St Lawrence.

I went over the road and had a chat with the verger, Nigel Nicholson, but barely recalled a word that he had said. It was no reflection on him. That day I barely recalled a word that anyone had said. I had been rung by my friend Peter Deeley, the news editor of *The Observer*, and been told some news which had broken my heart. My great hero and spiritual mentor, Canon David Watson, had died.

All deaths claw at our insides and some more than others but the loss of David was particularly shattering for me. Not only had he helped to lead me to Christ, he had also shown the way to hundreds, if not thousands, of others. In my view he was one of the great pilgrims of history and I counted meeting him as one of the great privileges of my life. The man seethed with honesty and integrity. I had long believed and prayed that he would be healed of his cancer so that he could lead our lost and fallen tribe back to God. Now he was dead. Why?

I trudged sadly onward. I came across a lovely old Saxon church in Compton and sat alone in a wooden pew, looking up at the stout round pillars fashioned out of chalk, the chancel arch and the strange, possibly unique double sanctuary. There was also a beautiful piece of stained glass – one of the earliest in the country, it said in the guide book. 'The green robe of the saviour was similar to the ancient glass at York Minster,' it went on.

It reminded me that I first met David in York, the city where his work had become such a symbol for renewal in the Anglican church. That church was far from dead and you had to come early to get a seat. Such beautiful moments, I remember – the swelling joy of the singing, the eddying flute in the communion, David's jokes.

On many occasions during my pilgrimage that year I felt that I had come close to the practice and presence of God. But sitting in the old Saxon church of Compton I felt that I knew nothing at all. I understood only the darkness of the dark night. God has told us that our thoughts are not his thoughts but, at times, I had felt close to his healing power though now he had clearly withdrawn again, leaving me shivering and chattering helplessly in the cold and the damp. He had withdrawn and, outside, a grey winter rain was falling on everything.

The real problem – the main jagged irony – was that I did not now think that I could turn my back on God either. I was not at all sure – even in my bitterness with him – that I could find the time and energy to stamp him out of my heart again. But I did, that day, understand his aloofness and what that old monk in Quarr had said: 'He's nothing like his created reality. The closer you come, the further he seems to be away. The more you know the more you realise that you don't understand at all. He is only like himself.'

To make matters worse my knee had ballooned up again and I was in the greatest pain when, later that afternoon, I came to Guildford Cathedral.

Question: which cathedral should you avoid at all costs if you are feeling low and believe that God has abandoned you?

Answer: the cathedral at Guildford.

As cathedrals go it is big and spacious enough but there is no love or prayer or even fine craftsmanship in it. There is no stained glass in the windows. The lines are straight and clean. The main vaulting is of concrete, sprayed with asbestos plaster to prevent echoes and externally covered with red brick. The communion table is built of fibre glass.

In the nave I met Arthur Smallpiece who said that they had to drive eight hundred and sixty-four chunks of concrete into the ground before they started building this thing in 1936. The architect wanted all the windows clear to let God's daylight into the church. Everywhere you looked the place stank of the modern world and, when a patch of damp erupted in the roof, they were told to leave it alone since it might give the building a look of maturity.

Arthur Smallpiece had a terrific zest for all kinds of facts

*Guildford Cathedral:
'There is no love or fine
craftsmanship in it. The
main vaulting is of
concrete, sprayed with
asbestos plaster. The
communion table is built
of fibreglass.'*

and figures. The cathedral cost four hundred and fifty pounds a day to run and the heating was provided by six miles of copper piping. There were three thousand kneelers – each individually designed and embroidered by local women. The altar carpet weighed a thousand pounds and was made by six old ladies of the Mothers' Union. The bishop's throne was built *in situ* by a local carpenter. One icon on the wall was found in a Turkish street market.

Yes, but where was the spirit of prayer? In which corner could I kneel and hide and ask God why he had taken David from us?

A lonely, stumbling journey into Guildford. Dark trees stared down at the howling in my knee. The empty dusk had no pity. The streetlamps and lights of passing cars sent my shadow dancing all around. Shadows ambled towards me when I approached the streetlamps. Shadows raced around me when the cars passed by. My breath came pluming around me in white vapours. I just wanted to lay my head down on the pavement, curl up and die.

The next morning I had woken up in Guildford to find that my get-up-and-go had well and truly got up and gone since I had clearly got some cartilage trouble in my knee. The only way I could now finish the Old Way was to hire a car. A car! What a rotten leg of the pilgrimage this was turning out to be. But there seemed to be no other option; I could hardly crawl those remaining miles.

So I hired a car and my first day back behind the wheel was hardly worth bothering about. I was now unable to finish the Old Way continuously and had to drive up here and double back around there picking it up where I could. To make matters worse I often took the wrong turning and ended up on the motorway which ran almost next to the Old Way, sometimes having to make a ten-mile detour to get back to where I wanted.

What could be more depressingly different to the journey of the pilgrims of old than driving down a motorway? One day I was wandering along catkin lanes, struggling through clouds of pilgrim prayer and memory, and now I was whizzing about in a little tin box, trussed up with a safety belt like a battery hen, with not a soul to pass the time of day with.

Where once I could sit and rest on a bank of dead fern I now sat looking at mile after mile of unwinding concrete, belting its way through the countryside at odds with everything. There was none of the society of those old coaching inns in the motorway cafes either – just people coming in for a quick bite, many so mesmerised by the constant movement of their windscreen wipers that they acted and moved like zombies, others queuing up for food with globby piles of chips stacked high on everything and coffee machines where you had to press a dozen buttons before getting half a cup of cold tea.

When I did finally pick up the track I came to St Martha's Hill, leaving the car and hobbling up through a wood, past an abandoned chalk pit, unsung and silent and given over to ivy, to find the church locked and the view of the surrounding countryside, said to be the finest in the county, obscured by rain mists.

Later in the day, mooching around some churchyard, I spotted scoops of earth flying up out of the ground. I went over for a chat with the gravedigger, a young art student with fine features and an even finer attitude, who was here making a bit of extra cash. 'I've got to go down really deep on this one,' he said. 'The husband's going down tomorrow and I've got to leave enough room for the wife. It's tough stuff this clay but not as wet as it is on the other side. Sometimes I get little turns when I come across some old bones but I just put them in that polythene bag over there and let the vicar deal with them. No, I don't know what he does with them. Myself, I want to be cremated. I've seen too much of the dirty side of this business to want to be put down here. And it's expensive, too. You've got to pay a basic four hundred pounds for the cheapest funeral and then you can go up to a thousand pounds with no problem.

I wouldn't want my family to spend all that just to get rid of my dead bones.'

I drove onwards, still rumbling with grief, past damp churches and pools where pilgrims would have stopped to drink. One man who lived near some lime workings said that around a hundred pilgrims a day came walking past his house in the summer. 'They're often knocking on the door asking for a drink of water. Lots of them do it on that mile sponsorship deal. I don't mind them asking for water. It's when they leave crisp packets and litter everywhere that I object.'

I visited the churches of Gatton and Merstham, jointly run now by a tall, tentative vicar who liked to stop talking in mid-sentence and put one hand on the top of his head. He gave me the keys to both the churches quite happily. 'I did once have a lovely old key for one of the churches but a German tourist made off with it for a souvenir.'

In Gatton two ladies were busy polishing the mass of elaborate woodcarvings which were piled everywhere. They'd been doing this every week forever, they thought, though thirty years might be more precise. One of them began polishing a brass lectern. 'You *can* lacquer it but it's not the same somehow,' she added with the precision of an expert.

I moved on again, coming to picture postcard villages flung down around ponds in which ducks dropped their yellow beaks into the water, heaving their behinds up into the air and making their yellow webbed feet waggle about, as they foraged for food. I walked around the back of a churchyard when a magpie flew across my path. I moved along country lanes which, in summer, had teemed with a tireless exuberance. Now there was just the damp sleep of winter with the earth waiting for the warming revival of spring. Like me.

Outside the church in Otford a man was sitting quietly in the back of his van, cap in hand, brewing tea. Charley from up Fulham way, he said he was, a retired businessman who now liked to spend his time travelling the country in his van. Where did he like to go?

'Some of the names escape me but, if I've time, I like Pembrokeshire the best. North Wales is nice too. I love old churches but I'm an agnostic you know. No. I won't change my mind now. I'll take my chances.

'I mostly travel on my own. I used to have a mate but he died. I often wish he was back 'cos I liked travelling with him. I've got a wife. Yes. She sometimes comes with me and we see one another occasionally. The problem is I won't travel abroad and she loves foreign travel. I gave up abroad after the war. I saw all I wanted then. She goes off on her own now. My wife's a teacher and knows exactly what she thinks. They're like that, school teachers are.'

Later that afternoon I signed into a Carmelite monastery, The Friars in Aylesford, a tangle of old buildings and stately archways, set around a bird-songed courtyard and just next to a peaceful sweep of the River Medway. Geese wandered unconcernedly on the main path leading up to the monastery. Doves warbled in the eaves and, out in front of the reception office, the leaves of a solitary acacia tree chattered in the cold wind.

Of all the religious orders the Carmelites, I read in my guide book, are perhaps most closely associated with the pilgrim cult. They first gathered as a disorganised band of pilgrims on the slopes of Mount Carmel in Israel where, in the tradition of the Old Testament prophets, they maintained a life of prayer and silence. Following repeated Moslem attacks a small party of them came and settled in Aylesford in 1242. They built hermitages here in a place which was also associated with St Simon Stock, an early Carmelite who was said to have inspired their change from an eremitical to a begging life and to have seen a vision of Our Lady who touched his scapular and promised protection to all who wore one.

The hermitages grew into this priory but, by the beginning of the sixteenth century, religious life was declining here. In 1535, the royal commissioners reported that the friars held eighteen acres of land with an annual value of forty-two shillings and sixpence. Considering that they had to pay twenty shillings and eightpence to the Provincial and two shillings rent to the Master of Hospital at Strood, that must have made them very poor indeed. In December 1538 the priory was dissolved and the community formally surrendered the house before setting off to seek employment as best they could. Some became parish priests or chaplains.

The building changed hands many times after that and was gutted by fire in 1930. It was put up for sale in 1949, but Carmelites throughout the world contributed to a fund to buy back their ancient house. In 1951 St Simon Stock's relics were transferred here from Bordeaux where he had died, thereafter attracting pilgrimages here which brought money and, with it, the possibility of building up this marvellous complex.

My guide around the place, another Brother Francis, was a man with a shy, quiet personality which sat strangely in his huge all-in wrestler's body. First he took me to the tremendous Pilgrims' Hall, probably the oldest building in the priory and now used for meals. It has two wooden upper galleries with neo-Elizabethan rafters and it would have been on these galleries that three to four hundred pilgrims a night would have slept on their way to Canterbury. Youth groups still sleep here when they make a similar journey.

Brother Francis also showed me the Prior's Hall with its series of paintings by the Polish artist, Adam Kossowski, outlining the history of the Carmelites from the days of Mount Carmel to their triumphant return to Aylesford. Adjoining the hall were the cloisters and the cloister chapel, now used for silent prayer and meditation. The stained glass window of Our Lady of Mount Carmel was a gift from the artist Moira Forsyth. The painted Stations of the

Even such reclusive orders
as the Carmelites are
dependent on the public's
charity and goodwill. In
return they offer care and
sanctuary for the casualties
of twentieth-century life.

Far Right: Stained glass
hours. Modern
ecclesiastical art ranges
from the sublime to the
shiftily trendy.

Cross were again by Kossowski who, here, has put together one of the largest collections of modern ecclesiastical art in the world.

We moved on over to the new shrine area with the choir chapel which was now used daily for the Mass and Office of the church. These days nearly a quarter of a million pilgrims come here each year – from Easter to October – to worship in the open-air church. Large groups have also come from Poland, Italy and Spain, though the Spaniards are not going to be allowed back. 'They left too much rubbish behind last time,' Brother Francis confided.

The main shrine, to which most flocked, was the Relic Chapel. On the altar stood a reliquary containing St Simon's skull and it was visible even now, sitting behind some thick plate glass, looking like a rough reddish coconut as it sat on a tiny white pillow put there, one suspects, to make it feel comfortable. 'It's not much fun being a saint,' said Brother Francis. 'Bits of you get scattered everywhere. As you can see, we got the skull.'

After supper I had a long chat with the Prior, Edward Maguire, a man with a puckish red face and silvery curling hair and such an attitude of having lived life to the hilt he might have been a Montmartre painter or a Greenwich Village drunk. He had been here for nine years but, being a Carmelite, he could easily be moved on at any time. Most of his work was to do with administration but it soon emerged that he was a man with a lively and shrewd intelligence who had long understood the difficulty of making up his mind in advance of any situation.

What they did here, he explained, was to take people in who needed help. 'Exhausted people, alcoholics, that kind of thing. We give them a warm room and feed them and give them time to reflect on their lives. We don't take in people who have just had a nervous breakdown, though, since the sense of quiet and isolation here wouldn't help that. There's always some sort of transient population here.

We never send anyone away. This is simply a place of prayer.'

The conversation drifted, inevitably in my present mood, to the death of David Watson. I explained that I too was exhausted and very angry with God.

'Well, anger with God is fine. That's a form of prayer too. If you are angry with him then you should always tell him so. It's even a form of passionate prayer. But remember that he is not as we are. We each of us have sparks that we hand on to one another. That's all I know for certain. Your weaknesses are always detected and become someone else's strength. In some strange way we are always looking after one another. Somehow there is a sense in which suffering always fulfils God's purpose. But how? I just couldn't even start to tell you why six million Jews were allowed to die.

'Your mind will not be able to help you with the loss of this man. You won't be able to think your way out of it. Neither is it so much a matter of time as a matter of acceptance when you will find a pattern, a reason. Then you can take it.'

They were the good, concerned words of a good, concerned man. That night in my bed they rang in my mind, as hard and true as steel, a poultice, at least, on the still suppurating boil of my grief.

Pilgrimage was clearly not just the acquisition of knowledge or experience or even new ideas. One had to grant that suffering must be part of the journey too, if it helped us to grow close to him who suffered much. One had to grant that there were times when the turning over of words and concepts would mean nothing and take you nowhere. One had to grant that there were times when one had to just sit still and know; that there was nothing easy about coming to terms with the mystery of God and the real nature of holiness. Did one? I don't know. We were all back in the shifting quicksands of the mind again, this moving jungle of ideas that we all somehow had to machete our way through.

The next morning, after a service in celebration of St David, whose day it was, I carried on my way again – passing the ruin of Boxley Abbey, on by woods of beech and box then on to the hamlet of Detling and Thurnham where, in the church of St Mary the Virgin, was the grave of Alfred Mynn, one of the founders of Kent cricket, who died in 1861. 'Four hundred persons have united to erect this tombstone,' it said portentously, 'and to found in honour of a name so celebrated the Mynn Memorial Benevolent Institute of Kentish Cricketers.' The sum raised, it added, was one hundred and twenty-one pounds, ten shillings invested in India five per cent stock.

Then to Hollingbourne and Lenham and the church of St Mary's where one altar slab celebrated the prolific Mary Honeywood who died in 1620, aged ninety-two, leaving three hundred and sixty-seven descendants – sixteen children, one hundred and fourteen grandchildren, two hundred and twenty-eight great-grandchildren and nine great-great-grandchildren. What a funeral that must have been. The memorial slab was rather reassuring somehow, redolent as it was of the way life keeps renewing itself.

A massive carved pulpit stood in one corner; in another, I found a medieval mural of St Michael weighing souls. There was also a graphic exhibition on church costs which cast a rather new light on that simile about being as poor as a church mouse – organ maintenance eighty-eight pounds a year; organist and choir two hundred and sixty-four pounds; hymn books one hundred and twenty pounds; heating four hundred and ninety pounds; candles, wine and communion wafers one hundred and fifty-six pounds; insurance eight hundred and eighteen pounds and electricity one hundred and seventy-three pounds.

One guessed, but didn't know for sure, that all this

was for a regular Sunday morning congregation of about twenty. One country vicar once told me that he had a regular congregation of eight and when I expressed some sympathy for this poor turn-out he said not at all since, for the past year, the congregation had been four so they were now undergoing something of a booming revival.

There were but a few miles left now on my pilgrimage. I took them slowly, pulling into a layby for a cup of tea and a rock cake from one of those doubtful caravan restaurants you see dotted along the roads of Britain. The lady was pleasant enough and served her tea in nice china cups but her rock cakes tasted of petrol. I stopped to read the local society notices in a shop window: 'Lady Monckton speaks about her year as High Sheriff of Kent,' and 'A Kent police crime prevention officer talks about how to deter the burglar and theft.' I passed curling oast houses and the gently rolling hop fields where the lines of wire stood, bare and quivering in the wind, patiently waiting for the hops to rise and engulf them.

A few miles out of Canterbury I stopped off at a stained glass studio run by Mike and Lynne Boothroyd in a shed in their garden. They did have some orders for church work, I discovered, but they found making small hanging terrariums to put plants in far more profitable. They used antique glass and expensive opalescent blue glass from Belgium and were now turning over fifteen hundred pounds a week.

The trouble with church windows was that they could be fifteen feet wide and a hundred feet long and, even when they made it in four-foot sections, it meant that the sections would take up the whole of their bench and nothing else could be made. It would be nice to create a great stained glass work, it is true, but there was, ah, the bank manager to look after. Well, we all had that problem.

It was, I guessed, as apt an observation on the state of ecclesiastical art in the modern world as I was likely to get.

People often ask me if I write about places in advance of actually seeing them. The answer is never. A writer who succumbs to his prepackaged notions will soon get into a load of trouble not to mention a further load of hard work changing them back around again.

But, just as I had often fantasised about this monk who was going to show me the Holy Grail, I must admit that I had often fantasised about my final few miles into Canterbury. The rough scenario – as etched out by imagination – went something like this:

It would have been a long dog of a tramp all day as I moved down The Old Way, with just the sheep looking at me. Just when my tired body and bleeding feet had announced that they were going to go no further, I would round a bend and my spirits would soar as I first spotted the spire of Canterbury Cathedral rising, majestic and mystic, out of flower-flecked fields. The land would be covered by low-lying mists too. Earlier that day, there had been a shower of rain which, even now, the sun was drying out.

I would have to decide, then, if I was to stop for the night just here so that I could tackle this spiritual queen of cities fresh, first thing in the morning, or if I should press on. Still unsure I would have knocked up a friendly vicar in a huge stone local rectory, full of damp and mildewed theological books, where he would have stuffed me with marvellous food and fabulous stories whereupon, suitably revived, I would have tramped off into the thickening dusk and straight up to the cathedral door where, with bats flitting about me, I would have slumped to my knees and given thanks for a safe journey throughout the year.

The reality was altogether different.

I did stop at Chilham, a small snooty English town six miles out of Canterbury and the last staging post on The

Old Way, only to find that the church was locked. I finally located the rectory – which was a modern, detached red-brick job with an integral garage and a dog barking somewhere inside it – only to find that no one was in. The nearby pub was closed too so, finally, I jumped into my car and drove to Canterbury and, rather than seeing that dreaming spire poking up out of steaming rose fields, I did not see it at all since, just on the outskirts of the city, I was stuck in a traffic jam for more than an hour since they were digging up the road.

Even worse the car had begun to show a distinct and worrying tendency to fall to bits in my hands. The clutch was travelling some six inches before it engaged. The radio merely screamed with static and now the lock had fallen out of the driver's door and was just hanging off the side like a detached eyeball hanging on the end of a bit of string. It confirmed all I had ever believed about these four-wheeled boxes which had conspired to imprison us and ruin the world.

On the same journey, on two feet as God had planned it, Belloc had written of his first sight of the vast building with its particularly immense spire. He said that it became the pivot for all they saw. 'Save perhaps once at Beauvais I had never known such a magic of great height and darkness.'

Then warming still further to the emotions released by his first sight of the spire he wrote: 'It signifies the history of the three centuries during which Canterbury drew towards it all Europe. But it stands quite silent and emptied of every meaning, tragic and blind against the changing life of the sky and those activities of light that never fail or die as do all things intimate and our own – even religions. I received its silence for an hour, but without comfort and without response. It seemed only an awful and fitting terminal to that long day I had come. It sounded the note of all my road – the droning voice of extreme, incalculable age.'

No such inspired philosophical musings for me, though. When we finally got over the bridge, past a clanking steamroller and a man waving a green flag, through that appalling smell of boiling tar and past men with shovels flinging asphalt around, we were detoured off the main road and through an industrial estate. When I did spot the cathedral's spire, it was poking up over the dowdy orange asbestos roof of a factory making kitchen fittings. I bet Chaucer and his gang didn't have this kind of trouble.

The sun was just setting as I signed into the Falstaff Hotel near the West Gate, an appropriate enough choice of watering hole, since the gate was always locked at nightfall in Chaucer's time. Visiting pilgrims had to wait out here in one of the inns or alehouses until dawn.

The West Gate is now the only gate remaining of the seven which once stood in the city walls of medieval Canterbury. Its huge twin towers are joined together by an arch which has a jutting terrace through which bricks and boiling oil could be dropped on the city's attackers.

The gate is no longer locked for the night curfew, of course, and the cars are now a greater danger than bricks or boiling oil, so I ventured out into the dark city streets for a night of quiet celebration now that I had finished my journey.

I found Canterbury an attractive and cheerful jumble of brick and half-timbered houses with moneyed, rather self-conscious fashion shops, a sprinkling of pubs without much life in their bars and sudden, surprising aspects of waterways flowing cold behind the backs of sloping houses built in the Middle Ages.

The next morning I ventured back into the city trying to locate The Chequers of Hope with its dormitory of a hundred beds. This was where Chaucer and his fellow pilgrims had stayed: that colourful, motley crowd which included a prioress, a nun, three priests, the monk and the friar. Then there was a scholar, a pardoner selling indulgences, a summoner, a cook, a haberdasher, carpenter, weaver and tapestry-maker not forgetting the miller, the parson, the reeve, the frankelyn and 'a verray parfit gentil knyght'.

There were no such persons out on the wintry streets of Canterbury that morning though there were some school-boys with starched butterfly collars, a sprinkling of American tourists and tradesmen carting their goods to the weekly trade fair. 'This is the worst fair of them all,' one trader was saying to another. 'They think it's just Woolworths. When did you ever make money in Canterbury?'

The Chequers of Hope no longer exists, though there are a few of its paving stones in a coffee shop beneath a new department store. I did, however, find one genuine curiosity – a huge red pump, pinned to a wall above the window of a leather shop. This pump, I had been told, commemorated the monks' practice of selling medieval pilgrims water which was red with rust. The monks claimed that the water was tainted with the blood of Thomas à Beckett.

The man in the Tourist Information Shop, Gavin Mac-Lean, did not know if this story was true but he did explain that increasing numbers of pilgrims – largely from America, France and Holland – were now coming here each year. Some thirty-two thousand came to his shop in the last year alone. Having ascertained the size of their wallets he would direct them to accommodation that ranged from Mrs Wainwright in South Canterbury Road who charged five pounds a night, to the four-star County Hotel where two nights of bed and breakfast would cost more than many people earn in a week.

Clearly times had changed since 1520, when a post was set up in the street to display the provisions made with 'letters expressing the ordering of vitell and lodging for pylgrymes'. Then pilgrims might have slept three to a bed with three beds to a room. Some would have slept on straw-filled palliasses and had to cope with fleas and mice.

Their welcome might not always have been very amiable either – or so we might deduce from one of the ancient byelaws which stated: 'No inn-keeper or host when any pilgrims or strangers come to the City, shall catch them by the reins, their clothing or their staves and try to make them come into his Inn, nor shall any cross over the thresholds of his Inn when shouting at said Pilgrims and strangers passing along, making him, under pain of imprisonment or fine.'

Had I been a medieval pilgrim I might not have found the pain in my knee so wretched either. One Archbishop Arundel once reported that pilgrims brought with them singers and also pipers 'that when one of them which goeth barefoot striketh his tow on a stone, and maketh it to bleed, it is well done that he and his fellows begin then a song . . . to drive away with such mirth the hurte'.

Indeed had I been a medieval pilgrim with a gammy knee I could also have signed myself free into the Eastbridge Hospital, just down the road a way, which in its original charter was obliged to 'receive wayfaring or hurt men' who might stay one night only, or more if they were too sick to depart, with beds for eight men and four women. The hospital was allowed twenty loads of wood each year and fourpence a day for each person with sixpence a week for the beer. Other costs included twenty shillings a year for a poor woman (who had to be over forty years) to wait upon them.

The building is still there and open to the public. The crypt where once they slept and the chapel where once they prayed were empty when I looked around. From somewhere just down the stairs came the odd drooling squawks of astonishment of American tourists.

A siren wind blew in freezing gusts around the flat lawns of the cathedral when I finally entered its precincts. I looked up at the great Norman arcadings and ornate stone traceries. Inside, I was immediately overwhelmed by the sheer size of the nave. There was little intimacy here but – as befits the Mother Church of Anglican Christendom – there was unmistakable authority.

Machines offering earphone commentaries for twenty pence were dotted around in white metal banks. Two students were sharing one earpiece. Tourists drifted past, one with a crying baby.

I laughed, you know, when the blood spattered in red and silent drops over that grey stone slab. I could never be sure why it was that I laughed when I held onto my arm and looked down at all that blood bubbling warm everywhere. I suppose I must have laughed since such a thing should be happening to me before my very eyes in a cathedral.

I saw a hiker with coloured badges stiched on to his rucksack – Monte Carlo, Morocco, Paris, Spain. On top of it all was a red and white Canadian flag. One supposes that such men, with their mountainous packs and legs like oak trees, are the modern pilgrims. Pilgrims of old would have gone to Jerusalem, Santiago de Compostela and Jericho, and they too would have brought back the special emblems peculiar to such places: the palms of Jericho or cockle-shells from Compostela.

It was an ice-dark day in winter, just like this one, and the monks were due to start vespers when the trouble began. I remember looking into Thomas' eyes when he gave me the kiss of peace. There was an angry sadness in them as if he knew what was to come. His lips were cold too. His hands clasped me tight on both shoulder-bones. 'Do not worry yourself Edward,' he said. 'God is with us in all we do.'

Footsteps and voices echoed around the stone columns of the crypt. A child dropped a sweet paper and was told to pick it up. Two black-gowned vergers were discussing a forthcoming concert. 'The children can change here but they mustn't go in that chapel over there or the one here. Let's make sure that's understood by everyone.'

The four knights – Reginald Fitz-Urse, William de Tracy, Hugh de Moreville and Richard Brito – burst into our chamber and were taken in to see Thomas where, for a long time, they just sat looking at him in scornful silence. When Thomas greeted them curses were spat at him and they told him that the king had ordered him to depart from all lands which owned his dominion. They were, they kept saying, the king's men.

'Cease your threats and still your brawling. I put my trust in the King of Heaven who for his own suffered on the Cross.'

The knights retired in a tumult of insults ordering us all to seize and hold Thomas lest he try and escape but Thomas ran after them shouting 'Here, here you will find me.'

A woman was praying alone in one of the small chapels. Squeals of distant laughter echoed around these old columns. I came to the cathedral bookshop and information centre. Just above were the steps, leading up to the Trinity Chapel, worn into curving waves of stone by centuries of pilgrims' feet.

Ere long the murderers returned in full armour. They found the doors locked so they broke in through a partition making some of the monks flee in terror. Commotions and threats travelled everywhere in the cathedral and we tried to get Thomas to leave with us but he would not. Thomas was always too proud to run from anyone and he merely followed us slowly into the church, driving us all before him, as a good shepherd does his sheep.

I glanced over the enormous range of merchandise on sale. That much of it might be, with no intrinsic spiritual significance, but I suppose a plastic key fob with a picture of the cathedral might momentarily jog someone's memory of times spent here in God's house.

Then the four men dashed in with drawn swords.

The stained glass in Canterbury was astonishing, perhaps the finest I had seen anywhere all year. It was so careful in

its detail, so brilliant in its texture, so certain in its faith it made me catch my breath. Hands stood out like beacons. Faces shone like the sun. One of the shafts of light caught on a flash of steel, creating a ferocious and murderous sparkle.

Thomas was on the steps leading to the choir when the knights shouted at him to restore those that he had excommunicated. He refused and long shadows slanted across the nave when they rushed at him, trying to drag him outside the walls of the church where they could kill him. Thomas held on to a pillar.

I was holding Thomas when the knight whirled his sword, cutting off the crown of Thomas' head and, in the same stroke, gashing right into my arm, almost severing it. That was when I laughed. It was the sight of my own blood that made me laugh. The sight of Thomas' made me weep. He was cut again and again falling to his knees, saying in a low voice, 'For the name of Jesus and the protection of the Church I am ready to embrace death.'

Thomas' hands did not resist one stroke. Nor when smitten did he utter a single word, neither cry nor groan, nor any sound at all indicating pain when one of them placed his foot on the neck of the holy martyr scattering his brains and blood about shouting mad violent boasts that the man would rise no more. When his body lay there, silent and still, I prayed in my own blood and tears.

At the far end of the cathedral Thomas' shrine stood as empty and as silent as the looted tomb that it was. They needed twenty-six carts to carry all the treasures away when it was Dissolved.

Christendom reacted with tremendous emotion to this savage murder and Thomas was made a saint within days of his death and long before his official canonisation. Miraculous cures were soon reported near the tomb, children were christened Thomas, stained glass windows proclaimed his glory as thousands upon thousands made

'Twenty-six carts were needed to carry away Canterbury's treasures after Dissolution and the looted tomb is the perfect symbol of the present church – a forlorn space echoing to the clatter of tourists and the flash of cameras.'

Canterbury Cathedral: 'There was little intimacy here but – as befits the Mother Church of Anglican Christendom – there was an unmistakable authority.'

holy water of St Thomas had, in some instances, made prisoners' shackles fall off. A man came here with a violent toothache and saw a vision of a man who asked him to open his mouth. Air was wafted into the mouth and immediately the man lost his pain.

In the high noon of medieval pilgrimage this shrine was covered with gold plate and jewels of every kind – rubies, emeralds, sapphires and diamonds. Monks would point out the truly outstanding gifts like the regale, a ruby given by the King of France. All this surrounded 'the brain pan of the holy martyr', according to one account, 'which was thrust quite through, all the other covered with silver, the overpart of the brain pan was bare to be kissed and therewithall is set forth a certain leaden table having graved in him a title of Saint Thomas of Acrese. There also hang the shirt of hair, and his girdle with his hairen breeches wherewith that noble champion chastened his body, they be horrible to look upon and greatly reprove our delicate gorgeousness.'

The relic trade underwent a boom. Parts of Thomas' clothing went to churches far and wide – his books and penknife to Bury, a tooth to Verona. A Florence convent claimed to have an arm, blithely ignoring Lisbon's protestation that it already had both of them.

The racket in indulgences prospered also. The Pope granted an occasional plenary indulgence, and this attracted extra thick swarms of pilgrims. By 1500 the church had to pay five hundred gold florins and a fat royalty from the proceeds to acquire an indulgence. It was Pope Leo's ready sale of indulgences that stoked up the angry fires of Martin Luther.

It was Henry VIII, the Defender of the Faith, who dissolved the shrine and so the Canterbury pilgrim's wonderland came to an end after four and a half centuries.

Dissolution was clearly just as well. It marked the end of a corrupt and decadent church which had become an offence to God. There was an historic inevitability, I came

their way here to be baptised in the font of their own tears.

'This citie hath been chiefly maintained by two things,' wrote the Protestant Lambarde. 'First by the residence and Hospitalitie of the Archbishop and Religious persons and then by the liberalitie and expense of such as either gadded to St Thomas for help and devotion.'

A madman was taken to the tomb and chained there throughout the night; his sanity returned. Cripples came and threw away their crutches. Swellings and ulcers disappeared. The blind saw again and it was reported that the to learn on my pilgrimage, in the arrival of men like Calvin, Knox and Luther. They were sent to purge the poisoned body.

But who now is going to purge this present church, which is not so much corrupt as fast asleep; not so much decadent as divided? Such a church is just as much an enemy of God as a decadent one, all as ineffective as that cordoned-off empty space that I now saw before me. In many ways this looted tomb was the perfect symbol of what we now have – a forlorn space echoing to the chatter of tourists and the flash of cameras.

Just behind me was the Chapel of Saints and Martyrs, its elegant altarpiece surrounded by a vivacious mosaic of purple stained glass. 'The blood of thy martyrs and saints shall enrich the earth, shall create the holy place,' it said on the tapestry. On a board on the other side of the chapel I read, 'A martyrdom is always the design of God, for his love of men, to warn them and lead them, to bring them back to his ways.'

I took a candle and lit it for that great canon, saint and martyr, David Watson. It shone a bright yellow with hazy, stammering smoke drifting up out of its tip before settling again. Light flickered on the brown marble pillar behind. The candle said a prayer for the saints and martyrs that are the lights of the world.

He had all the qualities of the saints of old, did David. Just like Swithun, who travelled around on foot, David only ever travelled around on a bicycle and ate the simplest of meals. Like Patrick, David also fought the demons of darkness with fervent prayer and fasting. Like Columba – 'tender in every adversity' – David was always prepared to teach even when 'hurting, wounded and vulnerable'. Like Cuthbert, he taught goodness by the impeccable lesson of being good himself. His spirit straddled the modern world just as surely as the spirits of those medieval saints straddled the old.

David's miracles were no less astonishing. He maintained the miracle of a deep and loving faith even when asthma kept him up through the night fighting for breath; even when he was beleaguered by depressions which got the black dogs yapping; even when his insides were being eaten away by cancer. Even in all that pain and suffering he kept showing glimpses of his greatness, still held up a light in the darkness.

Holiness abides. That's all I had really learned about holiness in my stained glass hours. Institutions may fall and decay and the loved old may always give way to the despised new but there will always be men ready to pick up the fallen torch, always another to pass it on and teach us again the way and meaning of holiness.

When I left the cathedral groups of visitors were hanging back in the porch. It was snowing. Huge fat flakes came whirling in over Canterbury, falling softly on my face and dissolving in my eyes like tears. I walked around to the other side of the cathedral and found a small frozen waterfall in some leafless wisteria. The snow fell into the canals, disappearing soundlessly as it kissed the water.

Two schoolboys rattled past me on bicycles. A rabble of noisy winds rose up and began spitting, harsh and angry, over the grey slate rooftops. Two birds were fluttering hard against the face of these furious winds, fighting to get back to their warm nests, perhaps, or merely just wanting to go forward. They fought harder and harder until, finally, one fell away behind the cathedral cloisters. But the other battled on bravely, fighting every inch of the way against the chill winds of God.